Computer Graphics for Theatre Design

Computer Graphics for Theatre Design: Practical CGI Techniques for Scenic, Costume, and Lighting Designers explores techniques and technologies for incorporating computer graphics in scenography.

The book offers practical guidance to create simple yet effective and attractive design work. It features instructions on producing professional-quality computer images, videos, and interactions using open-source software and other software that is available at no cost. Also included are tips on new means of collaboration, preparing a digital portfolio, and more. The text provides instruction in 2D sketching and painting for costume, scenic, and lighting design, as well as 3D modeling and rendering for scenic design and lighting visualization. Lastly, it discusses using computer graphics and simulations not only to produce and communicate traditional designs, but to be incorporated directly on stage in media-enriched productions.

Computer Graphics for Theatre Design offers instructions in all major areas of scenographic techniques and how skills used in one area can be applied to the others. By providing guidance useful to all three main areas of design, a single, comprehensive class on computer graphics can be offered to students, or traditional classes in each area can use specific sections, all in the same text. The book will also be of interest to professionals looking to introduce CGI techniques in their design work.

Mark Reaney is a scenographer and retired professor in the Scenography Program within the University of Kansas' Department of Theatre and Dance, where he taught classes in computer-aided design for over 25 years. He pioneered the use of CGI in scenography and virtual reality as a scenic medium and directed the Institute for the Exploration of Virtual Realities (i.e. VR). Beginning in 1988, he has written extensively on the subject and spoken at venues across the U.S. and Europe. Current projects include new VR recreations of historic theatres. Long afflicted with MS, Mark is always exploring ways in which digital tech can aid scenographers with disabilities. Documentation of the work in CGI/VR/Theatre projects, productions, and publications can be found at www.ievr.org.

Computer Graphics for Theatre Design

Practical CGI Techniques for Scenic, Costume, and Lighting Designers

Mark Reaney

Routledge
Taylor & Francis Group
NEW YORK AND LONDON

Designed cover image: Mark Reaney

First published 2026
by Routledge
605 Third Avenue, New York, NY 10158

and by Routledge
4 Park Square, Milton Park, Abingdon, Oxon, OX14 4RN

Routledge is an imprint of the Taylor & Francis Group, an informa business

ISBN: 978-1-032-94628-3 (hbk)
ISBN: 978-1-032-94627-6 (pbk)
ISBN: 978-1-003-57174-2 (ebk)

DOI: 10.4324/9781003571742

Typeset in Sabon
by Apex CoVantage, LLC

To Emma
Su and Vince
Billie and Norm
David and Sara

Contents

Acknowledgments

Thanks to Kerry Lafferty, John Ezell, and Del Unruh for building the foundation for this work.

1 Fundamental Principles

"The business of workers in the theatre is, as I see it, to express a timeless theme by the means of the tools of one own's time."

Robert Edmond Jones

FIGURE 1.1 A computer-generated scenic sketch and lighting study for *Talley's Folly*.

In today's rapidly evolving landscape, it's essential for scenographers to embrace digital tools in their creative process. The integration of technology into artistic practices has transformed the way designers conceptualize and execute their visions. Utilizing these technologies is no longer just a supplementary skill; it has become a fundamental part of the creative toolkit, akin to traditional drawing and painting – each as critical and legitimate in its own right.

DOI: 10.4324/9781003571742-1

Many emerging designers in scenic, costume, and lighting design are proficient in various computer skills due to early exposure to technology in education. This emphasis on digital literacy enables students to use graphic programs and design software for both artistic and academic tasks, positioning these skills as essential. Aspiring scenographers have typically invested in both education and the technology that supports their art, including computers, monitors, printers, and various peripherals. Integrating digital design into your workflow can leverage this investment and transform your creative practice, enabling greater productivity, effective collaboration, and broader sharing of your work.

This trend not only benefits artists but also fosters a generation that integrates technology into their creative expression, resulting in a more diverse and richer design landscape. As traditional and digital practices converge, scenographers can explore innovative techniques, such as virtual reality, projection mapping, and 3D modeling, to enhance their work.

FIGURE 1.2 Digital costume designs for *Macbeth* and *Ella Enchanted* by Lindsay Webster.

Traditional drawing and digital design can harmoniously coexist in a designer's workflow. Conventional hand sketches of costumes, figures, or scenery can be scanned, enhanced, scaled, and colored on the computer. Rough preliminary ideas can be digitized and refined. The refined graphics can later be presented and shared in a digital format or printed on high-quality paper and painted in a traditional manner. 3D modeling programs allow you to create renderings that can simulate hand-drawn effects, resulting in a hand-painted sketch with precise perspective. Additionally, parts of your 3D model can be sent to a 3D printer and incorporated into a conventional model box.

FIGURE 1.3 For this scenic rendering for *Much Ado About Nothing*, a sketch rendered with a 3D modeling program was printed on suitable paper and painted in watercolors.

Modern theater practices require designers to use digital workflows for seamless integration into productions. Computer drafting is now the standard, and lighting and stage control systems are completely dependent on computers. The design process can begin with a sketched ground plan or elevation and move through drafting, digital sketches, and 3D models. Modern lighting boards can upload these lighting plots and scenic models, enabling cue writing and visualization before the construction phase. If immediate access to the lightboard isn't conveniently available, a simulated version can run on a personal computer, allowing for flexible cue writing.

DIGITAL STAGECRAFT

Exciting new integrations are transforming the design landscape in theatre and visual arts, particularly through the rise of online marketplaces for fabrics, wallpapers, and other building materials. Designers can now easily explore various materials and incorporate detailed fabric representations into their costume sketches, thereby enhancing their creativity. This technology also benefits scenic designers by allowing them to visualize patterns effectively, streamlining the design process.

Digital scenic models enable designers to represent their work dynamically and produce graphics for the quick creation of painter's elevations. These can be sent electronically to production teams and print shops, facilitating a smoother transition from design to physical production of drops and drapery for live performances with minimal lead time.

Collaboration is crucial in theatre productions, and technology has made it easier through platforms like Zoom and Microsoft Teams. Effective digital communication allows artists to share visual ideas and updates efficiently, ensuring everyone is aligned. File-sharing services also enhance access to the latest designs, enabling rapid adjustments during discussions.

Furthermore, advancements in technology enable the sharing of virtual sets and models in 3D, allowing teams to visualize and manipulate designs collaboratively. The accessibility of computer resources and affordable software fosters innovation among aspiring artists and designers. As we embrace these changes, the arts will continue evolving toward a more interconnected and dynamic creative community.

Using CGI On Stage

Acquiring skills in scenographic CGI is essential as digital imagery has become central to modern theatrical production. Today's audiences, steeped in popular culture and accustomed to rapid-fire visuals from movies and social media, expect rich, engaging experiences that resonate with their multi-sensory lifestyles.

Traditionally, theater relied on static stage pictures that limited creative possibilities. In contrast, contemporary plays often employ a cinematic flow with frequent scene shifts, reflecting the complexities of modern life. When employing traditional stagecraft for these dynamic narratives, we often resort to unit sets and lighting changes, which fail to capture the essence of modern storytelling.

To engage today's audiences, our stagecraft must evolve in tandem with the narratives we present. This means embracing technology not only for innovation but also to keep the art form relevant. Integrating CGI and digital elements thoughtfully can create immersive experiences that honor theater's legacy while also ensuring its future.

The goal is not to replicate cinema, but to redefine theatrical identity by crafting stories that resonate with today's viewers. The evolution of stagecraft is an artistic necessity and a commitment to the future of storytelling.

As Robert Edmund Jones said, "to express a timeless theme by the means of the tools of one own's time."

FIGURE 1.4 VR-based imagery was generated in real-time and projected onto the scenes using various methods in this production of Mozart's *The Magic Flute.*

Learning the Tools

This book is more than just a collection of tutorials; it aims to provide a deeper understanding of digital graphic design concepts and skills. While tutorials are valuable, particularly for beginners, they can become outdated as software evolves, much like recipes that limit creativity in cooking.

Relying solely on tutorials can lead to a narrow understanding of software, leaving you unprepared for different versions or unique projects. By learning how graphics programs handle tasks like outlining and shading, you develop the skills to critically evaluate your work and adapt techniques from various sources to suit your artistic vision.

The ability to transition between different applications enhances your creativity, allowing you to explore various media and achieve your desired outcomes. This book focuses on crucial skills for creating scenographic sketches, detailed renderings, and lighting solutions, equipping you with a versatile toolkit to thrive in diverse creative environments.

The instructions presented are not meant to be exhaustive or definitive. They are intended to impart basic procedures that can be used to create workman-like design sketches using a computer. The software being used has hundreds of additional tools that are not, and may never be, needed. With further use and exploration, one can advance from journeyman to expert, learning new techniques as needed. However, the goal is not to become an expert with CGI, but to utilize digital tools efficiently and effectively to create outstanding designs for the stage.

The lessons do not need to adhere to any one specific software or computer platform rigidly; instead, they prioritize underlying principles that transcend individual applications. Fortunately, the tools and techniques for accomplishing desired tasks exhibit striking similarities across numerous programs. While these features may present themselves with slightly different visuals, be located in distinct areas of the user interface, and bear varying names, they ultimately serve the same fundamental purpose. For example, to select parts of an image characterized by similar colors and brightness, one might utilize the "Magic Wand" tool in *Photoshop*, the "Fuzzy Selection" tool in *Gimp*, or the "Contiguous" tool in *Krita*. Similarly, to create a smooth, curvy hose shape, you could use "Loft" in *Cinema 4D* or *3DS Max*. *SketchUp* refers to a similar function as "Follow Me", while *Blender* offers options like "Profiles Along Path", "Array Object Along Curve", or "Bridge Edge Loops".

Each part of a project may require specific software, but it's important to understand how tasks can be performed across different programs. This flexibility enhances your ability to apply general principles of software operations, allowing you to adapt to any suitable application for the task at hand.

Being knowledgeable in multiple programs not only broadens your skill set but also enables smooth transitions between applications, optimizing your workflow and variety of outputs. This adaptability is especially useful in collaborative environments where colleagues may use different tools.

In situations where specific software or file types are required, having a diverse skill set helps you navigate challenges effectively. For students, familiarizing themselves with various software options prepares them for diverse professional settings and fosters an adaptable mindset.

The Book's Structure

This book is loosely patterned after a course I taught at the University of Kansas for over 20 years. Each chapter represents a week's lecture and study. An assignment was given that served as an exercise of the covered skill set.

Time permitting, additional lessons were added to provide variety and fill the semester. There was always time to experiment with the unusual 3D creator, *SketchUp*. Additionally, an alternate paint program may have been introduced, or a 3D character creator such as *MakeHuman* or Autodesk *Character Generator.* Creating a fantastic landscape with a terrain generator such as *WorldMachine* or *TerreSculptor* was always a popular project.

Following a good deal of discussion and practice with virtual sets for TV and film, the semester concluded with a final project that involved creating a virtual set for a TV news show, a sports halftime show, a children's program, or anything else the students could conceive. The "exam" consisted of the entire class meeting at a local TV studio, where they utilized the green screen to "perform" within their sets. More of a party than a test.

For the sake of continuity, most of the demonstrations here are for a small-cast version of *My Fair Lady*. This was a summer production that the director referred to as one of his "Jewel Box Productions" (read: small budget). The cast was small with the usual doubling of the chorus parts. The production featured a unit set with revolving wall units and slip-stage wagons for fast changes. Because of its compactness and the fact that it included painted wings and a rear-projection screen, it serves well as a subject for demonstrating CGI techniques.

Scenographic CGI: Software

Budget is a crucial factor for freelance designers who must balance various business costs while keeping their fees competitive. Costs include software, equipment, marketing, and office space, making it essential for newcomers to optimize these expenses.

While educational discounts are beneficial for students and educators, not all software developers offer this, and some provide limited savings. Designers need to be resourceful, exploring various applications that meet their needs without breaking their budgets. Learning multiple software platforms can provide flexibility and access to low-cost or free alternatives, enhancing profit margins.

Companies like Autodesk offer entire product lines free to students, including programs such as *3DS Max* and *AutoCAD*, which are essential for design work. Maxon also provides free products for students, including *Cinema 4D*. Adobe offers significant discounts and bundles its Creative Cloud, which includes essential tools like *Photoshop* and *Illustrator*, while Corel provides discounts on its graphic design software.

It's essential to note that student discounts typically expire upon graduation. This, in turn, leads to higher costs as freelancers transition to subscription-based models. However, many budget-friendly and open-source alternatives are available, allowing designers to minimize expenses without sacrificing quality. By exploring a mix of established and emerging tools, freelance designers can maintain creativity while ensuring their business is financially sustainable, supporting a successful freelance career.

Open-source software encompasses a vast spectrum of applications, ranging from basic utilities designed to enhance daily tasks to highly sophisticated programs that can rival, and in some cases surpass, their commercial counterparts. This diversity means that open-source solutions can be found in almost every area of technology, including operating systems, productivity tools, graphic design software, game development frameworks, and much more. Developed entirely by users, who are often passionate about their projects, open-source software is generally made available to the public at no cost, democratizing access to powerful tools that may otherwise come with hefty price tags.

A successful open-source program can give rise to numerous offshoot projects or "branches," which not only expand the software's functionalities but also cultivate a space where creativity flourishes. Many of these projects have stood the test of time, demonstrating their reliability and effectiveness across various user bases, thanks to the continuous contributions from their communities.

In addition to documentation and tutorials, many user communities gather and curate a wealth of valuable resources that can be used freely by anyone. These typically include extensive libraries filled with templates, patterns, and textures. Some include 3D objects and materials, and most provide plugins and program extensions, which can be instrumental for designers and artists looking to enhance their projects.

2 Drawing, The Start of a Sketch

FIGURE 2.1 A costume sketch can be started using a variety of methods, rough drawing, template, or research.

Creating costume sketches on a computer can be quite a challenge. Costumes and the figures they adorn are inherently organic, while computers often struggle with anything that isn't geometric. We all know that computers thrive on straight lines and flat shapes, but costume design demands a fluidity that traditional tools naturally provide. This disconnect can be frustrating for costume designers, who rely on intuitive, organic drawing processes.

DOI: 10.4324/9781003571742-2

Drawing by hand allows for the beautiful imperfections and graceful curves that perfectly capture the essence of fabric and motion – a mathematically perfect straight line can feel rigid and lifeless when we're trying to express so much more through our art. So, when transitioning to digital design, it's essential to find tools that mimic that organic feel.

The pursuit of this more organic drawing is perhaps subject to small differences from one program to the next. Although software programs generally share similarities, those subtle differences can significantly impact how a designer works, ultimately influencing their choice of tools.

Drawing and painting software typically falls into two main categories: raster graphics and vector graphics. The oldest style of painting on a computer is raster graphics, with Adobe *Photoshop* being a classic example, having been around since the dawn of personal computers.

Raster graphics programs manipulate the color of the pixels in the workspace. In painting, a "brush" alters the pixels it touches. Each brush has a specific pixel pattern, and additional modifiers such as "Flow" and "Opacity" regulate how it paints.

FIGURE 2.2 a) "Airbrush" paint brushes and pencils are defined by the pixel patterns moved around the drawing area. b) Those patterns can be seen and edited in the Brush editor panel. c) Vector graphics are manipulated by moving points. Curves are manipulated by moving the control points at each endpoint.

In vector graphics, you select points on the screen and then connect those points with straight lines or curves. These form the outline of shapes that can be filled with colors, patterns, or gradients. Programs like Adobe *Illustrator* are based on vector graphics, which are commonly used in graphic design and advertising. These graphics have a more mechanical look, perfect for creating clearly defined shapes.

There's also a variation of raster graphics that uses procedural technology, moving a mathematical formula rather than just a brush pattern of pixels. "Procedural" painting simulates traditional art tools, producing subtle differences in line quality and effective paint textures. For instance, simulated watercolor brushes can create complex color interactions, leading to effects such as colors bleeding together or settling at the "bottom" of the painting.

In the few programs that accomplish this type of sophisticated color mixing, the layer on which wet paints are applied will remain wet until you explicitly

FIGURE 2.3 Procedural paint programs create marvelous imitations of real art mediums.

command it to dry. Typically, the program will not allow you to merge layers together if one of them is still considered wet. The program that best typifies procedural painting is *Corel Painter*.

Each program style works in noticeably different ways, and designers' preferences are based on their work style. Combining different programs in a design workflow can be beneficial, as it covers various tasks such as sketching, coloring, and texturing.

Adobe *Photoshop* has long been the leader in photo retouching and 2D graphics, evolving through user input and regular feature updates. Its extensive features set a standard for other programs, leading to many alternatives that emulate its workflows.

One prominent alternative is *GIMP*, an open-source raster graphics editor used for image manipulation, editing, and free-form drawing. *GIMP* includes many *Photoshop* features and is highly customizable, benefiting from user contributions in software development and documentation.

Inkscape offers functionality similar to Adobe *Illustrator*, serving as a vector graphics editor for artistic and technical illustrations. With the ability to create precise shapes and sketches, *Inkscape* can feel intuitive for users of *Illustrator*.

Krita, similar to *Corel Painter*, focuses on replicating traditional painting tools and techniques. It specializes in realistic painting styles and emphasizes a user-friendly experience, embodying its name, inspired by the Swedish word "krita," meaning "crayon" (or chalk), and "rita," which means "to draw."

The intention of this book is to focus on techniques rather than specific instructions for any particular software. As previously mentioned, once you understand the techniques and what you want to achieve with each step, it's simply a matter of locating the corresponding buttons in any software and understanding how different techniques are named and functions are labeled.

For our costume rendering demonstrations, we will use *Krita*, which offers many features similar to those found in Painter and Photoshop, while also supporting vector graphics. It's powerful yet lightweight, available on mobile devices, and best of all, it's free.

TABLETS, PADS, AND TOUCHSCREENS

To design costumes digitally, you must tackle one fundamental yet challenging task: drawing. Using standard input devices is far from intuitive; moving a

FIGURE 2.4 Professional workflows typically use a pen-style input device. A graphics tablet, display tablet, or touchscreen.

mouse lacks the tactile familiarity of holding a crayon. The fine motor skills of traditional drawing don't easily translate to this new medium. An additional disconnect occurs as you move your hand on the desktop while seeing the result projected on the computer's screen. This challenge requires not only skill but also patience and adaptability.

This struggle brings to mind the precision of surgeons who expertly navigate procedures while monitoring results on a video screen. Their adaptability highlights the remarkable human capacity to overcome challenges.

Graphics Tablets

The most effective and often used solution to the problem is the use of graphic tablets, which offer a more intuitive interface that mimics the physical act of drawing. However, many users still experience a disconnect between drawing in one place and observing it somewhere else. It's a love-it-or-hate-it technology; some find it appealing, while others give up before exploring its potential. Experimentation is key; don't just try it for 10 minutes. Dive in repeatedly with various setups and software.

There are many tablets available, ranging from display tablets costing several hundred dollars to standard drawing tablets under $50. Many people give up on graphic tablets, leading to a plethora of barely used options available online. If possible, borrow one first to test it out for a week or two before making a purchase.

Standard graphics tablets are most common, a flat surface with a stylus. While they all have similar features, focus on finding one with express buttons for shortcuts and ensure that one is configured for "Right Mouse button" clicks, which are essential for accessing drawing tools.

Look for a pressure-sensitive stylus, as this feature distinguishes tablets from mice. The harder you press, the darker the line, mimicking real drawing tools. Quality tablets also sense stylus angle, rotation, and movement speed. Many styluses toggle to an eraser function when flipped upside down, and some models have additional buttons for reprogramming various functions.

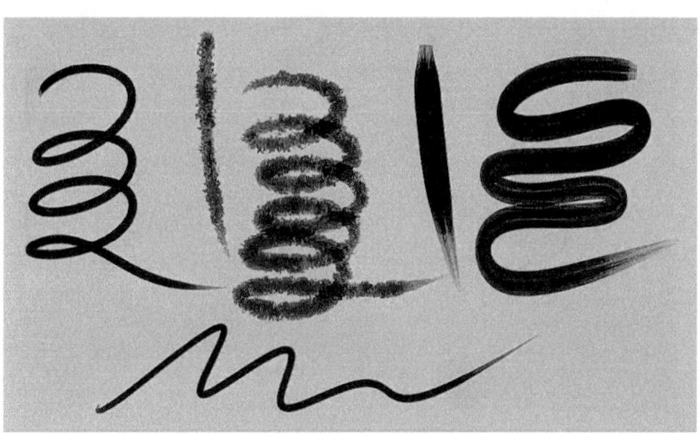

FIGURE 2.5 The pressure, rotation, and angle of the stylus can be adjusted to produce different qualities.

Pressure-sensitive styluses have become the standard and have been for quite a while now, making it hard to find a graphics tablet that does not come equipped with one.

Display Tablets

Display tablets have a built-in screen that mirrors your computer's display, thereby allowing you to draw directly on a graphic program's viewport. This creates a natural drawing experience but comes at a higher cost than standard graphics tablets. Some advanced laptops may have detachable touchscreen monitors, simulating display tablet functionality. Such laptops have a higher price tag, and the sensitivity and resolution of a touchscreen usually can't match that of a display tablet.

Mobile Devices

Mobile devices, such as smartphones or tablets, can also serve as drawing tools, offering a similar experience to display tablets at a lower price. However, their precision and computing power are limited.

Investing in a pressure-sensitive stylus can enhance working with a mobile device and typically costs around $40 to $50. Check your tablet's specifications to ensure it supports advanced input, as you'll need compatible apps to leverage pressure sensitivity.

While touchscreen tablets host good programs, high-powered graphics software is often limited to desktops or laptops. Some laptops with touchscreen capabilities can act as display tablets, but this is rare and typically more expensive.

You can also connect mobile tablets to computers via USB or Bluetooth, but compatibility varies. Direct connections may only support file transfers, not real-time data swapping. For real-time use, appropriate software is often required on both devices – consider using bridging apps like *Virtual Tablet, AstroPad, Super Display*, or *Weylus* to enhance compatibility.

FIGURE 2.6 Tablets and touchscreens have the advantage of allowing users to create sketches beneath the point of the stylus.

Stylus

Any graphic tablet is ineffective without a stylus. This pen-like input device mimics traditional tools such as pencils, pens, markers, paintbrushes, and airbrushes. Styluses vary in type, reflecting different technologies. Some tablets require a specific type, while others work with more generic sorts.

The simplest option is the passive capacitive stylus. This basic pen connects your hand to the drawing surface, allowing a touchscreen to detect input as if your finger were touching it, but focused on a small point. Therefore, it is much more precise, giving the sensation of using a pen.

Using an Android or iOS tablet as a graphics tablet is convenient and affordable, although setup can vary depending on the software and stylus used. You can use a capacitive stylus on an iPad like you would on your phone.

In contrast, an active stylus resembles a standard pen but contains internal electronics that provide a charge to the tip. This clarifies the drawing and allows for palm rejection, so you can rest your hand on the surface without making inadvertent input. Active styluses need charging through a USB port.

Universal styluses, which are also capacitive, don't require your hand to make a connection. They have rechargeable batteries and can provide adequate palm rejection. If your palm interferes, consider wearing a glove or using an insulating pad.

Not all apps are created equal for stylus use, so you may need to experiment. Universal styluses usually work fine, but may not be compatible with all applications and their various brush types.

Pressure-sensitive styluses, ranging from $30 to $50, are available for mobile tablets but may not be supported by all devices or apps. Check the specifications and reviews to ensure compatibility. You'll need both the app and the tablet to support pressure-sensitive input for the best experience.

Using a Graphics Tablet

There are several effective ways to enhance your experience with graphics tablets and make drawing feel more natural. A great first step is to cover the tablet with a sheet of drawing paper. The magnetic field of the stylus will operate through the paper, providing a surface that mimics traditional media and significantly improves your comfort while drawing.

A screen protector with a paper-like surface is another valuable addition, protecting the tablet while providing the right amount of friction to mimic drawing on real paper. This added texture improves control and accuracy.

If you have a rough sketch, such as an initial idea for a costume design, you can place it on the tablet and trace over it with your stylus. This not only helps in refining your ideas but also captures intricate details without losing the essence of your concept.

Some advanced tablets, like the iSKN Repaper, allow you to use a real pen or pencil. This system tracks the pencil's movements, providing an authentic drawing experience. You can start by putting a blank paper on top of the tablet or drawing over an existing rough sketch, generating both traditional and digital sketches simultaneously.

When setting up your tablet, ensure it's directly in front of you and aligned squarely. If it's misaligned, even by a few degrees, it can lead to frustration and inaccuracies. Maintaining a consistent relationship between your position, tablet, and monitor is essential for an optimal drawing experience. Many users prefer keeping the tablet and monitor in a straight alignment for a more intuitive workflow.

Watch your posture while drawing, especially during long work sessions. Sitting upright, with your feet on the ground and arms comfortably resting, can help reduce fatigue. Regular breaks are also beneficial for maintaining focus and comfort.

Many mistakenly think they need to press the side switch on the pen to activate its functions. This is generally not the case. The side switch's functions can vary, but they often default to features like "Right Click" or "Pan/Scroll". A light tap of the pen on the tablet is all it takes for a simple click. The tip of the pen is your clicker.

Focus on the screen rather than your hand or the tablet. Your hand doesn't dictate where your drawing goes; the screen does. By training yourself to look at the screen, you'll improve your accuracy and overall efficiency in creating artwork.

WORKING FROM A FOUNDATION

Sketching is not much different whether you're doing a traditional painted rendering, a digital painted rendering, scene painting a large drop, or anything else. You first need to start with a sketch to provide the outlines, the basic foundation for the rest of the painted rendering. Many designers prefer to invest a great deal of work in the sketch, allowing it to support the rest of the rendering. In this workflow, the details are depicted primarily in the drawing, and the subsequent painting mainly provides color information. In this way, they work similarly to artists like Andrew Wyeth or Degas.

Others prefer to have a very light sketch in the background and do more opaque painting over the top, resembling the work of Rembrandt or other similar artists. Interestingly, or unfortunately, just getting the sketch going and entering the digital drawing process can be one of the more challenging tasks. Starting off with a blank canvas and drawing in a fluid manner to initiate the sketch can be quite challenging. Again, this simply takes practice and a certain amount of confidence. Creating a freehand line drawing in a computer program can be a bit difficult, which is where having a graphics tablet offers a significant advantage over using a mouse or trackpad.

Pencil Sketches

There are several ways to get the costume sketch started. The first is to mix media: start with a pencil sketch on paper. (Yes, a piece of paper.) While having skills in digital media is fantastic and up-to-date, and has all the advantages mentioned earlier, possessing basic studio skills, such as drawing, is invaluable. Being able to draw with a pencil can be liberating; it also enhances your communication skills and your eye for various details that you observe in the world, rather than just looking down at a monitor. Additionally, it is simply an enjoyable pastime.

Starting a costume sketch with pencil work is a standard technique that has been widely used for several decades. It is still probably the most common way to get things started. You might create some early sketches while in conference with your collaborators or do it privately with your research materials around you. In any case, you can decide how far you want to take the first sketches – whether it's just the rudiments, the very rough bones of a costume design, or if you wish to flesh it out considerably by adding more detail.

When you're ready to move it into the digital realm, there are some obvious methods for doing that. One is to use a flatbed scanner. Once considered a rare piece of equipment, scanners are now standard in most workspaces. Often, printers come with a built-in scanner, which is very convenient and usually results in high-quality scans. The resolution may depend on the initial cost of the scanner. If that method appeals to you, it will inform how much you want to invest in that kind of equipment in the future.

Scanning software is typically built into the computer's system and is supported right out of the box, making it just a matter of opening a window and clicking a few times. A typical scanner will handle letter or even legal-sized documents, though there are scanners available that can accommodate larger sizes.

Another option is to use a cell phone. Cell phone cameras are very good for this task; they typically have higher resolution than you would find in a flatbed scanner. While it can be a bit inconvenient, taking a moment to set up before you start can make a significant difference in achieving a perfectly clean photoscan.

Once you have several pencil sketches ready to be entered, find a spot with very good lighting, preferably sunlight coming in at a forward angle of about 45 degrees. Make sure there are no dark corners in the pencil sketch to be scanned. Even a small difference may not look like much to the naked eye, but once scanned, it can be fairly obtrusive.

It's worth the time and money to use a tripod. A tripod attachment that will hold a smartphone is easy to find and inexpensive. These typically fit most sizes and brands of phones and are quick and easy to set up. With the tripod, it becomes much easier to ensure that the phone is positioned directly over the center of the sketch and perpendicular to it, avoiding any keystone distortion.

Taking pictures is then a matter of capturing two or three shots of each pencil sketch, perhaps with the light coming from different directions. Start by taking a set of pictures from one direction, then turn the sketch and tripod setup to a slightly different angle and take another set. This process doesn't cost anything but a bit of space in the phone's memory.

There is scanning software designed explicitly for this task. These apps can automatically straighten unusual angles and rotations in the images, resulting in a polished final product with no further action required on your part.

For Android phones, you can use Google's *PhotoScan* software. However, be aware that Google's *PhotoScan* may not work at a high resolution. There are some modded versions available for download that do scan in full resolution, as well as some commercial third-party products that scan directly. These apps are often designed to automatically upload images to a cloud server, such as Google Photos or iCloud, but you can easily bypass that if desired.

Always aim to scan at the highest resolution possible, as you will want to work on the sketches on the computer at that same high resolution. Remember, while the resolution can be lowered at any time, raising it will not improve its quality.

FIGURE 2.7 Sketches can begin with pencil sketches, templates of research images.

Templates

Many costume designers begin their sketches with a figure template, which is an outline of the body that provides the correct proportions as a starting point. Numerous templates are available online or in books, and you can create your own by sketching the outline of a figure using the seven-head-tall rule, then scanning it for digital use.

After downloading a template, open it in *Krita* or drag and drop it onto an open sketch. An option dialog will open, asking if the template should be added as a layer of the sketch or a new, separate document. Either can work. If the open sketch is set to the right size, resolution, and aspect, add the template as a layer. Start your pencil sketch on this outline, then scan it back to your computer for further editing. It's smart to have a variety of templates with different poses to avoid a rigid look in your sketches.

Search for templates that showcase a diverse range of body types. Be careful not to select overly stylized fashion figures. Instead, opt for templates with standard proportions for most projects. Having a stock of templates with realistic body shapes will speed up the workflow.

Costume sketches often depict youthful characters, but it's essential to represent a range of shapes: short, tall, overweight, or skinny. For instance, you need a template for overweight figures for characters like Falstaff, and one resembling an older woman for Juliet's Nurse. Templates for children are also necessary; you can't design "The Music Man" without Winthrop.

An unusual yet useful source for figure templates is the works of Renaissance Masters like Michelangelo, Da Vinci, and Raphael. Their drawings feature unique characters and outstanding line quality. Although a "Michelangelo" template may not end up in your final design, his exceptional drawing can inspire your work in a truly fantastic style.

Research Templates

In using templates as a drawing aid for initial sketches, additional methods can help jump-start your work. Research images can serve as a foundation for your drawings.

Before sketching, you've no doubt researched the historic period, milieu, or style of the production. Use these research images to support your initial sketches. Research is crucial in the design process, especially in costume design. Don't try to reinvent period costumes from whole cloth (pun intended), use your research.

As we craft a message for our audiences – a concept – we must recognize that both designer and audience share cultural conditioning. No production exists without a style, rooted in these cultural norms. The right research gives you a basis for making choices that align with that style.

Without research, the design may feel lost, meandering from scene to scene and character to character without a cohesive aesthetic. Once you settle on a specific style, whether a historic period or a distinct set of textures and colors, the production gains the glue needed for a unified look.

Developing research skills takes experience. You'll learn where to look and which sources are most useful. These may include books, museum photographs, or inspiring finds online. As you compile references for your costume, cut these research artifacts into smaller pieces when necessary and use them as an underlayer for your drawing to achieve the right silhouette.

Graphic programs can trace the edges of selected objects, while AI tools can convert photographs into line drawings or sketches. If this suits your needs, upload a picture, turn it into a line drawing, and integrate it into your custom sketch as necessary.

Complete research should also include colors and textures. This will influence choices of fabric, prints, and patterns that will go into your sketches and ultimately, into your designs.

Posable Figures

Another method of starting a sketch is to use a poseable figure using software designed specifically for that purpose. There are posing programs that can be downloaded and run on your computer, as well as several online sites where you can pose figures and then either download an image or make a screen capture. While some online sites may require membership, many also offer free versions that are more than sufficient for our needs.

Some of the best posing software includes mobile apps, and there are actually more posing apps available for mobile devices than for Windows and iOS computers.

The best posing software often provides options for altering body shape, allowing you to make characters shorter, taller, heavier, or thinner. They typically come with a menu of preset poses, and some even feature preset scenes with multiple characters and furniture props. All posing software allows you to click on various joints in the figure's body, enabling you to rotate the joints and create figure templates tailored to your project.

You then export an image of the figure, download the results, and build up an entire stash that you can pull from in the future. Examples of some good software include:

TABLE 2.1 There are many available applications/sites for posing human models and creating figure templates.

Application	Type	Source
PosemyArt	Online	https://posemy.art
Just Sketch Me	App and Online	https://justsketch.me
Elldrich Foundry	Online	https://creator.eldritch-foundry.com
Make Human	App	http://www.makehumancommunity.org/
Mixamo	Online	https://www.mixamo.com/#/
Phone Apps		
MagicPoser		
Poseit		
Pose Maker Pro		
JustSketchMe		

BASIC PRACTICES

As you work, it's important to save multiple copies of your project for safety and to allow for experimentation without compromising your progress. Make it a habit to save your work every time you start something new or every

15 minutes. Additionally, save a copy of the project with a version number or the date in the file name.

As you hone your design skills, you'll also hone your computer studio skills. It is important to be able to turn out a costume sketch in around two hours. If you are working on a large-cast musical like My Fair Lady, with all the changes, the costume count comes to 150. That's 300 hours of sketching. You can anticipate that when you're first getting accustomed to computer sketching skills, it will take a bit longer, but with practice, you will quickly work up to speed.

Customize the Workspace

With any software that involves using a workspace, it's important to configure that workspace right off the bat in a way that works best for you. This may involve placing settings, toolbars, and palette sets in locations that you're accustomed to from using other programs in the past, or it may mean setting up configurations that align with your individual workflow. You may have certain habits and tools that you use more than others, and these may not be reflected in available presets, so it's crucial to learn how to customize. Every program made today has a configurable workspace and a customizable graphical user interface that you can arrange for comfort and, more importantly, to make working as fast and efficient as possible.

If there are certain tools that you use more frequently, consider placing those on the side of the workspace closest to your dominant hand. This way, you won't have to constantly cross over the entire drawing surface to grab a favorite tool. Additionally, if there are certain commands and menu items you use often, consider bringing those commands to the workspace in the form of buttons or palettes to avoid pulling down menus repeatedly. Most graphic programs are divided into the drawing area or viewport, accompanied by a toolbar that runs across the top or bottom of the screen, housing major commands as well as system commands for opening and saving files.

Furthermore, programs will have their main features divided into categories of function and organized into palettes and toolbars. While names may change from program to program, their functionality is essentially the same. In most programs, you can arrange the palettes and toolbars by moving them to the edges and docking them to keep them fixed in that position, or you might prefer leaving them floating to easily move them out of the way. Palettes can often be arranged in sets of tabs so that they share the same space in the workspace but open one after the other rather than all at once.

Your choices regarding how many palettes and managers are open at one time may depend significantly on your screen size. Using a laptop may prompt you to make more palettes that can be closed, while a large desktop monitor might call for having all the palettes you need open simultaneously. Toolbars vary slightly from program to program in size and the items they carry. Typically, they are divided into segments with dividers or spacers interspersed between sets of tools.

Always Work in High Resolution

You can always reduce the size later, but increasing it won't improve the quality. Working in a high-res sketch will allow you to zoom in and work on details. Adding filters to sharpen or blur areas works much better when the program has more pixels to work with. Even brightness and contrast are more effective in high-res.

Get Accustomed to Using Multiple Layers

If you create lots of layers, you will be able to edit every step in the process individually. Make a new layer for every step of the sketching process and for every piece of the costume. Later, you can turn layers on and off as you see fit. You can reorder the layers to bring certain colors or tints on top of others, certain parts of drawings or textures over others. Also, each layer can be controlled in terms of its opacity or the method of blending over the layers that are below it.

Using multiple layers is a good backup practice as well. You can create copies of layers, lock them, and make them invisible. This way, if something goes wrong with your current layer, you can simply discard it and revert to the original copy to continue your drawing.

Always make a copy of your initial sketch so you can refer back to it later.

There are various methods for copying layers, but the simplest way is to click the "Duplicate layer or mask" button at the bottom of the Layers docker (Ctrl + J).

Since you're working at a high resolution, feel free to zoom in on certain areas to make it easier to work. Just remember not to stay zoomed in for too long, as you might end up focusing on tiny details that won't significantly impact the overall appearance of the sketch and may waste valuable time. A general rule to keep in mind is to work quickly to maintain your momentum.

THE KRITA INTERFACE

When you first open *Krita*, you'll see an arrangement similar to other drawing and painting programs – a basic set of tools on the upper left side where you can choose brushes and tools for drawing geometric shapes. The selection tools are there as well, along with tools for easily moving, rotating, or cropping images. Below that are the "Brush" presets, featuring many predefined brushes that come with the first installation of the program. These can be divided into tags or subsets of brushes so that not all of them have to be open at the same time. Brushes can also be downloaded from the *Krita* website or from the libraries of other users. There's a certain amount of pride and creativity involved in creating optional brush sets.

On the upper right side, you'll find several usual palettes and windows. Some are already arranged in tabs. There's a color selector, which you can configure to whichever type of selector you prefer, along with another window for tool options. Every time you select a tool from the sets on the left, the various options for that tool will appear in the tool option palette. Below on the right side are crucial windows showing a graphic representation of all the layers you create while making a graphic image, with a channel tab next to it to display individual channels like the red, green, and blue channels, along with any special transparency or overlay channels that may be created. This layout is inspired by *Photoshop*.

All of this is customizable. On the upper right of each individual palette is an icon that, when clicked, will float the palette or detach it from its docking position. All of these individual palettes or workspaces are called dockers in *Krita*. Once free from its position, a docker can be moved around to another part of the workspace and redocked by holding it up against the desired position until a white line appears. If you position a docker directly over another docker, the highlighted docker will become a tab of the first docker when you release it. All dockers can be resized through the usual method of grabbing an edge until the resize icon appears and moving back and forth.

The Brush Tool

So much of achieving the look you want in digital painting comes down to the simple selection of a brush or a brush setting. In the most basic terms, brushes are configurations of pixels that you'll be moving around the screen to change the color of the pixels they interact with. You can change the brush's size – how many pixels wide or in diameter is the area you want to use? What is the shape of the brush? Is it round, rectangular, or a scattered collection of dots?

Then there are variations: circles can be transformed into ovals or ellipses, and the squares into rectangles with variable heights and widths, or different ratios? How many variations of the collections of dots do you need? Following that, the basic controls for a brush will affect the outcome.

Opacity

The first is opacity: will the new color completely cover what was underneath, or will it be set to a certain level of translucency?

Flow

Most brushes can also be controlled for their flow, which indicates the speed at which the paint is released. How quickly will the translucency turn into opacity?

Smoothing

Next up is a very useful setting for smoothing. Smoothing will convert the jittery lines that come from using an input device into more graceful arcs. While smoothing can be extremely helpful, it needs to be used moderately, as it can slow down the process. The program has to see where you drew the line, figure out what you were aiming for, and then decide how to smooth it out.

In *Krita*, there are three different smoothing settings available. In the tool options for each brush, you'll see options for normal, weighted, and an additional setting that can be modified with various variables, ranging from no effect at all to a significant amount.

Delving deeper into brush specifics, you'll find that they can deliver color in a variety of ways, often mimicking natural art materials, allowing your lines and colors to emulate pencil, ink, acrylic paint, oil, or watercolor. Before diving into serious sketching on the computer, it's a great idea to spend some time trying out all the different options in the brush palette.

The first set of brushes features lovely, colored icon graphics to give you an idea of their functions. When you hover the cursor over them, the name will appear.

Then, there's a middle set of tools, which includes the erasers. Different types and shapes of erasers yield different effects.

The blending tools come next, which will affect the colors already on the surface, using stumps, smudges, and similar techniques.

There are also tools for stamping or sliding that create various cool effects, and others that apply patterns in a scattering manner – great for creating floral designs. If you don't find what you need, you can select a similar tool, then open the brush editing window by clicking the "Brush Editor" icon in the toolbar or shortcut F5.

The Brush Editor

At first glance, the brush editor may seem quite daunting, but keep in mind that *Krita* is primarily designed for use with a tablet. Therefore, the majority of brush settings are tablet-specific, allowing for various interactions based on parameters like brush pressure, tilt, and more. Many of these settings will depend on the type of tablet you're using and your own personal preferences. It will take a good amount of trial and error, along with some slight tweaks to each parameter, to find the formula that works for you. **There are dozens of options and parameters that you will never need.**

Of course, one should at least be familiar with the main parameters that define the brush shape and characteristics.

- Select a brush in the presets panel.
- Open the "Brush Editor" by clicking its icon in the toolbar (or F5).
- The editor is divided into three columns.
    - The first is a small version of the brush presets.
    - The second column is a list of categories of editable options.
    - The third is an interactive panel where each individual setting can be manipulated.

The first category of settings is the general category, including color, texture, and masked brushes. The first setting in the General category is the most important:

- "Brush Tip". Here you will see a footprint preview of how the brush will touch the painting surface and many options for customizing it.
- "Blending Mode". Blending modes can be applied to individual brushes, not just layers. In the options, you'll see the usual settings that you would also find in the layer settings. Once again, trial and error can lead to some surprising results.
- "Opacity".
- "Flow". Here, you can create interesting effects by tweaking the curve graphs, but remember, most of these settings deal with input from the graphics tablet and depend on the capabilities and settings of that tablet.

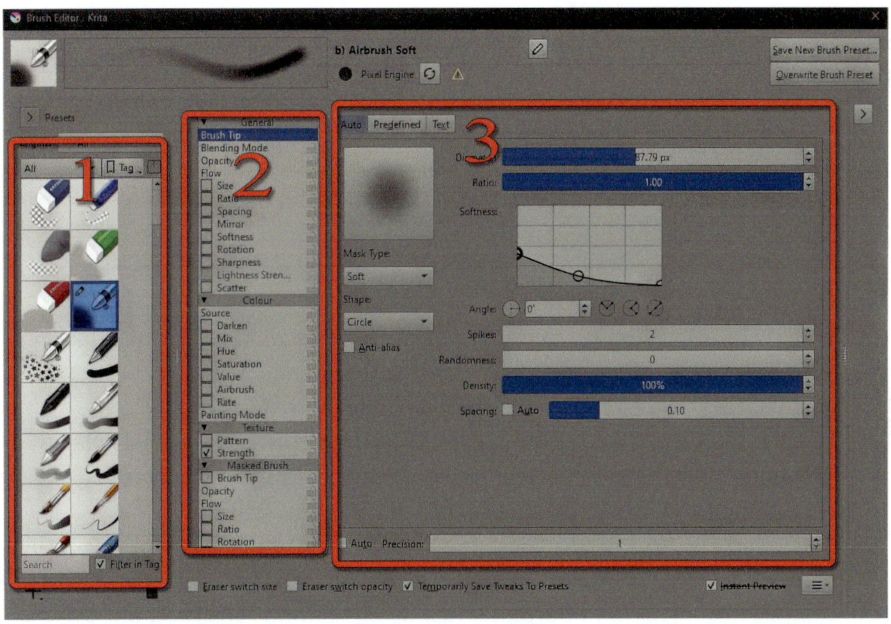

FIGURE 2.8 The Brush Editor's settings.

When you want a new brush, it's still more efficient to start with an existing brush that's close to what you're looking for. After that, you can edit and save it as if it were a new brush.

- Select a brush in the presets panel.
- Select a brush that is most similar to the brush you are looking for.
- Start with the first and most perceptible of the brushes' attributes, the brush tip.

General Settings

Brush Tip

- Properties panel tabs.
  - "Auto" is for customizations.
  - "Predefined" opens a palette of useful brush tip presets.
  - "Text" – Don't bother.
- Take a look at the bush tip presets. Select the most useful.
- Reopen the "Auto" panel.

At the top is the footprint preview of the tip.

- Go down to the "Shape" dropdown and select "Circle" or "Square".
- Click "Anti-Alias" to give the brush a slight blur at the edges that will remove the "jaggies".
  - Jaggies are the jagged edges that result from painting on square pixels. (When working at high resolution, neither the Jaggies nor the Anti-Aliasing are noticeable.)
- The "Diameter" slider controls the size of the brush tip.
- "Ratio": flattens or elongates the shape, changing a circle to an ellipse or a square to a rectangle.
- The "Fade" sliders make the edges of the shape gradually softer and more translucent.
  - This is the property that gives the airbrushes their distinctive quality.
- "Angle": turns ellipses or rectangles to a designated angle.
  - This is key to setting up a calligraphic pen or brush.
- "Spikes": changes a circle to a star shape. A simple ellipse has 2 spikes.
- "Density": determines if all the pixels in the brush tip shape deliver paint or if the shape consists of bristles spaced apart from each other.
- "Spacing": In *Bforartists*, brushes deliver paint to the surface with a curious stutter. Spacing sets the distance between the paint stamps. Zero is a continuous flow. This is important when using "Stamp" brushes, but can yield interesting effects with any brush.

Now select the "Predefined" tab of the properties panel.

A palette of eccentric brush tips appears.

- Select a good profile.
- Use the settings to the right for:
  - "Size".
  - "Rotation".
  - "Spacing".
  - These can be changed as you work with the Brush Tool Options, or with the pop-up (right-click) widget.

The additional settings for "Brush Mode" only work with brushes of the RGBA type. That type of brush can be identified in the presets by the small multi-color tag in the upper-right corner. Or they can be isolated in the previews by changing the dropdown at the top to RGBA.

Those settings are used to alter the grayscale of those brushes with the usual "Brightness", "Contrast", and "Neutral Point".

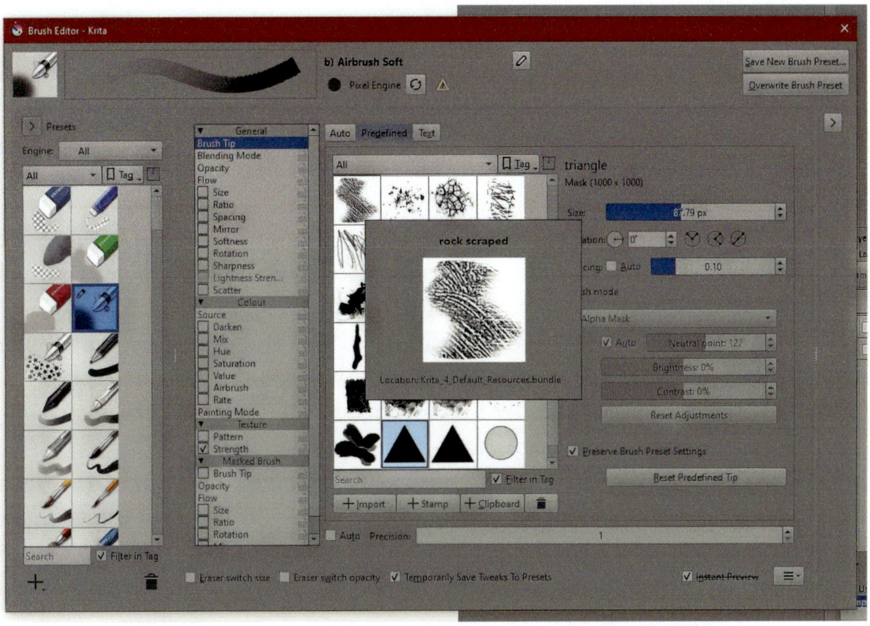

FIGURE 2.9 The Predefined brush tips offer options that would be difficult to make with the "Auto" tools.

Blending Mode

In *Krita*, brushes can have a blending mode similar to that of layers. If you know you're going to use a brush specifically to darken, lighten, or overlay material beneath, you can assign a blending mode to the brush. Once the blending mode has been set, changing it requires you to reopen the editor and repeat the process. Also, you can't easily change the blending of any painting that has already been done with that brush.

- It's generally more useful to open an empty paint layer, set that layer to your desired blending mode, and then paint on it with any brush you choose.

If you later decide to make a change, it's much easier to change the blending modes of layers than it is for brushes.

Color Settings

Source

In the color category, the first entry is "Source". There are six sources to choose from. Each option is toggled on and off with a checkbox.

- The default setting is "Plain Color", and it does exactly what you think it does.
- "Gradient" allows the brush to paint in whichever gradient is selected in the toolbar.
  - Because it uses more than a single color, the "Mix" parameter must be checked. The Mix variables are largely tablet and stylus-dependent, so you will need to experiment with different stylus movements and switch configurations.
- "Pattern" scores a 12 on the cool-o-meter!
  - This is the magic that turns a regular brush into a pattern brush.
  - You don't need to choose a specific pattern when you create the brush; it will paint whatever pattern is active in the Pattern Docker.
  - Any fabric swatches or textures added to the Pattern presets can be painted onto costume pieces instead of being dumped with the Paint Bucket.
  - This can be used not only for patterns, but also for textures, distressing, background paper, or canvas – anything you wish.

Next to the pattern selections, there is a version of the pattern palette. Adjoining that is a tab with options for changing the pattern's scale and rotation, giving you greater control over the pattern brushes you're creating.

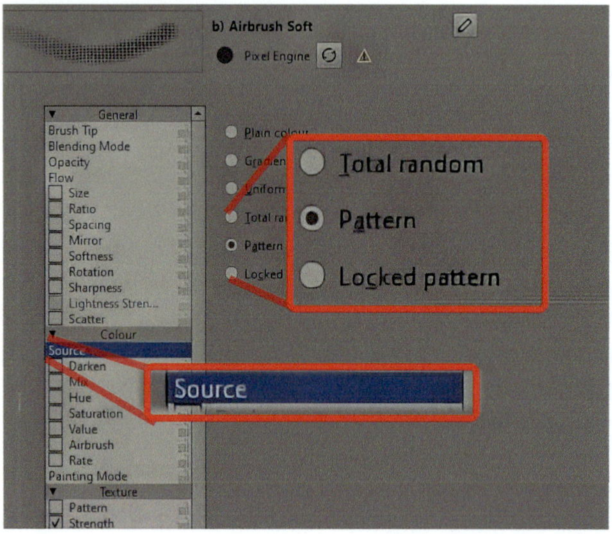

FIGURE 2.10 The "Pattern" option enables a brush to utilize patterns, textures, photos, or any other graphic file.

Texture Settings

Pattern

The first and most useful texture option is "Pattern". This shouldn't be confused with the pattern used in the color settings. When this is checked, a selected pattern creates the appearance that the paint, chalk, pastel, or charcoal is being applied to a textured surface. This brush option is fantastic for giving the illusion of using real traditional drawing tools on textured surfaces.

In the options panel for "Textures" is the small version of the "Pattern" presets. There are many useful choices, like canvas and paper. And just as with color patterns, you can always import your own. The patterns usually used as texture are presented in grayscale because that's all you need to indicate a rough surface over which to paint.

Once again, there is an adjoining tab with options for changing the pattern's scale and rotation. Just like any other pattern, it can be customized for scale and rotation. And there are additional settings for "Brightness", "Contrast", and "Neutral Point". These settings affect the brightness and intensity of the pattern, and therefore determine how rough and three-dimensional the texture appears.

- "Texture" > Check "Pattern".
- Properties Panel > "Texture" tab > Select the pattern you want to use.
- Properties Panel > "Options" tab > Set the "Scale", "Brightness", "Contrast", and "Neutral point".
    - **With every adjustment, test the brush on the drawing.** You don't need to wait until after the brush is saved or the brush editor is closed.

If you wish to edit the pattern in the texture settings, you must reopen the brush editor. Simply clicking on another texture in the Pattern docker won't do the trick.

Save the New or Edited Brush

Save any changes by overwriting the brush's default settings or creating a completely new brush.

- Select one of the "Save" buttons in the upper-right corner of the editor.
    - "New Brush Preset" opens a save dialog.
- Give the brush a descriptive name.
    - The lower-case letter preceding the name determines where the new brush will be located among the other preset icons. Similar brushes are grouped by sharing the same letter.

- Select an option to reuse the existing icon, load an image from your computer, or open the Icon Library that contains many basic images.
    - The new icon image will open in a scratchpad.
- Adjust the hue, saturation, and gray level of the new icon.
- Apply stickers from the palette or paint with a brush.
- Click "Save".

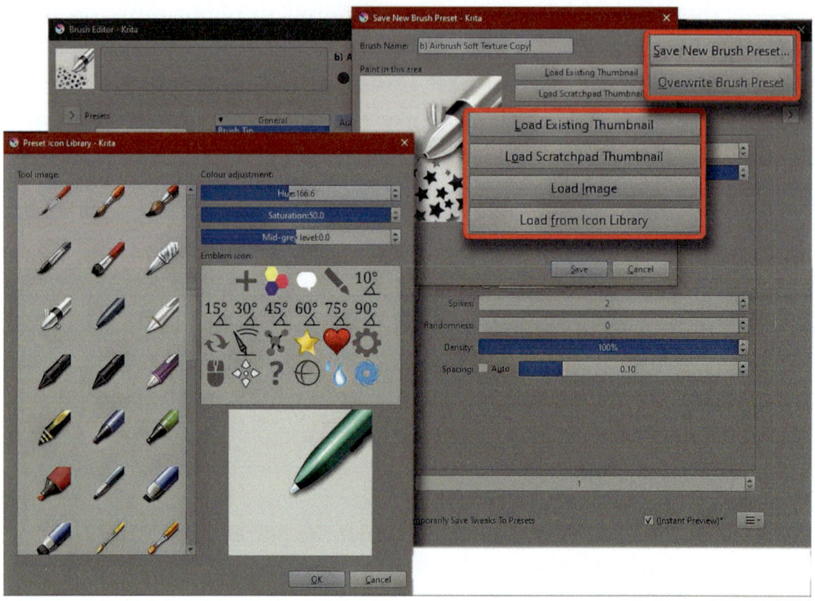

FIGURE 2.11 As you save brush presets, your custom library will grow.

The Pop-Up Palette

Right-click anywhere in the viewport to open the pop-up palette. This incredibly useful and convenient tool brings many of the most-used settings together and saves having to search and select buttons spread around the workspace. You have quick access to:

- Right-click on the canvas.
    - A color selector and color history.
    - Current foreground and background colors.
    - Brush presets.
    - Zoom, rotate, and mirror the canvas.
- Open the additional "Brush Options".
    - Resize and rotate the brush.
    - Flip the brush angle horizontally or vertically.
    - Adjust the brush's "Flow", "Spacing", and "Opacity".

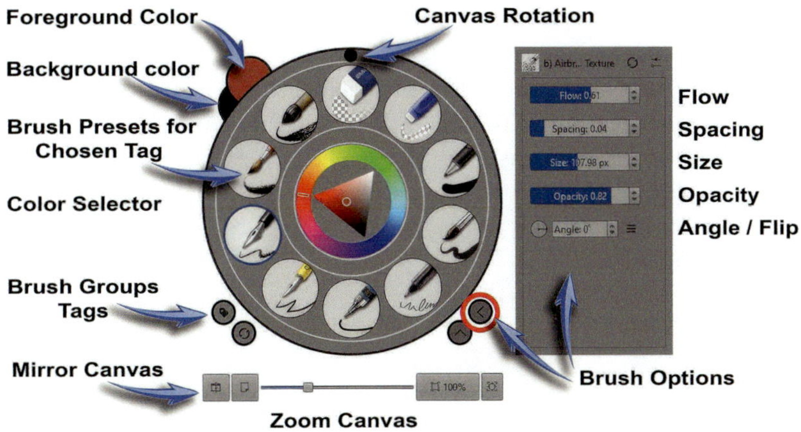

FIGURE 2.12 The pop-up palette with the brush options opened.

START DRAWING

Setting Up a New Sketch

On opening the software to start a new drawing, you'll see a window for setting the new drawing's size. There are many presets for standard documents and fields for entering custom dimensions. Use the custom field, a ratio of approximately 4:7. Try 3,400px by 6,000px for a start. This is a handy size because legal-size paper is around that ratio. Therefore, sketches can be printed on standard-size paper.

Open your pencil sketch or template with menu commands or drag-and-drop, and it's time to start editing, adding, and making changes. Before drawing over the rough draft, template, or research items, save a backup.

- Duplicate the layers.
- Group them.
- Turn off their visibility.
- Make a new paint layer.
- Select a brush to begin your drawing.

Choose a tool that has an interesting line quality, preferably one that resembles calligraphy. This type of tool typically starts with a thin line, becomes thicker in the middle, and then tapers off as you lift the stylus. These variations will be more pronounced if you're using a pressure-sensitive stylus, but they should still be noticeable to some degree regardless of the stylus you choose.

Using a calligraphic pen nib, you'll notice that the width of the line changes depending on the direction you move. When you draw in one direction, you create a thicker line, and when you shift at a 90-degree angle, the line becomes thinner. This is essential to avoid producing a dull, uniform outline in your sketch that resembles a bent coat-hanger.

Study the works of the masters, like Michelangelo and Leonardo, the delicate drawings underlying Andrew Wyeth's watercolor landscapes, and the rich line quality evident in Edgar Degas's paintings. Their work highlights how engaging and varied line quality can elevate a drawing. It's crucial that your drawing doesn't appear as if you simply held a crayon and traced around the figures like you were stirring a pot.

FIGURE 2.13 The drawing styles of a) Rembrandt, b) Degas, and c) Michelangelo.

Work with confidence and move briskly. Quick strokes will help you avoid the little wiggles and shaky lines that often occur when you're overly cautious. Developing confidence with your drawing tools will enable you to draw quickly and fluidly without hesitation.

Just like in traditional drawing, avoid approaching the line timidly by using many small, tentative strokes that create a fuzzy outline. This "hen-scratching" may keep the line moving in the right direction, but it can appear insecure and unprofessional. It's perfectly fine not to hit the line perfectly. As you draw, feel free to adjust the line if you think it needs to shift a bit to one side or the other. Having multiple lines is completely acceptable; it reveals the artist's hand and can even create a subtle, rounded, three-dimensional effect. Look at the multiple lines in masterpieces, such as the sketches of Michelangelo.

You might start with a lighter, more transparent line or one with less opacity. As you refine your drawing, you can make the line darker or thicker where needed. Remember to work quickly and avoid trying for perfection. Don't constantly switch to an eraser. Graphics tablets make it very tempting to flip the stylus and begin erasing. Program a tablet pad for "Undo", but it's better to forge ahead, then create a new layer to hold a more refined drawing.

Not everything needs to be outlined with a hard, definitive line. Some elements can be left more open-ended, allowing the viewer's eye to fill in the gaps during the painting stage.

There are no drawing weaknesses that can't be fixed with practice. With pencil and paper or computer and monitor, you'll be drawing with confidence in no time. Until then, if you don't have the confidence, fake it.

3 Painting the Sketch

FIGURE 3.1 Efficiently painting a sketch can be broken down into a few uniform steps: drawing, blocking, texturing, and toning.

Before painting over the template or any research items, create a new layer to preserve a clean version of the source material. Once the drawing is well in hand, make a copy of it. If there are any parts of the template or research that are being used in the final drawing, select those sections, copy, and paste them

DOI: 10.4324/9781003571742-3

into new layers. Group all the old layers together and give that group a suitable name. Make it invisible and lock it, so it can't be opened unintentionally.

MAKING A TRANSPARENT SKETCH

To simplify your workflow, merge any drawing, template, and research layers that are still being used. Copy that layer and convert it to a transparent layer that only shows the lines. Having a copy of your sketch, particularly a pencil drawing that is either transparent or translucent, can be incredibly beneficial. If you maintain a layer that consists solely of the pencil and no background, you can overlay it on top of any new layers that follow. This approach ensures that everything stays perfectly aligned, no matter how many layers you create. Separating the pencilwork as its own layer allows you to enhance the drawing aspect of your sketch, whether you want to emphasize it boldly or subtly, all depending on how you adjust the brightness, contrast, and opacity of that layer.

Incorporating this pencil layer into your final rendering can impart a beautiful watercolor effect to the surrounding colors and patterns, giving the sketch a more precise appearance and adding intricate details to costume pieces that might otherwise be challenging to manage. Think about the works of Degas and Wyeth – though the drawing isn't overtly prominent, its presence provides an edge to the colored areas, rendering them controlled and thoughtfully composed.

Take all the layers that are to be included in the final sketch and merge them into a single layer. Make a copy of this layer; it will be the one you begin working on. You can create more copies if needed.

- Start with your initial sketch, whether it's scanned or created digitally. If there are multiple layers, merge them using right-click options or the Layers Options menu at the bottom of the Layers docker.
- Make a copy of the layer.
- Adjust the brightness and contrast with the Color Adjustment Curve filter to get the desired level of black and gray in your outline.
- Select All and copy the image.
- With the "Add Layer" button, add a transparent mask to the layer.
- Paste your image.
    - Edit menu > "Paste into Active Layer".
    - This transparent mask will generate an alpha channel where blacks appear transparent and whites opaque, the opposite of what is needed.
- Invert the colors after the transparent mask loads.
- Filter menu > Adjust > "Invert" (Ctrl + I).
    - Now, only the blacks and grays are visible, and you can see through your drawing to the artwork beneath while continuing to paint.

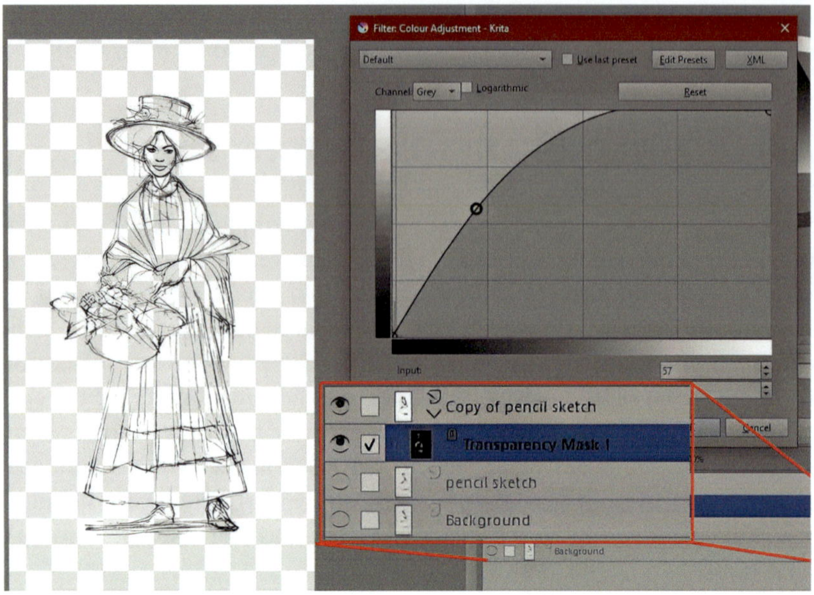

FIGURE 3.2 A transparent mask is one way to make a transparent overlay of the initial sketch. Even a rough sketch of Eliza's costume for Act I, scene 1, can add to the look of the final rendering.

Optionally, convert a layer directly to a transparent mask.

- Make a copy of the drawing layer.
- Make another copy to become the Transparent mask.
- Layer menu > Convert > "Convert to Transparency Mask".
  - The layer will become a mask and attach itself to the next layer below it.
- Invert it, and it's done.

There is a third option. While quick and easy, it is not quite as controllable as the Transparency mask. You can make a quick test to see if it works for your sketch.

- Make a copy of the drawing layer.
- Filter menu > Colors > "Color to Alpha".
  - A color picker triangle will appear.
- Pick the background color that you want to be invisible.
- The "Tolerance" slider sets the number of shades close to the chosen color that will become transparent.

That's it. No masks, just a layer containing the lines of your drawing.

COLORS

Now it's time to start adding some colors to your artwork. The first crucial step is to fill in sections of color and texture roughly. In watercolor painting, this process is referred to as "Blocking" or "First Wash." If you're working in oils, you'll know it as "Underpainting." In the realm of scene painting, it's commonly called doing the "Lay-in." At this stage, our focus should not be on highlights, shadows, or subtle shading. We are simply aiming to get the basic colors of the materials applied to your sketch.

To begin this process effectively, try working freehand. Select a brush from the large brush palette; a good starting point might be the basic "j) WaterC Flat Decay Tilt" brush. Upon selecting the brush, you will notice it comes set for default opacity and flow. Keep in mind that you can alter these settings at any time to fit your needs. Start brushing into an area that represents a single material. Initially, you may find it challenging to stay within the outlined shapes, but that's perfectly okay. Remember, painting strictly inside the lines can be quite monotonous. Whatever notions you learned about that in third grade may not apply here.

As you begin painting, you might start with a lighter touch. However, instead of adjusting the brush to a lighter opacity, adjust the entire paint layer to control the transparency. It's crucial to create a new layer for each costume piece you are working on; this will help keep your work organized and make adjustments easier down the line.

Consider zooming in on the picture to enlarge your shapes and thicken the outlines, making it easier for you to paint those intricate details. However, remember that zooming in can make it tricky to fit the entire area on your screen at any given time. This may require some practice as you grow accustomed to working with different magnifications, especially when using a graphics tablet. Finding the right balance in your view can help manage your workflow and improve your painting efficiency.

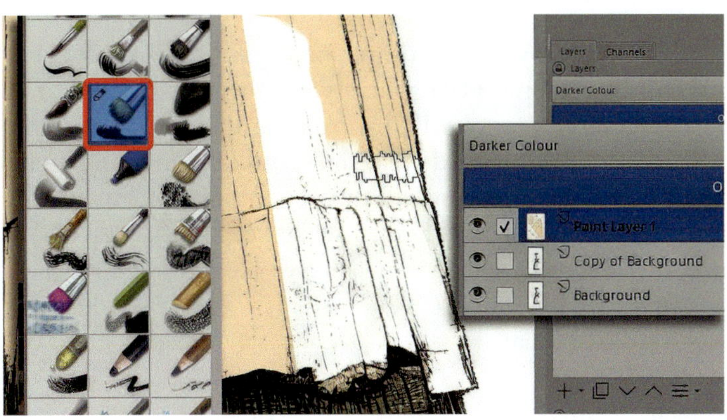

FIGURE 3.3 Color blocking can be done in multiple layers and with different blending options to better control the final color balance.

Depending on the medium you choose, whether it's watercolor, simulated acrylic paint, or oil paint, the color may exhibit some grain from the brush strokes. Pay close attention to this aspect and actively work to keep it under control; we want to avoid brush strokes that seem illogical or unnatural to the viewer.

The primary goal here is to learn to work quickly and efficiently. To achieve this, find techniques that allow you to lay color into an area rapidly. While building up several translucent layers of tints can create depth and texture, it tends to be slower than applying a color all in one go. Experiment with different brush shapes and sizes; try something circular for soft edges, horizontal for broad strokes, or flat vertically for sharp lines. Each brush may yield different effects, so test them out to see which best suits your intended style.

USING MASKS

After exploring the application of color, the next step is to begin using selections as masks. Selections are incredibly useful, allowing you to isolate areas for editing. Selections are routinely used in digital environments for tasks like moving objects, performing cut-and-paste operations, or copying layers. In the context of painting, selections are utilized as masks for controlling where paint is applied.

Instead of relying on traditional methods like masking tape, frisket liquid, or frisket paper, we will utilize the easy-to-apply, easy-to-remove masks and selection functions that many digital tools offer. This approach not only simplifies the process but also allows for greater speed and flexibility in the work.

This mimics the techniques of the skilled airbrush artists of the 1980s, like Hajime Sorayama and others. These artists created their stunning illusionary works by spending a considerable amount of time creating and removing masks, often more than they spent applying paint with the airbrush itself.

Selections can serve as either positive or negative masks. When you select an area, it will be the only place where you can paint on the surface, allowing for precise control. Conversely, by inverting the mask, you can block any paint application in that selected area, similar to how masking tape functions. Everything outside this selection will then be available for painting, allowing you to focus your efforts where needed while keeping the rest of your canvas untouched. This technique can greatly enhance accuracy and reduce the risk of unwanted color spills.

To invert a masked area:

- Filter menu > Adjust > "Invert" (or Ctrl + I).

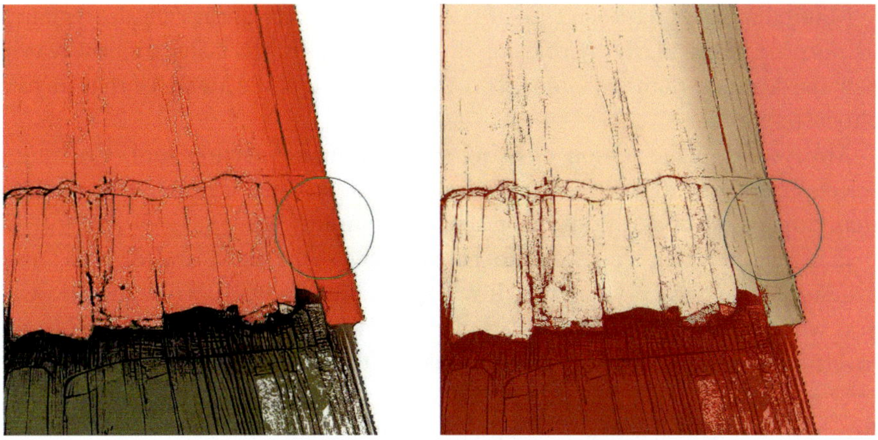

FIGURE 3.4 a) Use a positive mask or invert it, and b) Use a negative mask.

In all 2D programs, there are several varieties of masking tools: rectangular and elliptical (or circular), as well as polygonal and freehand, which will have different, eccentric shapes. Once the selection is put on the page, simple edits can be made quickly.

- Select a simple Selection tool, "Rectangular" or "Elliptical".
- Click-Drag to select an area in your sketch.
- **Hold down the Shift key** while overlapping a new selection shape to ADD TO THE SELECTION.
- **Hold down the Alt key** while overlapping a new selection shape to SUBTRACT FROM THE SELECTION.

Very complex masks can be formed by manipulating basic shapes. After creating a basic mask:

- Check Menu > "Show Global Selection Mask".
    - o The odd-looking red mask filter will appear in the viewport, making it easier to see and edit the mask shape.
- Select the "Transform" tool (Ctrl + T).
- Rotate, scale, or move the mask.

  Or,

- Use the many options in the Transform Tool Option docker to make "Perspective", "Warp", "Cage", or "Mesh" transformations.
- Uncheck "Global Selection Mask".

Manipulating a mask isn't just for editing the selection; it can also enhance its purpose, particularly by rotating it. In many cases, it's faster to just create a new mask rather than scale or distort the existing one. Be aware of that in your efforts to save time.

Always weigh the option of using the Polygonal Selection tool. Creating a selection mask by making multiple clicks around an area is nearly always faster than doing a lot of additions, subtractions, rotations, etc.

Pick the area that you want to paint, such as the skirt, and draw a mask around it. Now, when you paint, it will go where you want, while the area that you want to keep clean is shielded. Then, place a mask outside one edge and invert it. Now, you have a masking shield that can be moved around the sketch over and over. You can try using it while painting with a flat color and a paint brush, or use it with a wider, less focused tool like an airbrush.

Saving a Mask

If there's an area that has taken quite a while to mask right because of a highly complex fit, you can save the mask for later use. When it comes time to add more textures or do some shading to the same area, you can easily access your saved masks.

- While the mask is active, make a new layer.
- Right-click on the new layer.
- Add > "Add Local Selection".

A mask layer will appear below the paint layer with an icon that resembles the selected area. The small circle icon to the right is bright, indicating that the selection is active.

- Click on the small circle to deactivate the selection.
- Make a new selection and save it as another Local Selection.

You can save many sections to a single paint layer. If you do, give them distinctive names.

- Activate them one at a time by clicking the circle icon in the layer panel.
- Click on the "Selection Mask" layer while it is active.

It will show the selection in the drawing space as a Global Mask (with the Pepto-Bismol pink background).

- Now you can edit it with the Transform tool or by adding and removing bits.

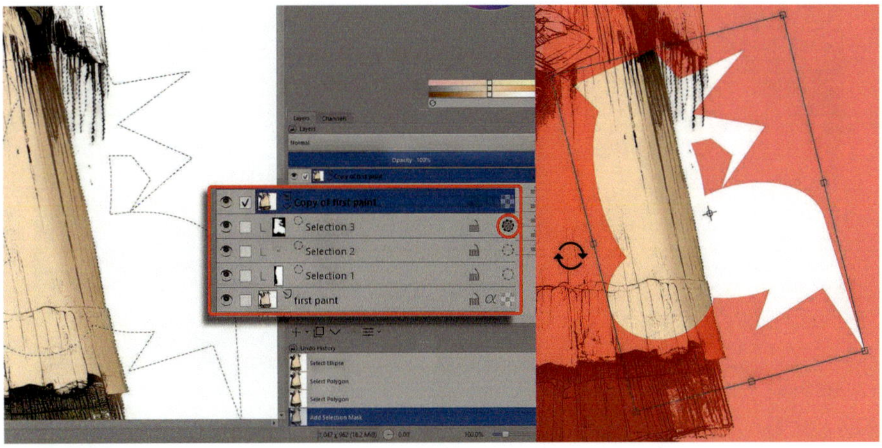

FIGURE 3.5 a) A layer with Multiple Local Selections. b) Selection editing.

SHADING

Look how cool it is to mask the edge of a costume piece and use the airbrush to give a toning effect as it goes from center outward – very sweet!

Toning the edges of your costume pieces creates a compelling illusion of three-dimensionality. This technique can significantly enhance the perception that the costume is wrapping around the figure, adding depth and realism to your sketch. To achieve this effect, you can use any brush that you prefer, but setting it to a low opacity will give you the best results. This allows for a more subtle application of color, enabling you to build up layers gradually for a more refined finish.

Start by making a new layer, which will allow you to experiment freely without altering the layer holding the selection masks. Don't hesitate to try out different blending modes such as "Darken" or "Multiply", by using the pull-down menu in the layers panel. These can dramatically change how the colors interact with one another. Each blending mode has its unique way of mixing the colors of overlapping layers, and exploring these can lead to unexpected yet delightful results.

Here, a quick mask has been applied to tone a fold in Eliza's skirt. After a few paint strokes, the mask is simply moved over to the next fold. Move it over, rotate it if needed, paint, and repeat. It can be used again on the next piece or wherever. Unlike masking tape or pasteboard, it won't get soggy or become impossible to see through. You gotta love virtual tools!

Color selection is a matter of personal preference. Some use individual colors when toning each piece. In that case, a quick trick is to sample the area with

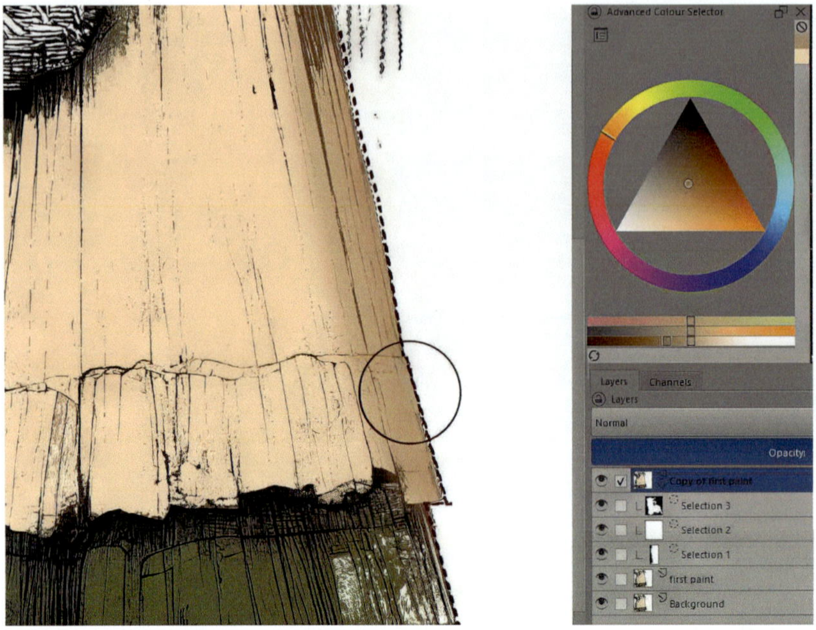

FIGURE 3.6 Toning the skirt with masks and airbrush.

the eyedropper tool, then just lower the value in the Color Selector docker. You might adjust the saturation while you're at it. Other artists prefer to use a single shading color for everything. Try picking one of the darker shades already in the sketch or a darker gray, or a gray tinted with something that matches your color palette. Try reducing the opacity of the toning layer, then experiment with changing its Blending modes. "Multiply", "Darken", and "Hard Light" are often useful options.

Highlight colors can be chosen using the same methods. A soft eraser can also be used to create highlights. Place a layer filled with a suitable light color beneath the layer being highlighted. ONLY USE AN ERASER ON A **COPY** OF THE WORKING LAYER. BETTER SAFE THAN SORRY.

If you need guidance on techniques like adding folds and pleats to your costume pieces, refer back to the previous section, where you'll find helpful tips on how to create convincing fabric textures. Remember that details like folds not only contribute to the realism of the costume but also enhance the three-dimensional effect you're aiming for.

You can layer both shadows and highlights thoughtfully. Some designers prefer to alternate between the two, while others do all the shadows first and the highlights later.

- Sometimes, making two translucent passes works like a charm.
- Try increasing the airbrush size and just graze the edge of the area you're working on, trusting the selection to contain the color in the right spot.

- You can also open the airbrush settings to tweak it for a larger, softer edge.
- Experiment with positive and negative masks.
  - Positive: Select only the area you want to paint.
  - Negative: Select the area to be protected from paint and invert it.
- If you have a transparent drawing layer, try keeping it on top and painting below it. It may give you a better sense of where the masks should fall.

FIGURE 3.7 Eliza's costume with most of the shading in place.

4 Patterns and Textures

FIGURE 4.1 These sketches by designer Linsay Webster for a production of *Trojan Women* show the use of pattern in the material of the denim jeans, the green cardigan, and the brown coat. Textures are heavily deployed to render dirt, mud, and wear.

DOI: 10.4324/9781003571742-4

PATTERNS

Filling the sketch with basic color fields is the first option to consider. The second is to fill it with patterns. One of the great advantages that computers have over traditional drafting and painting is the ability to replicate real materials perfectly, adding depth and richness to your designs. The patterns you incorporate into your sketch can be fabric swatches downloaded from the internet, scanned, or photographed.

If you have already made fabric choices or at least narrowed down options among real, existing fabrics, you can efficiently find swatches of those fabrics online. Websites dedicated to fabric sourcing or fabric retailers often have high-resolution images available for download. If you have fabric swatches in hand, scanning them and using their inherent patterns on the computer is a straightforward task. It's very helpful to look for swatches or photographs that include an entire repeating pattern, but this is not absolutely essential for your sketching process.

Patterns can also be invented. They can emerge from your own creative designs on the computer or be sourced from other visuals, such as photographs, artworks, or abstract designs. Anything that can be adapted in the service of achieving the texture or pattern you need can be used. When selecting patterns, consider what will fit the costume and how they might later be created through fabric painting, weaving, or other techniques.

If you haven't done any actual fabric shopping yet and are not ready to commit to a particular fabric choice – especially before you've had a chance to confer with your colleagues about your design – be cautious about spending too much time searching for the exact fabric this early in the process. As you sketch, remember that the goal is to keep your time to two hours or less. This time frame includes the time spent online looking for patterns to incorporate into your sketch, ensuring you remain efficient in your workflow.

In addition to being visual elements, patterns can serve as textures. You can find various types of knits, weaves, and brocades to use in the sketch as an underlayer. Later, colors can be layered on top for additional depth. Depending on the character or mood of the costume, you may want something rough and pronounced or something silky smooth. Consider taking a printed pattern and overlaying it on a particular texture, using the former for color and the latter to introduce light and shadow definition to your design.

In many cases, you might need to use a single instance of the pattern. In other instances, you may wish to repeat that pattern several times across the garment, much like wallpapering a wall. If you decide that repetition is necessary, adjust your online searches to include the word "seamless." Sometimes, textures specifically designed for 3D modeling are useful, as they are typically truly seamless and allow for smooth transitions.

Remember, you are not limited to the color palette bound within the pattern; that color can always be edited later on. However, the specific pattern may provide significant insight into your final choices. Try searching for PBR materials (physically based rendering materials), which are commonly used in contemporary 3D modeling.

When you have imported a swatch, you can lay it into an area of the sketch and scale it to the exact proportion that the original fabric would appear on a human figure in actual use. This scaling capability is a significant advantage of working digitally. You can also scale it larger or smaller than the original if you think that would better suit the character or costume design you are working on. Ultimately, your objective is to determine how best to visually recreate that fabric before it is incorporated into the costume concept.

Drag and drop the image onto your sketch and indicate in the pop-up that you wish to use it as a new layer. After that, use the transform tool to adjust its dimensions to your desired size. This can result in a realistic version of the material, as if it were being used straight off the bolt, or it can be stylized to reflect a more theatrical approach, perhaps much larger or decidedly smaller than the actual pattern might suggest.

Working with a repeating pattern can significantly elevate your sketch. First off, you've got to determine whether a repeating pattern is indeed necessary for your drawing. For the purposes of a sketch, an indication of the pattern may suffice. You can simply scale or rotate the swatch to effectively cover the designated area. If the costume piece is small or contains folds or pleats, a pattern would likely be broken up and doesn't need to actually be seamless. Instead, a single motif can just be applied several times within the contour of your costume design to maintain visual interest. This method enables you to strike a balance between complexity and clarity in your sketches, ensuring they effectively convey your ideas.

MAKING A REPEATABLE PATTERN

Most 2D graphic programs have built-in tools designed explicitly for creating repeating patterns. In Krita, for instance, you'll find several effective tools available, as this software is a commonly used and popular choice for generating repeatable motifs.

Before you begin, ensure that the pattern you have is indeed repeatable. The image you're working with needs to contain at least one full motif of the pattern. Carefully examine the edges on one side of the image. Scanning horizontally, look for a section within the pattern that matches this edge. It's also important to check from the top down to confirm that the design aligns correctly.

When you identify a material or texture that could serve as a good pattern for your sketch, try to find a copy in the highest resolution available. This provides a clear foundation for your work. Ideally, the image should include at least one complete repeatable pattern, along with some extra parts of the pattern present around the central important area to give you more flexibility in editing.

Next, you will need to edit the image to ensure it is repeatable. This involves adjusting the edges so that when multiple instances of the pattern are placed side by side, they will line up seamlessly. Use the editing tools in your graphic program to trim and blend the edges, carefully ensuring that the pattern flows consistently from one tile to the next. Pay close attention to any markings or features that must align, as these will be crucial for achieving a polished and professional-looking seamless pattern.

- Drag and drop the pattern image onto the Krita workspace.
- A dialog pops up asking how you want to add the image.
- Select “Open in New Document”.
- Click the button “New Layer”.
- Click on the top ruler and drag a Guideline down onto the pattern.
- Place it over a landmark in the pattern and its next repeated double to determine if it needs to be rotated to be level horizontally and vertically.
- If necessary, use the Transform tool to rotate the image to level and press “Enter” to accept the transformation.

FIGURE 4.2 Scale the pattern one side at a time until it matches its adjoining twin.

The pattern may look distorted because it wasn't scaled evenly in both directions. If so, then

- Turn off "Wrap Around Mode" to see the seamless pattern.
- Make the background layer invisible or delete it altogether.
- Select the layer containing the pattern and use the Transform tool to scale it down either horizontally or vertically until it looks correct.
- Select Image menu > "Trim to Current Layer" to eliminate the leftover, empty canvas area.

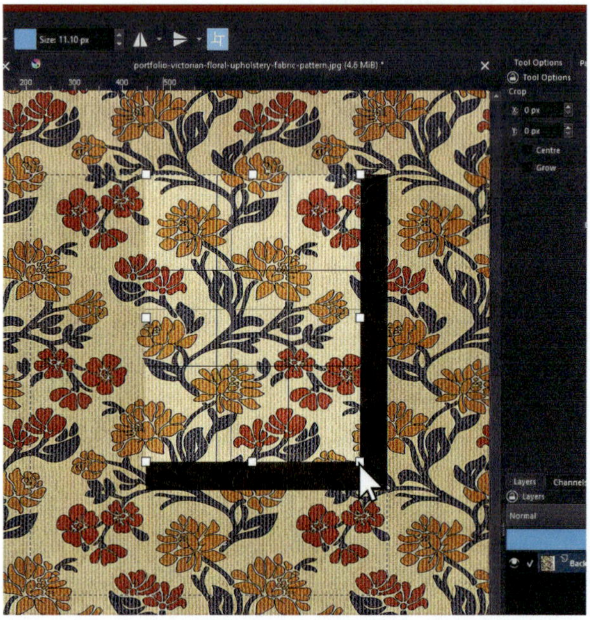

FIGURE 4.3 Scale the pattern to return to its original aspect.

- Open the Pattern Dropdown. (In the toolbar, not the Pattern Docker).
- Click Custom > "Update".
  - You should see a thumbnail of the contents of the current layer or a selected area on that layer.
- Click "Use as Pattern" for a temporary fill pattern or "Add to Predefined Pattern" to save it in the pattern resources.

Import Patterns

You can also create patterns from any image file.

- Click the "Add Resource" button at the bottom of the Pattern Docker.
- Browse to a JPG or PNG file and select it.
  - The image will be immediately added to the pattern resources.

Using Patterns

One of the easiest ways to incorporate repeating patterns is by using a separate layer below the existing sketch layer and revealing it where needed.

- Create a new, empty paint layer.
- Select the rectangular area tool.
- In the tool options, set the source to be a pattern, and make sure the pattern you've created is selected in the Pattern Docker.
- Draw a rectangle that's large enough to cover the area where the material will appear in your sketch.
    - o You can rotate a shape while drawing if you drag the shape and press Ctrl + Alt before releasing the mouse button. The shape will then rotate around the active corner until the mouse button is clicked.
- Use the rectangle as a preview of how the pattern will look. This is your chance to tweak things.
- In the tool options, adjust the scale and rotation to fit the angle of an arm or leg, and so on.
- Now hit the (always faithful) "Undo" command (Ctrl + Z) and draw a new rectangle.
- The transform tool can be used to further refine scale and rotation, but be careful; this can be a rabbit hole. **Don't spend time on fine details that no one is going to notice.**

FIGURE 4.4 Scale and rotate the pattern to align with the costume piece.

Placing this layer beneath the sketch layer is usually a good move. It might be a good idea to make a copy of your sketch onto a new layer and then position it above the pattern layer. Now, you can use an eraser on the sketch layer to reveal parts of the pattern beneath, or if you are using a transparent sketch, you can use an eraser on the pattern layer to trim it back to the outlines.

You can do this, revealing or trimming using either selection tools or an eraser brush. The rectangular selection tool is fantastic for clearing out large spaces efficiently. Remember, when you place a rectangle or any other shape selection onto your sketch, you can rotate it to align with the area you intend to clip.

- Drag the selection shape as usual, but press Ctrl + Alt before releasing the mouse button. The shape will rotate around the corner that was dragged.
- Or, switch to Select menu > "Show Global Selection Mask". The selected area can be manipulated with the Transform tool.

The ellipse selection tool is particularly good at maneuvering around curved edges. However, nothing beats the irregular polygon selection for cutting around eccentric shapes with full control. Just click around the area that needs attention, and don't hesitate to zoom in! The outline will enlarge, making it easier to hide the Polygon selection behind it.

Whichever method you use to select unwanted parts of the pattern, as with all painting programs, tapping the "Delete" key finishes the removal.

The other method for fitting a pattern is to use an eraser brush. Keep in mind that the eraser can function much like a drawing tool. Use a small eraser for intricate areas and a larger one for broader spaces and to remove material quickly. You'll find that the eraser has a slightly soft edge. You can tweak this in the brush editor to best suit your needs.

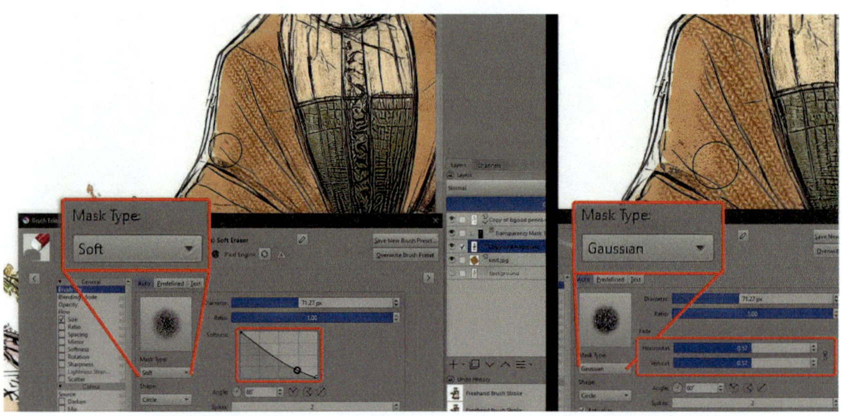

FIGURE 4.5 a) Brush settings for "Soft". b) Brush settings for "Gaussian".

Deforming the Pattern

You can do so much more than just rotate the pattern! Once you have the pattern on its own separate layer, you can manipulate the entire layer and the pattern itself to adapt to any unusual bends or viewing angles of the specific costume piece.

- Select the pattern layer.
- If you only want to transform part of the layer's image, select that area with one of the standard selection tools.
- Select the Transform tool.
- In the tool options, you have access to a full array of deformers.

The common ones, position, shear, and scale, are at the top of the docker. Below are more exotic options: Perspective, Warp, Cage, Liquify, and Mesh.

Position and scale will do exactly what you'd expect. Just activate those options, and then select a handle on the layer to push or pull it for various effects. With Shear, you can transform a regular rectangle selection into a parallelogram by simply adjusting the top or bottom offsets or shifting the sides. This gives you a distorted view of the pattern that can mimic the perspective distortion when you're looking at a pattern from an unusual angle.

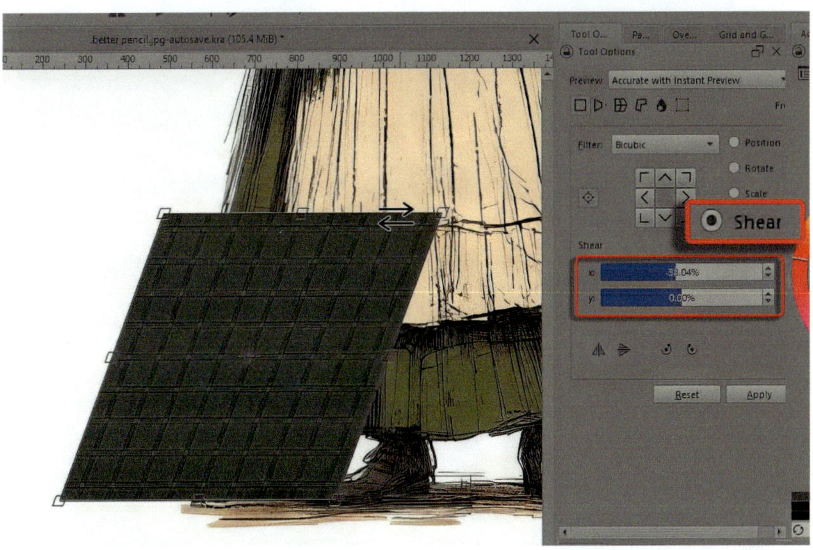

FIGURE 4.6 Applying "Shear" to a selection.

Warp controls are also fantastic for this. They break the pattern into multiple sections, and by sliding the control points, you can create smooth, curved distortions. The Subdivide value breaks the image into more sections for more detailed control. As usual, pressing the Ctrl key allows you to select multiple control points. This is great for giving the impression that a pattern is wrapping around a cylindrical body part.

The Cage deformer is another powerful option; it lays a grid of points over your pattern. The number of points is determined by the values entered in the column and row fields. You can then select individual points to adjust the pattern, making it appear as if it's adhering to a bumpy surface, which can lead to some truly unique effects.

The Liquefy option enables a more freeform approach. Instead of manipulating regularly spaced points, it uses a brush that is painted over the drawing, sliding bits of the pattern in whichever direction, similar to a smear tool in other software. There are two modes here: Build Up and Wash. Typically, Wash is more useful because, as it shifts a part of the pattern, it influences the surrounding areas right next to it. On the other hand, Build Up allows you to slide one part of the pattern directly over the adjoining sections.

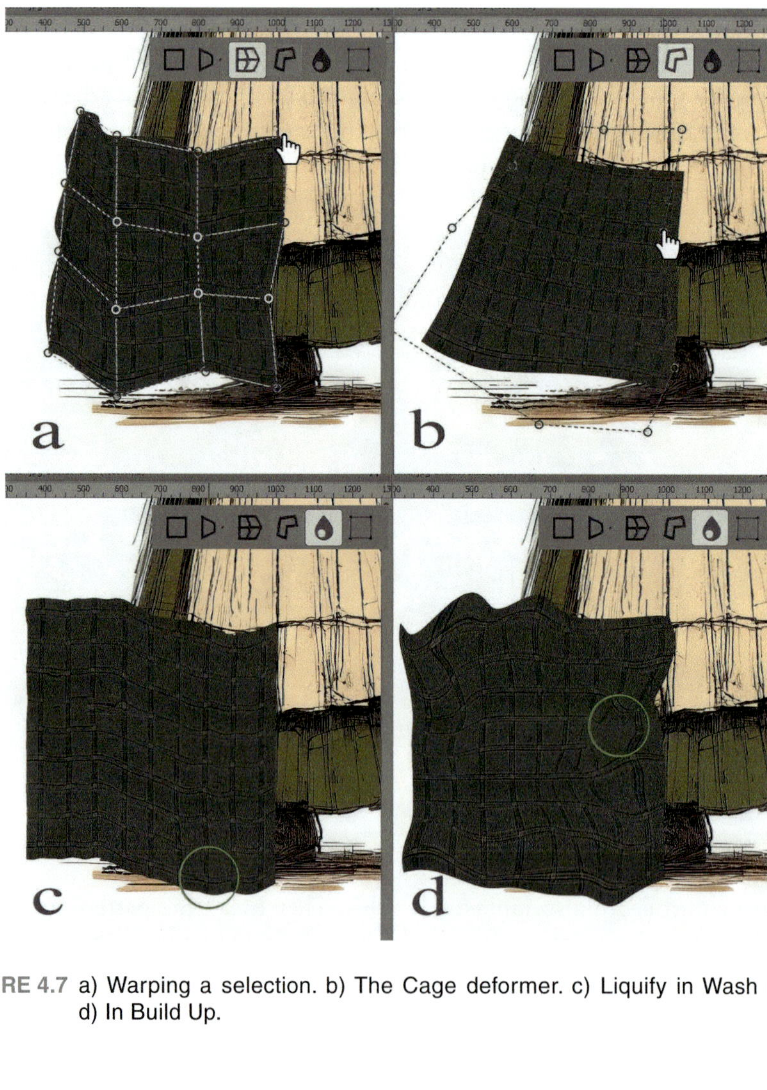

FIGURE 4.7 a) Warping a selection. b) The Cage deformer. c) Liquify in Wash mode. d) In Build Up.

Blending Patterns

Keep in mind that when we see someone on the street wearing a patterned garment, the print typically blends into their overall look without being too overt. Similarly, you want patterns in your sketches to be recognizable but not so loud that they overpower the rest of the sketch. Develop methods of toning down patterns so they blend into the overall "look" of the costume.

1. Erase
   - Use one of the eraser brushes to make the pattern fade here and there. A layer of underpainting may be needed, placed below the pattern layer. Or, preferably:
   - Create a new layer.
   - Set this layer's blend mode to "Erase".
   - Paint with standard paint brushes (not erasers).
   - Now, you can hide the erasures or adjust the opacity of the layer.

FIGURE 4.8 Fading parts of Eliza's skirt with an eraser.

2. Darken
   - Set the color selector to a shade of gray and paint with low opacity.
   - Or select areas first, then paint with grays.
   - Or better yet, create a new layer and paint. Adjust the opacity and blend mode.

- Or select areas and open Filters > Adjust > Color Adjustment Curve and tweak the brightness and contrast.
- Or even cooler, select areas to darken. Create a new filter layer with the Color Adjustment Curve option. Now click on the properties button at the bottom of the Layers docker and adjust the darkness, hue, and saturation of the selected areas. The opacity of the layer can also be adjusted.

3. Saturate or tint/shade
   - By using the HSV Adjustment filter instead of the Color Adjustment Curve, the same methods used to darken areas of the pattern can be used to alter the hue and brightness. Reducing or increasing the saturation of colors can be particularly effective on costumes that will be distressed to show age and wear.

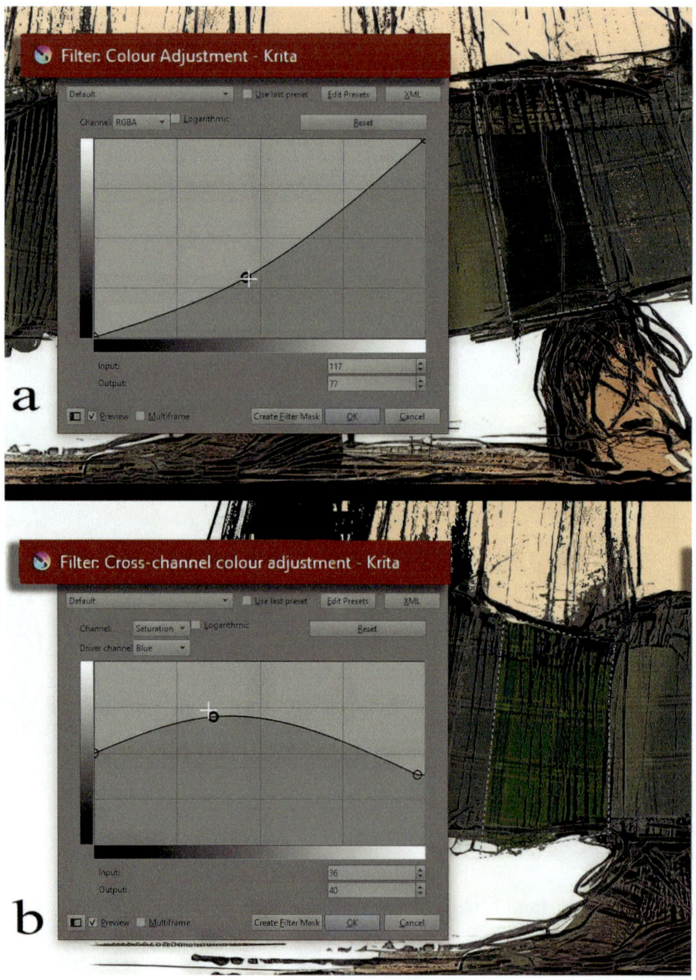

FIGURE 4.9 a) Darkening a selection drawn with the Lasso selector. b) Deepening the color of the selection.

When using the eraser tool, you can customize its strength for a softer or more defined edge. Zooming in a bit will help with that precision, making it easy to coax the underlying pattern to the top.

When finished, combine those two layers and then create another layer with a rectangle tailored to a different body part. Keep refining until you have just what you need.

Pattern Brushes

But it gets even cooler! Patterns can also be applied using a brush instead of shapes or the bucket tool. This allows for more precise application of the pattern exactly where it's needed. You can adjust the rotation and scale of the brush while working, further enhancing your design capabilities.

First, select the brush that has all the qualities that you want in terms of size, opacity, softness, and flow. Any brush will work. It can be watercolor, textured, or a stamp. Airbrushes work very well with patterns. Next, open up the brush editor by clicking the button in the toolbar or keypress F5.

In the Color section:

- Color > Source > Select "Pattern".

If you want to change the spray pattern or brush texture:

In the texture section:

- Texture > Check "Pattern".
- Select a pattern from the palette.
- Click the "Options" tab.
- Set the default Scale, Brightness, Contrast, etc.

Save the New Brush

- Click the "Save New Brush Preset . . ." button at the top of the editor.
- Give the new brush a name. The letter prefix (a), b), c) . . .) sets its position in the Brush Presets docker.
- Give the new brush an icon from an image file on your computer ("Load Image") or from the icon library ("From Image Library").

All of these painting techniques, whether you're using fill patterns or pattern brushes, can be adjusted for their opacity. It's a good idea to lay down a base color underneath the pattern that will complement the varying opacity of the fill pattern. However, remember that you can also set the fill pattern for the entire layer. Therefore, it may be better to apply the paint a little more heavily than you initially think is appropriate and adjust the layer's opacity later on.

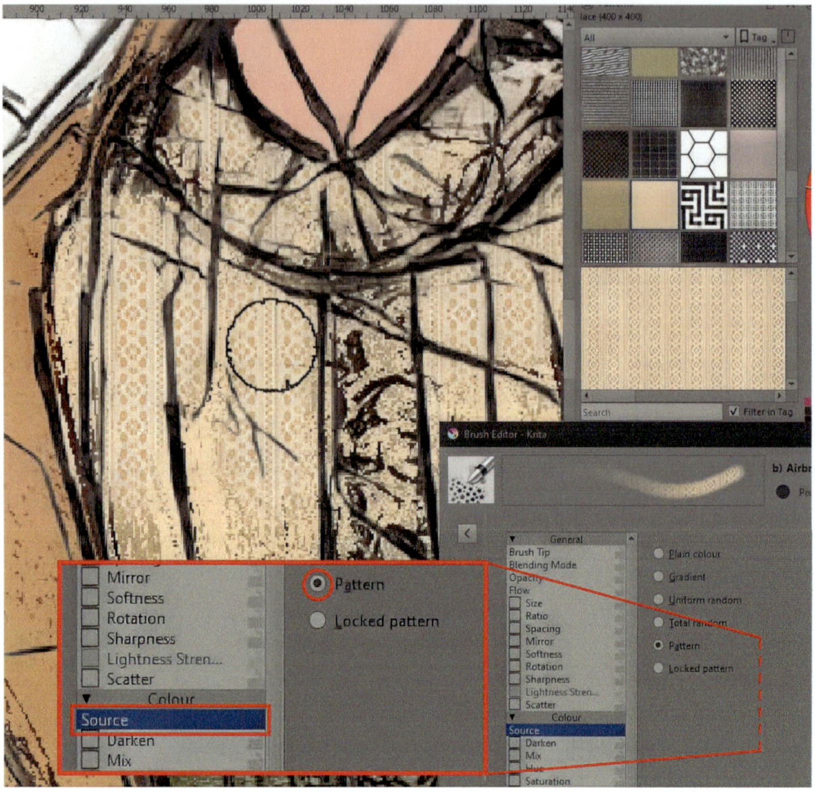

FIGURE 4.10 Painting with a pattern brush.

Texturing With a Brush

Once the areas are filled with color, it's time to dive into some targeted toning and texturing for those individual costume pieces! You've got a wide array of brushes at your disposal, each boasting unique spatter patterns and speckles.

- Make a new Paint layer.
- Select a Brush.
- Select an appropriate color.
  - Often, it is effective to use the eyedropper tool to sample a color that is already present in the sketch.
- Tweak the darkness and saturation in the Color Selection Docker.
  - The Hue, Saturation, and Value sliders at the bottom of the Color Selector docker offer greater control than picking points on the color triangle.
- Set the opacity to approximately 40% and begin spattering the costume with gentle taps of your mouse button.

While there are dedicated stamping tools in the brush palette, virtually any brush can do the trick if you apply it with single taps instead of sliding it across the surface. Try different opacity settings. Remember, you can always adjust the layer opacity later.

Selecting the area to tone is a breeze with the magic wand tool. Since there's already color in place, you can also infuse some texture by importing an interesting find from the web. **Dirt, rust, or grunge textures (yes, grunge is a type of texture) are great for distressing a costume.** Make one of these a new layer and apply it to your selected area, adjusting the opacity as needed to blend it smoothly.

If you need to merge two layers, simply right-click on one in the Layers docker and select a merge command, or press Ctrl+E.

Texturing the Entire Sketch

You can also tone the entire drawing to unify its appearance or to give it a classic texture, such as canvas or watercolor paper. Several paper and canvas textures are available in the Patterns resource and the Pattern Docker.

- Start by creating a new layer.
- Choose one of those pre-made, preset patterns.
- Select the Paint Bucket and fill the empty layer by simply clicking on it.
    - You can adjust the scale and rotation of the pattern after previewing it. Keep using the undo command. Remember, you can only apply scale and rotation adjustments before the pattern is filled, not afterward. It may take some trial and error to get it just right.

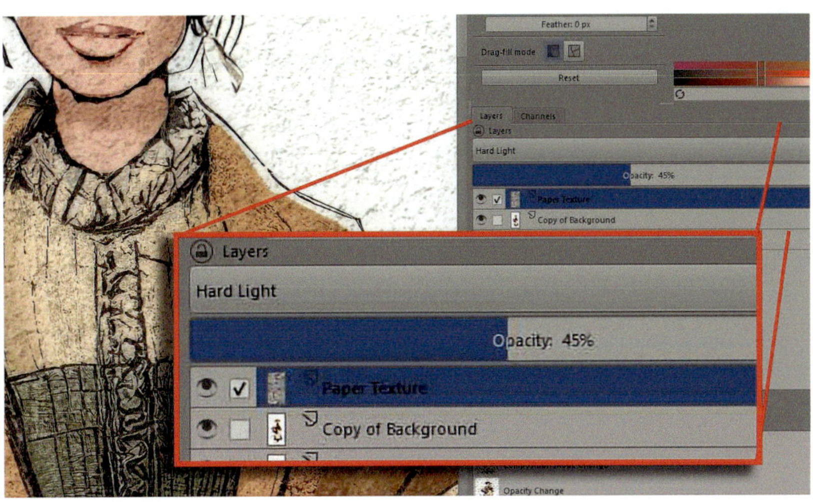

FIGURE 4.11 Fill a new layer with a paper texture.

Once your pattern covers the drawing surface,

- Adjust the layer opacity.
- Try different blending modes.
- Use Filters > Adjust > "HSV Adjustment" to tinker with the color.

In the deeper crevices, you can use texture drawing tools and paint brushes to add more depth. There are two or three texture drawing tools in the brush docker; by selecting them and rubbing them across your drawing area, you can reveal a texture beneath the charcoal and graphite. It's worthwhile to look at the brush settings, particularly the blot property, to understand how that effect is achieved. If you like, you can apply those same settings to any other brush you wish.

And if you're in the mood for something a bit more unique, consider searching online for antique parchment, cloth, or canvas textures. Once you find what you're looking for, skip ahead to the next chapter, where you'll learn how to transform an image into a repeating pattern.

As an option to using the Paint Bucket, you can easily fill the entire space with a fill layer.

- Add a fill layer.
- A dialog will pop up asking if you want a solid color, a gradient, or a pattern. Choose "pattern".
- In the first tab, scroll through the available options until you find the one that catches your eye.
- In the Transform tab, you set the scale, rotation, offset, and shear.
    - This dialog can be reopened by clicking the "Layer Properties" button at the bottom of the docker.

Just like any other layer, you can adjust the opacity and tweak the color and density with the Color Adjustment curve and HSV Adjustment filters.

5 Scenic and Lighting Sketches

FIGURE 5.1 A digital scenic sketch that captures a dramatic moment in the play and shows off the shape of the space, colors, and materials. The sketch also depicts lighting that creates the mood and atmosphere, while highlighting the action.

Sketching scenery on a computer parallels the process of crafting costumes, utilizing similar tools for the same intent as previously discussed. This demonstration uses *Krita*, which boasts features akin to *Photoshop* for drawing and photo manipulation, coupled with advanced painting capabilities reminiscent of painting programs. It excels at recreating the look and feel of traditional art materials, offering a remarkable experience.

One significant advantage of digital scenic sketches is the ease of making adjustments without the tedious task of redrawing from scratch. During the creative

DOI: 10.4324/9781003571742-5

process, designers can effortlessly modify elements, experiment with different silhouettes, or adjust color schemes to evoke various moods and fulfill the vision for specific scenes. Textures can be swapped seamlessly, traversing from the smoothest surfaces to the most rugged, from organic feels to sleek, high-tech appearances. Patterns, such as tapestries, upholstery, and drapery, can be integrated into the scene at the correct scale, truly mirroring the real-world materials.

Furthermore, alterations may be made after discussion with collaborators. Different perspectives can greatly influence the overall design. Collaborations with lighting designers can also shape color schemes, enhancing or muting various patterns through colored lighting, necessitating careful pre-planning.

Digital sketches of scenery can be organized into multiple layers, which can be manipulated in various ways, whether hidden, revealed, or rearranged as needed. Each layer can hold vital information regarding set shifts, accommodating significant changes in the scene's configuration. If a scene shift necessitates the addition or removal of smaller subunits from the main set, each can be placed on its own layer, allowing for independent editing without the hassle of redrawing the entire set each time.

Layers can also contain furniture and other scenic elements, enabling individual modifications without starting from scratch. Moreover, these layers can portray actors in different costumes or positions. If costume designers provide sketch information that can be scanned and incorporated into the set, it facilitates decisions about color harmony or contrast between the two design elements, allowing designers to determine which approach strikes the right chord for their shared vision.

PERSPECTIVE GRIDS

Krita has some tools that are unique, unlike anything offered by other drawing programs. These tools are incredibly useful for sketching scenery.

Like most drawing programs, *Krita* has a variety of assistant tools for placing guidelines and measurements on the screen. However, the *Krita* assistant tools can also create a perspective grid as a guide for sketching.

- Make a new layer.
- Select the "Assistant" tool in the Toolbox (just above the Selection tools).
- In the "Tool Options", set the assistant to "Perspective".
- On the sketch, click on "4 points" to form the corners of the grid.
    - It doesn't have to be perfect; you can straighten it next.
- Select and move corner points to level the grid, raise or lower the viewpoint, or shift the view to one side.
    - This offers a lot of flexibility, including the possibility of having the perspective twist or shift to odd angles. Better to keep the horizontal lines level.
- Select one of the center points and drag it up or down to create elevation grids.

A vertical grid along the upper edge or on either side helps you align and determine the height of objects and keep them straight up and down, ensuring that they remain plumb visually. Using the floor grid and an elevation grid together allows you to create objects with the correct dimensions and raised to the proper height for raised platforms, ceiling pieces, or hanging scenery.

When kept as a background layer, this perspective grid can serve as a visual reference that you can draw over. If you have a ground plan, it can quickly be transferred to any perspective grid.

OLD SCHOOL METHOD!

- Draw a flat grid over the plan with lines every 2 or 4 feet.
- Set the Subdivisions of the *Krita* perspective grid to match those across the width of the plan.
- Transfer landmark points, such as the corners of walls and platforms, from the flat grid of the plan to the perspective grid. Such as 20 ft left of center and 4 ft upstage of the plaster line, next 15' left 5' up, 12' l 9' up, etc.
- Drawing lines to connect the points will result in a perspective version of your ground plan. It is then quite easy to work up from there.
- Other set pieces, like furniture, can be plotted the same way.
- The height of objects can be gauged by drawing horizontal lines to a side grid and using it as a scale ruler for objects at a distance from the picture plane.

NEW COOL METHOD!

Import a copy of your ground plan (rough sketch or neatly drafted) and fit it to the perspective grid. You can then draw vertical lines upward from key points to correctly place the various scenic elements.

- Scan your rough plan, or if using CAD software, export an image file.
- Drag and drop the plan into *Krita* and make it a new layer.
- Trim it, keeping only the major parts of the design.
  - "Crop" Tool (Tool Options: "Applies to Layer").
  - "Selection" Tool: Select the waste bits and delete them.
- "Transform" Tool: Scale the plan to fill the width of the perspective plane.
  - If the grid's divisions equal 2 or 4 feet, you can guesstimate the size.
- Move the plan to approximately align with the bottom of the perspective grid.
- "Transform" Tool: Tool Options > Click the second option icon, "Perspective".
- Drag the top corners downward until the distance to the plan's most upstage elements matches that distance on the grid.
  - Again, use the supposed dimensions of the grid units to make an estimate (Ballpark it).

- Now, move the top corners toward the center until the perspective matches the grid.
- Any lines running directly up and downstage should parallel those of the grid. If there are no such lines in the plan, add two or three before transforming it.
- Pretty cool, right?!
- Hide the grid.
    - Each grid has a widget with a hide/show button.
    - Sometimes, it's easier to go to the "Transform" Tool's Tool Options and move the "Opacity" slider to 0%.
- Make any adjustments needed until it looks right to you.

Drawing aids can be very helpful, but they are no match for your eye. It has to look right to you.

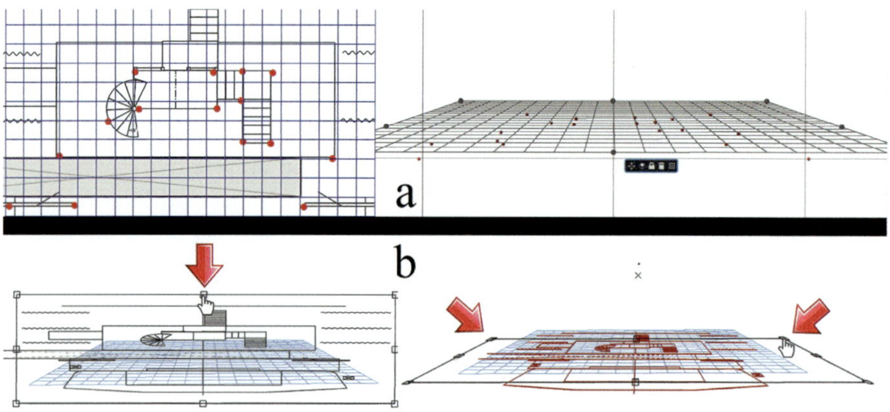

FIGURE 5.2 Both methods begin by drawing a grid over the ground plan.

a. Old school – Transfer key points from the pan to the perspective grid.
b. New cool – Place the plan in a new layer and transform it to fit the perspective grid.

The perspective grid in *Krita* can also act as a snap plane. Drawing lines over such a grid will snap into alignment with it and its vanishing point. This can be somewhat limiting, as many lines in a scenic design do not lie perpendicular or parallel to the proscenium or the plaster line. Walls are often angled in a somewhat cavalier manner, but the snapping perspective grid allows you to place points representing the landmark positions of corners, walls, scenic units, furniture, and any units that are at a 90-degree angle to the viewing plane, enabling precise alignment and elevation.

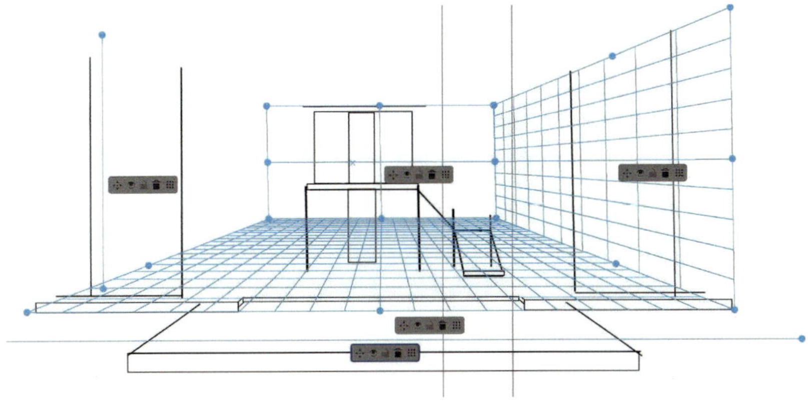

FIGURE 5.3 Lines automatically align with the perspective grid, horizontally and vertically.

If some segments of the set are parallel and at 90 degrees to each other, you can use the perspective grid to align those objects on the perspective grid.

- Choose a drawing brush.
- In the Tool Options, check "Snap to Assistants".
- Draw a line on the floor and see what happens.

If the line starts on the grid, it will snap to the vanishing point or run horizontally, parallel to the picture plane. You can still draw without constrictions if you start a line off the grid. In order to draw vertical lines, you need to create a vertical grid by dragging one of the center points of the floor plane. Then, when you start with the cursor on the vertical grid, it will snap to the orientation of the grid lines.

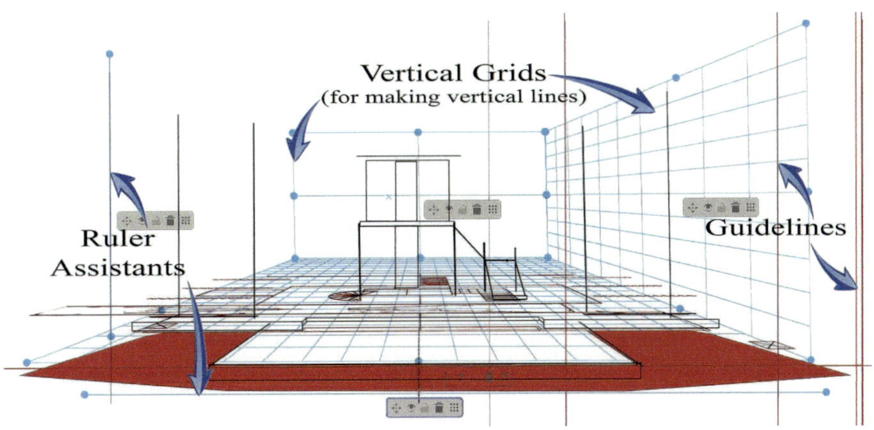

FIGURE 5.4 Lines automatically align with the perspective grid, towards the vanishing point or parallel to it horizontally. Use a vertical elevation grid to draw vertical lines.

You can skew the grid to shift the apparent viewpoint to the side or set up a second grid oriented for a specific scenic unit. From there, you can commence drawing anything that is similarly oriented, ensuring that all elements that are parallel to it are accurately represented. For example, if you have a wall with furniture placed against it, or one with a staircase attached, or parallel backing flats, etc.

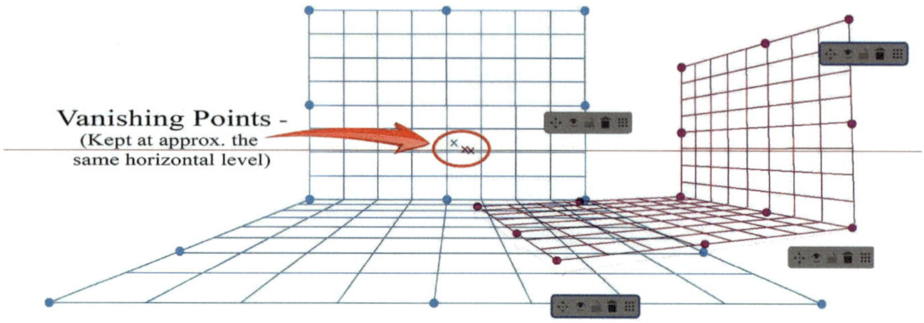

FIGURE 5.5 Add a second grid with a new vanishing point. Take care to match the height of the two vanishing points.

2-point Perspective Grids

If you think that's impressive, consider this: another option in the drawing assistant tool is the two-point perspective. With the two-point perspective, you only have to set opposite X and Y vanishing points in the viewport, then drop a third point to place the centerline.

- "Assistant" Tool: Tool Options > "Perspective" > Add: Dropdown > Select "2 Point Perspective".
- Place one vanishing point far to one side of the sketch.
- Place the second vanishing point far to the other side.
- Hint: Hold down the "Shift" key, and the second point will snap to constrained angles, including the HORIZONTAL.
- Click again to set the direction of the grid.
- The two-point perspective grid may look somewhat distorted as though being seen through a "Fish-eye" lens.
  - Adjust the "focal length" by moving the vanishing points further apart.
  - **The vanishing points do not have to be inside the drawing space!**

Now, you have gone from using a one-point to a two-point perspective grid. This transition is evocative of the movement from the Renaissance to the Baroque period – shifting from the classical, rational, mathematical precision

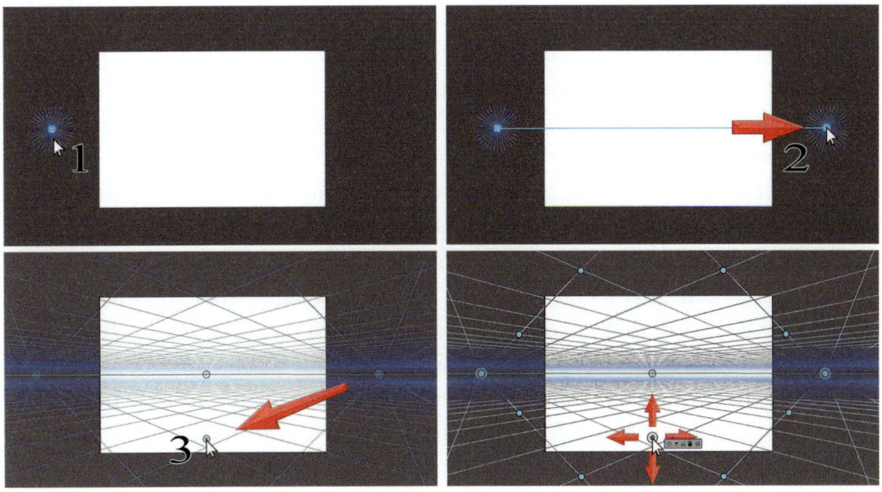

FIGURE 5.6 Making a two-point perspective grid is as simple as placing the two points.

of Serlio and one-point perspective to the complex, dynamic, and emotional stagecraft of Bibiena.

You can take a hint from Bibiena and other Baroque artists and use the two-point perspective to your advantage. Two-point perspective is inherently more dynamic and visually interesting. As perceived by an audience, your scenery will seem to pop out in three dimensions. One-point perspective works best when the scene is kept behind the proscenium and viewed as close to the center of the house as possible.

The "angled scene" or *scena per angelo*, credited to Bibiena. First used in Bologna, Italy, in 1703, it allowed more spectators to enjoy the stage illusion, rather than confining it to those seats along the theatre's centerline.

FIGURE 5.7 a) One-point perspective of the Renaissance. b) The two-point perspective of the Baroque period.

a: *Stage set for Comedy*, wood block print from *On Perspective* by Sebastiano Serlio, early 1550s; Metropolitan Museum of Art. b: Stage design, Palace Interior by Giuseppe Galli Bibiena; Smithsonian Institute.

A set placed at a 90-degree angle to the viewer can seem more realistic in many ways. It opens up to all sightlines while maintaining walls at 90 degrees to each other, typical of what you would find in a real room. With one-point perspective and the traditional box set, the walls must be opened up at unusual cavalier angles, which doesn't happen in real rooms.

Sets built with a 90-degree angle to the viewer tend to promote diagonal traffic patterns, which are generally considered to be more dynamic and visually interesting than simply moving straight across the stage from right to left or up and downstage. When actors enter through the angled sides, they are already positioned in a direction that encourages diagonal movement. Stairways realistically line up with walls and force actors to begin exits and finish entrances by moving diagonally. Even furniture can be expected to align with the room's architecture and will induce traffic to continue in interesting directions further downstage.

Even if used only as a rendering technique, adopting a two-point perspective can make a sketch look more interesting and dimensional. If you take a straight-on view of a traditional box set and shift it to one side or the other, turning the set to present itself at an angle other than flat, things become much more interesting and engaging to look at.

FIGURE 5.8 A forward-facing set can be rendered a few feet to the side of the center of the house, making it appear slightly more dynamic, as seen in this sketch for *The Importance of Being Earnest.*

TEXTURING THE SKETCH

There is a wealth of materials out there for scenic design. You can search for photographs of textures such as asphalt, concrete, grass, or wood. Try browsing catalogs of wallpaper, fabric, tiles, or many other building materials. Often, the most profitable sources of texture images are sites that host materials used in 3D modeling. They typically have well-organized, extensive collections of materials designed for architecture and design. You'll find all sorts of fabrics and wallpapers neatly organized and prepared to be seamless. Some sites offer textures alone, including both photographic and invented ones. Others provide texture maps as part of materials packages that contain several maps needed for 3D modeling. You need to find just the basic, obvious presentation of the material. Look for the files in the package labeled "base color", "diffuse", or "albedo".

Chapter 3 contains a discussion on using patterns, making seamless patterns, and setting up pattern brushes. In a scenic sketch, the additional technique of transforming their perspective is needed. Typically, the most straightforward way to accomplish this is to make a new layer, create a pattern-filled shape large enough to cover the surface you're working on, and cut or erase any overspill.

- Make a new layer.
- Select a shape tool.
- Tool Options:
  - Set Fill to "Pattern".
  - Outline to "No Outline".
  - "Rotation" and "Scale" to fit the size and position of the surface in your sketch. This may take some trial and error.
  - Select the pattern in the Pattern docker.
- Draw the shape over the area you are working on.

At this point, if you have a transparent version of your base drawing, moving it to the top of the layer stack and editing any patterned shapes in layers below it can be very useful.

- Select the "Transform" tool.
- Click on the "Perspective options" button at the top of the docker.
- Control handles will appear around the new shape.
  - You can refine the control by first selecting the precise area to be edited and then activating the Transform tool.
- Adjust the handles so that the pattern maintains the correct dimensionality for the sketch. Be sure to expand it where necessary to cover the area completely.
- Select and delete any parts of the shape that fall outside the intended area. You can also use an eraser, particularly where you want the pattern to fade rather than end abruptly.
  - HINT: If an eraser is selected in the Brush docker, the area selection tools will automatically delete any selected areas.

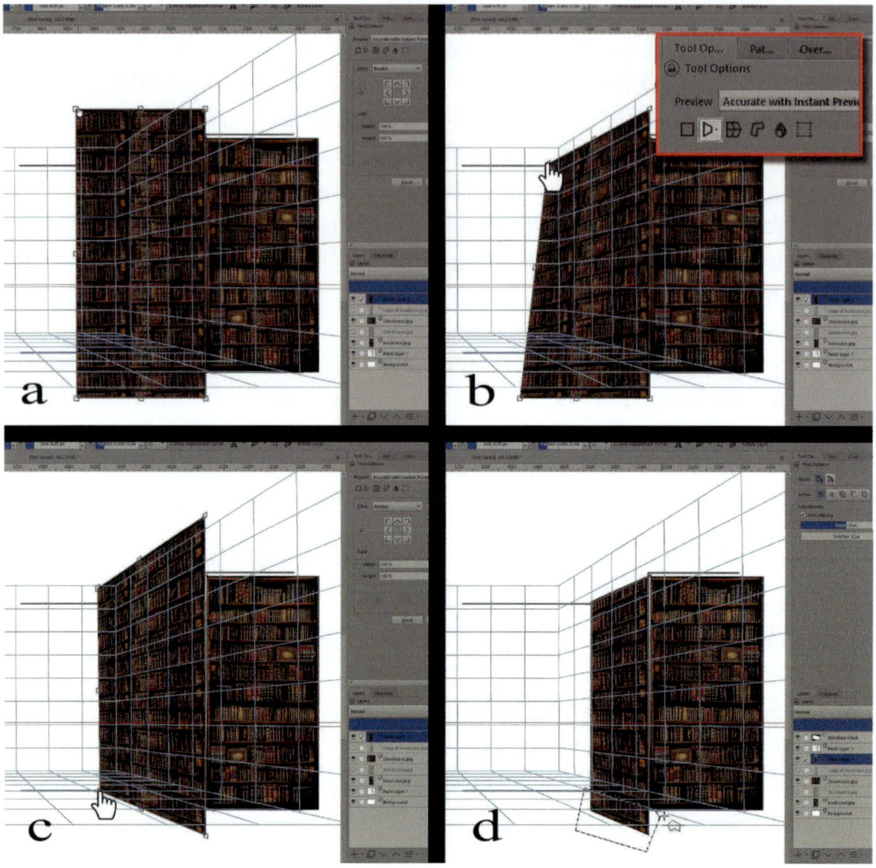

FIGURE 5.9 a) Create a patterned shape. b) and c) Give a pattern the proper perspective with the Transform tool. d) Trim the pattern to fit the area.

LIGHTING STORYBOARDS

No sketch is truly complete until it's illuminated with dramatic lighting that captures a moment in the show. Various lighting effects can be layered one at a time and adjusted in intensity or color until the perfect effect is achieved. The ability to simulate lighting on a sketch to explore all its different aspects is one of the most compelling reasons to embrace digital rendering. Once the lighting designer has a basic sketch of the set in hand, they can begin crafting a series of lighting storyboards. These storyboards become invaluable tools for the lighting designer, often serving as the only means of pre-visualization available.

Pre-visualization is just as crucial in lighting design as it is in any other facet of production. Set designers and costume designers flesh out their ideas through sketching and model-making, visually experimenting until they find a design solution that resonates. These sketches serve as a tangible means of communication among the production team, allowing for discussions that go beyond mere words.

Lighting storyboards function as a collection of smaller sketches that illustrate the lighting effects for each major cue. Throughout this collaborative process, sketches can be redrawn and re-imagined as many times as necessary. After all, a picture is worth a thousand words, and without visual representation, the entire design process stalls. This is equally true for lighting design, an integral part of the visual tableau on stage, requiring development through visual means such as lighting storyboards.

FIGURE 5.10 Designer Lindsay Webster combined color in addition to black and white in her lighting storyboards for *The Shape of Things.*

Just as one wouldn't expect a scenic designer to kick off the design process by drafting scenic units complete with all their dimensions, nor would a costume designer begin by drafting the patterns for each piece. Similarly, it's unreasonable to assume that a lighting designer would start their process by diving straight into a light plot. What informs the placement of the lighting instruments if the visual concepts haven't been brought to life? That's where lighting storyboards come in. They take an initial impulse or intention and help the designer figure out where the lights should go, how they should be focused, what intensity they should have, and the colors that will be involved.

Creating lighting storyboards isn't as complicated as some might think. Some lighting designers resist the notion of visualizing their design process, often claiming they can't draw. This argument simply doesn't hold water. In fact, it's almost laughable. Anyone can learn to draw! Typically, just one or two lessons from a skilled instructor or colleague can do the trick. While you might not emerge as an art prodigy overnight, anyone can certainly acquire the skills necessary to visualize design concepts. Plus, it doesn't require extraordinary drawing talent. With a rough outline of the set from the scenic designer, it's akin to a coloring book, simply color by numbers.

We've all colored in a coloring book at some point, and while the debate about staying within the lines is ongoing, the principle remains the same: take an existing idea and add color to it. The essentials of a lighting storyboard include highlights, shade, and shadow. Lighting design has often been described as painting with light, and that's exactly what you're doing in a lighting storyboard.

Highlights demonstrate how light affects the people or objects it touches, while shade represents the unlit sides that recede into dimness and darkness. Shadows can be incidental or meticulously crafted. In either case, the lighting designer is in charge of where those shadows fall and how they appear, just as designers are responsible for illuminating the entire scene from edge to edge, top to bottom, ensuring even the parts of the stage picture that fade into darkness are thoughtfully considered, alongside the key elements that demand attention and visibility.

Storyboards can start off in grayscale, and later, as you find you need more detail, you can add color. Generally, it's a good idea to kick off your storyboarding process on a medium to medium-light gray surface. This gray acts as a baseline for ambient light, making it easier to use brighter colors for highlights, showing how light interacts with your scene, while darker colors can nicely depict shade and shadow. If you begin with a pure white surface, you'll have to work much harder to create that middle ground and get your highlights to pop against the background.

On the flip side, starting on a pure black background can create some striking effects, but it also demands significantly more effort to render the scene. You'd begin with highlights and then have to fill in all the mid-tones, which can be quite the task.

FIGURE 5.11 A rough sketch is all that is needed to begin storyboarding the lights.

Initially, you'll want to have some sort of sketch or rough draft depicting the size and shape of the scenery for each act and scene, provided by your scenic designer. That sketch needs to be digitized if it isn't in a digital format already. You can do this by either fitting the drawing to your scanner or, if that's not practical, scanning the sketch in sections and then assembling them digitally. Alternatively, a smartphone camera is an excellent option, especially if you have good lighting, natural sunlight works best, and a tripod to keep your shots steady.

With a phone camera, it's effortless to snap a photo and send it straight to your computer, send it in an email, or upload it to a cloud account for easy sharing. Once it's on your computer, you can straighten any keystoning, rotate the image, and make adjustments to any scaling errors in the drawing. If you prefer, there are scanning apps for your phone that can automatically handle most of those corrections, making the whole process a lot smoother.

Start by creating a duplicate layer of your imported sketch. You can achieve this by either clicking the "copy layer" button or using the classic "select-all", "copy", "paste" command. It doesn't hurt to do it twice just to play it safe. The sequence in which you tackle the steps is entirely up to you. For now, let's dive into the highlighting. We're going to "paint with light" or use paint that mimics light.

Choose a brush or sketch tool that has some character – something that produces an interesting line quality, not just a basic circle. Aim for a tool that has that calligraphic flair, something wide in one direction and narrow in the other. This variation will allow you to create fascinating lines as your sketch tool shifts direction, enabling you to make thick lines when drawing in one direction and thin lines when drawing in the other.

This method evokes an old scenic artist's trick for rendering light in a painting (or the trick of a very old scenic artist). The go-to brush for scene painters is the fitch, a tool with long bristles that delivers an engaging line. The bristles are wide on one side and narrow on the other. A standard one-and-a-half-inch fitch, for instance, features bristles that are an inch and a half wide and half an inch deep.

When you paint with a scenic fitch, you create a calligraphic line, wide when you brush in one direction and narrow as you angle off to the side. Old-school scenic artists used to render light in a scene by angling the bristles toward the light source, high right, high left, medium right, low. If the brush is angled to indicate light from high left (the standard unless instructed otherwise), the illumination will emanate from that direction.

As you brush across the top of an object, such as a brick, you'll leave a bold line along the top and a thinner line down the side where the light hits. As the light source moves to a lower position, the line on top will thin, while the one on the side widens.

FIGURE 5.12 A scenic fitch and the line variation it produces.

You can apply the same technique for painting cast shadows on objects like bricks. Using a transparent, dark, cool color (think blue or purple) while maintaining that high left sun positioning, drag a bold line along the bottom of the brick and a thinner line on the opposite side, the right side. When the light is exactly 45 degrees to the brick, the top and sides receive even illumination. As the sun sets or the light dips lower, the shadow on the side will become broader than that on the bottom.

You can replicate this process when lighting a sketch. Treat a building or piece of furniture just as you would a brick. Angle your brush toward the light source and, without rotating it, glide it across the surfaces where the light strikes. This technique can make quick work of indicating the direction of the key light in a scene.

This is where it really helps to visualize in your mind how the light interacts with the object. One obvious option is to place an object in your workspace under a desk lamp. It doesn't have to be a model sofa; it could be any object that has a lumpy, sofa-like quality. As you adjust the desk lamp up and down, and front to back, you'll get a clear idea of how strong the highlights need to be. Is the light primarily hitting the front? Grab your painting tool and apply highlights there. If the light source is distant, making it less intense and more diffuse, instead of dulling down all the highlights with lower opacity, try painting them brightly from the get-go, then use the layer's opacity and blending modes to refine the image later. This method allows for easy adjustment.

How sharp is the focus in your scene? If it's very hard and sculptural, stick with a solid brush that has well-defined edges. On the other hand, a softer focus calls for a brush with a gentle edge. You might want to select a different brush from your palette or tweak the one you're using, following the brush editor instructions. For those dreamy, misty moonlight scenes, consider an airbrush instead of a traditional bristle brush or a dry-brushing tool. While an airbrush won't give you a calligraphic line, it will allow you to blend colors smoothly over a larger area.

When using an airbrush tool, you will need to utilize masks. For more detailed guidance on masking objects before painting, check back to Chapter 3. For now, stick with simple black and white tools. The beauty of digital art is that if you want to shift from black and white sketching to color, it's totally doable, as long as you're working with multiple layers. Remember to always start a new layer before diving into highlights. And while you're adding highlights, don't forget to illuminate the surfaces surrounding the lit object – think floor, walls, stairs. It's all too easy to get caught up in lighting your main subject and overlook the ambient light effects, but in real life, that overspill happens, and it should reflect in our storyboards too. If you need to light an object while keeping nearby pieces free from excess light, raise the light's position and angle accordingly, and sketch that out in your lighting storyboard.

Cast Shadows

Starting with cast shadows, pay attention to how the highlights direct the shading. If your highlights are coming from the right, that means the shadows will fall to the left. A highlight will cast a short shadow on the floor, while a low-angle light will produce a longer shadow. If the light is coming from the side, expect shadows to stretch across the stage. You can create cast shadows by erasing patches in the highlight pool or the overshoot area, or you can start a new layer and paint in a dark shape that mirrors the lit object.

This information can prove invaluable if you're intentionally using cast shadows as part of your dramatic statement. For instance, if you want to evoke the power and presence of Don Giovanni, casting a striking shadow on the wall behind him might be just the ticket. In such cases, it's wise to paint in the shadow first, which can help you determine where the highlights should go. It often requires you to position your lighting instrument so that it creates the desired shadow. While deciphering a lighting instrument's position based on highlights can sometimes feel subjective, the cast shadow often provides a more definitive clue.

FIGURE 5.13 *My Fair Lady* storyboards previsualize the making of a plot.

The storyboard will give you visual clues to the placement of instruments. To find the right position for the lights, draw a line from the end of the cast shadow to the top of the object casting it, and extend that line outward. This will give you a close approximation for placing the lighting instrument. To help you see the cast shadow more clearly, you might find that exaggerating the floor plane in your sketch is necessary, even if it doesn't match the perspective plane or the scenic designer's drawing. All's fair in love, war, and lighting sketches!

Shading

Shading can be tackled with whatever tool you prefer. Decide on the effect you're aiming for. Do you want a hard, painted shade that aligns with the crisp focus of the highlights or something softer that wraps gracefully around the figure, lending it a more three-dimensional look while downplaying its sculptural traits? Shading is often the most effective technique for communicating the quality of light and the amount of ambient light, or fill light, in a scene.

Start a new layer and adjust the transparency or opacity to around 70%. Typically, the placement of shade mirrors that of the highlight. On a rounded surface, don't let the shading reach the highlight; maintain some of the background mid-tone between them. This way, with less work, you'll create a smoother gradient.

For lighting with a hard focus, you may need the highlight and shade to be closer together. A soft focus suggests leaving more space and more middle tones between the two. Zooming in on your picture makes it easier to use a soft focus or soft-edged painting tool without straying too far from the lines. Since you're working on a separate layer, it's efficient to use something like an airbrush tool and paint over the outline and beyond. You can then come back with an eraser to refine your edges. Remember, the eraser is a drawing tool, too! Often, this approach is more time-efficient than masking everything off.

FIGURE 5.14 Shading objects with hard and soft shading.

6 Introduction to 3D Modeling

FIGURE 6.1 A computer model for the production of Steven Sondheim's *Assassins*.

Modeling is the process of creating representations of three-dimensional objects in a two-dimensional format. Unlike two-dimensional drawings, 3D models can be viewed from various angles, allowing for detailed observation and interaction. In modeling programs, this viewpoint is called the camera, which can be adjusted similarly to a real camera, including focus and zoom settings.

For example, if an actor is positioned behind a sofa, changing the camera angle can reveal both the actor and the sofa from different perspectives, enhancing understanding of the scene.

Creating 3D objects involves constructing a mathematical model composed of polygons, simple shapes such as triangles and squares. Imagine a mirrored

DOI: 10.4324/9781003571742-6

disco ball. It may look smooth from a distance, but up close, it's composed of many small square mirrors. The more facets a model (or a disco ball) has, the smoother it appears. Each facet is defined by the coordinates of each of its corners in 3D space (X, Y, Z). A modeling file is a list of these numbers for each of thousands or tens of thousands of facets of each of the hundreds of objects in a scene. Think about how all these objects, facets, points, and coordinates are smoothly being recalculated as you change your view of the scene. This is why we let computers do it.

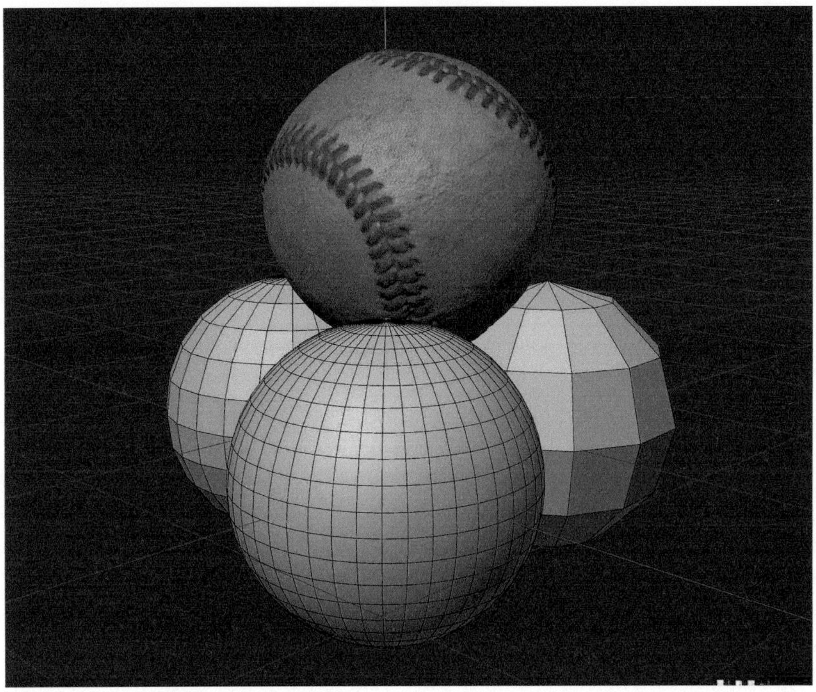

FIGURE 6.2 Four versions of a simple sphere object, varying in complexity and the resulting appearance.

That these objects appear to possess volume is ultimately an illusion. Any drawing or painted representation of a stage space creates an illusion, but when we utilize computer-generated imagery, we add a remarkable dimension: the ability to inhabit a 3D space or a virtual environment that can be viewed from any position and at any angle. This computer-generated space is commonly referred to as a virtual world, or in this case, a virtual stage.

3D objects can be enhanced with realistic textures, such as wood grain and fabric patterns, resulting in detailed representations that are difficult to achieve manually. By adding virtual lighting instruments, you can simulate how real lights work in a theater, casting shadows and adjusting color temperatures to create ambiance.

Additionally, virtual sets can feature projected images for dynamic backgrounds, allowing for quick scene changes. This flexibility surpasses traditional models, enabling multiple renderings to demonstrate various scene transitions and lighting effects.

Ultimately, these 3D representations come to life just as your physical stage set does when the work lights are turned off, the curtain rises, and the performance begins.

FIGURE 6.3 A digital scenic model, hidden-line, flat-shaded, with texture and light.

Working in an accurately scaled virtual space means that you can observe your virtual set from precise angles, which is crucial for effective staging. You can set up specific viewing positions such as the far house right, far house left, mezzanine front, balcony rear, and even from the lighting grid. (Why, I don't know, but you could.) You can visualize sight lines without approximate guesses. You can know exactly what the audience will see when they look through the window and see the backdrop, or through the archway toward the stairs.

You can assess whether the actors are visible from key audience perspectives. It's vital to determine if the lights can effectively illuminate them and assess how these elements interact with one another. Additionally, you can verify if the stage manager can see what needs to be seen.

The placement of lighting instruments can be demonstrated. For instance, it will be known if lights will cast unwanted shadows in certain areas or highlight elements that should remain unnoticed. Questions about how the yellow light will appear on a blue dress are easily answered in this environment.

After making these discoveries in the viewport, you can create dramatic full-color, lit renderings that effectively illustrate your work to colleagues or stakeholders, demonstrating the dynamic qualities of your scenery. During production conferences, you can present videos that depict light or set changes in real-time, which can help clarify your intentions. Furthermore, you can integrate your virtual set into a virtual reality program, allowing people to experience the environment in real-time. This not only enhances collaboration but also makes you look like a wizard!

FIGURE 6.4 The *My Fair Lady model*, viewed as from the balcony and directly above.

3D MODELING PROGRAMS

There are numerous 3D modeling programs available for creating scenic models, even though they are designed for other fields. 3D modeling software generally specializes in specific uses, with some focusing on animation and others on CAD/CAM or construction industries, enhancing design visualization. Many programs are suitable for beginners, offering limited features and simpler interfaces. Online 3D modeling platforms have also emerged, offering a range of capabilities.

While proprietary software used by large animation studios is often unavailable to the public, Renderman from Pixar stands out as an exception, offering versions that are free for all users.

Commercial software tends to be expensive, though more affordable and even free open-source options exist that can be functional for projects like theatre stage models. Finding user-friendly software with a shallow learning curve is crucial, as it allows for gradual skill development through incremental learning with each project.

Autodesk offers notable programs, such as *3ds Max*, which is known for its comprehensive features but features a steep learning curve. *Maya*, also from Autodesk, excels in video integration and special effects. *Revit* integrates modeling with construction and manufacturing, providing organizational tools for efficient project management, including timelines and specifications.

Cinema 4D, developed by Maxon Corporation, is my preferred modeling program due to its intuitive interface and sophisticated features beneath the surface. I often teach it to others because of its shallow learning curve.

SketchUp is another well-known modeling program, particularly popular for its free version during its early years. While it offers a unique modeling process, it lacks native support for advanced lighting and requires additional software for quality rendering, making it less versatile for those transitioning to other programs.

The 3D modeling landscape continually evolves, with options such as *Spline*, *TinkerCAD*, and *Onshape*, which come with limitations in file management and may require paid storage options.

Specialty software exists for specific aspects of 3D design. *Rhino* uses a NURBS modeling system, ideal for organic shapes. *ZBrush* excels in sculpting, which can be fantastic, particularly for character modeling. However, it has a steep learning curve and a higher cost. For a more accessible introduction to sculpting, *Sculptris* offers a free version.

Adobe's *Substance 3D* suite provides free access to its products for students, making it an attractive educational option. Other notable tools include *Shapr3D* for product design, *LightWave* for animation in film, and *FreeCAD*, which combines modeling and drafting capabilities.

Vectorworks is a favored drafting software for scenographers, offering the capability to convert 2D drafting into 3D models, streamlining the design process. While its modeling and rendering capabilities are limited, its built-in integration with *Cinema 4D* allows for seamless export for advanced 3D work. For better modeling, it's a better idea to start directly in *Cinema 4D*.

Another notable feature of *Vectorworks* is its ability to create light plots and export instrument data in various 3D formats, such as DWG or DAE. This enables the inclusion of crucial lighting properties, such as position, color, and beam angle, in scenic models. Later, intensities can be set, creating simulated lighting cues.

Blender, an open-source software, is highly popular and compatible with many modeling and virtual reality programs. While it offers a wealth of features and materials, its interface relies heavily on keyboard shortcuts, which can result in a steep learning curve.

To counter this, *Bforartists* has been developed as a more user-friendly alternative to *Blender*. It retains *Blender's* functionality but features a simplified interface with fewer shortcuts, enhancing accessibility for artists and designers.

Bforartists makes navigation and task execution intuitive, allowing users to focus more on creativity. The 3D modeling techniques demonstrated in subsequent chapters will utilize *Bforartists*.

BASICS FOR 3D MODELING WITH ANY APPLICATION

When using any application, 2D or 3D, it's essential to back up your work to a different location on your computer, an external hard drive, or the cloud. Many cloud storage services are free and offer software for automatically backing up your files or folders, protecting your work from unexpected issues.

Take advantage of your software's auto-backup features by adjusting the settings to suit your needs. Set backup intervals for approximately 15 to 20 minutes and retain around five backup versions to safeguard your latest work. Additionally, cultivate the habit of saving your progress frequently; pressing Ctrl + S every 15 minutes or after a break can help. When making significant changes, save multiple versions labeled with dates or times to easily revert if needed.

As highlighted earlier, the goal is not to create elaborate renderings or sketches. Models, whether created on the computer or by hand, serve primarily as preliminary notes guiding you toward the ultimate goal: designing a finely crafted stage production. Avoid getting lost in minute details. Focusing excessively on minor details, such as the intricacies of a table lamp's pull chain, may hinder your progress. It is crucial to establish efficient practices. Efficiency is speed multiplied by quality. While you may create a stunning model, if it's completed two days after opening night, it's neither efficient nor practical. Conversely, if you manage to produce a model quickly but the result is unrecognizable, it serves no purpose.

Begin your modeling process with basic shapes and layouts, akin to the practice of making a traditional white model. Subsequently, refine these models as you work up the design. Unlike traditional rough or white models, with digital tools, there is no need to start from scratch after making initial shapes. You can continue to enhance and develop your model incrementally, maintaining momentum and keeping the project on track.

3D SPACE

The first and most important skill to master when using 3D modeling programs is navigating within the virtual space. First, you need to become accustomed to using various types of views. Unlike a 2D graphics program in which you merely have to pan back and forth, up and down, and zoom in and out, a 3D modeling program uses a simulated 3D workspace. There is an extra dimension of movement in that creative process.

Orthographic Views

To describe this, programs represent the 3D space with the same views that we use when drafting a three-dimensional set piece, such as a staircase or a stage set as a whole. Namely, the orthographic projection, which involves using a top view, a front view, and at least one side view.

When modeling, there may be four views open simultaneously: three for orthographic projections (front, top, and side), and a fourth for a perspective view. This occupies a significant amount of screen space. As a remedy, not all four views need to be open at the same time. A simple keystroke will switch the views between top, bottom, back, and either side. Views can also be changed by clicking on the colorful widget in the top-right of all views. This is particularly useful when using a smaller screen, such as those found on laptop computers. Optionally, you can use other configurations. Rather than using all orthographic views, you can open just two, perhaps the top and one side. The screen can be split horizontally or vertically. You can arrange views any way you want. Finally, 3D programs utilize an additional view, known as the perspective view, which is used when rendering the scene.

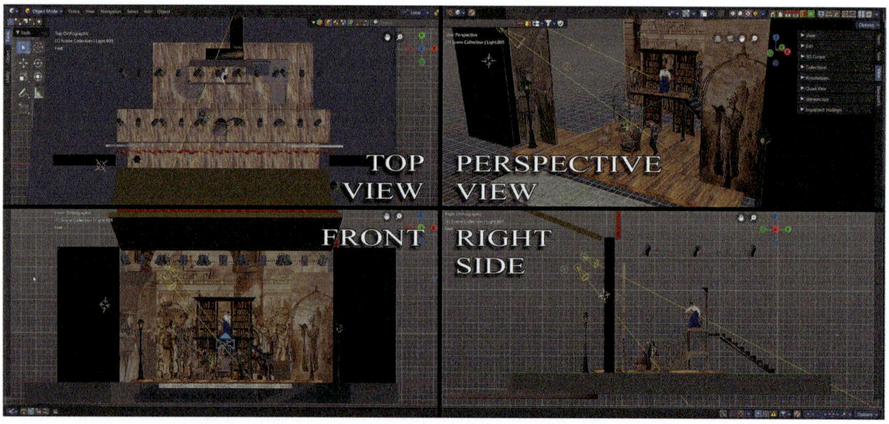

FIGURE 6.5 Orthographic views: Top, Side, Front, and Perspective.

Some programs are designed to work primarily with the perspective view. *Cinema 4D* is one that does, *Blender* or *Bforartists* is another. SketchUp also works primarily in that view. However, working solely in the perspective view can lead to some very serious misperceptions. Significant errors in the placement of objects can occur because you are seeing a flat, two-dimensional representation of a 3D space. Depth perception is not possible.

When working with orthographic projections, you know precisely where things are located. Checking the side and front views will ensure that all elements are positioned correctly in the 3D space.

TABLE 6.1 The default shortcut keys for changing views in the workspace.

Front	Number Pad 1	
Back	Ctrl + Number Pad 1	
Right	Number Pad 3	
Left	Ctrl + Number Pad 3	
Top	Number Pad 7	
Bottom	Ctrl + Number Pad 7	
Toggle View	Number Pad.	Toggle Between Orthographic and Perspective
Frame Selected	Number Pad 0	Move the view to frame the selected object
Frame Selected – Quad View	Ctrl + Number Pad 0	Frame the selected object in all four views
Frame All	Home	Frame the entire scene
Frame All – Quad View	Ctrl + Home	Frame the scene in all four views

Opening an orthographic view is always very easy. All programs use buttons or hotkeys for this. In *Bforartists,* the buttons are located at the right end of the main toolbar and feature icons resembling different views of a small house. The hotkeys for the views are listed in Table 6.1.

You can zoom and pan orthographic views in the usual way. View Rotation is locked by default. If rotation is unlocked, rotating in an orthographic view converts it to the perspective view.

To unlock/lock the view rotation:

- Viewport Tabs (Right side of the viewport) View > Quad View > "Lock Rotation".

To lock all views together so zooming and panning in one is mirrored in the others:

- View > Quad View > "Sync Zoom/Pan" locks all views together so zooming and panning in one is mirrored in the others.

To use all four main views:

- Viewport Menu View > "Toggle Quad View" or Ctrl + Alt + Q.

Other useful view commands are:

- Viewport Menu View > Area > “Horizontal Split”.
  View > Area > “Vertical Split”.

In addition, the multi-colored axis widget at the top-right of all viewports serves as a switch for orthographic views. Clicking on the circle at the end of any axis will activate the view related to that axis.

View Controls

- Select Orthographic views using the buttons in the toolbar.
  - Option 1 Front = Num Pad 1, Right = Num Pad 3, Top = Num Pad 7, Toggle Perspective = Num Pad, Frame the Selected Object = Num Pad 0
  - Option 2 Click on one of the direction nodes of the Viewport Axis widget.
- Select viewport shading using the buttons in the toolbar.

Viewport Shading

In addition to the various views, you can also select the display style. The most complex is a fully featured shading that will show objects with all textures in the scene’s lighting. “Display render preview” in *Bforartists*, “Gouraud Shading” in *Cinema 4D*, and 3ds Max, “Realistic”. The displayed scene will be partially rendered, incorporating light, shade, and shadows. One problem with full shading is that details in shadows may not be clearly visible. It is also more processor-intensive, slowing view changes.

Another display option is “flat shading,” which shows materials and basic lighting but no cast shadows. The “Hidden line” display shows you the shapes of the objects without textures. Everything defaults to a base color, typically gray, unless you make a change. In *Bforartists*, display styles are changed by selecting the buttons in the toolbar, which feature icons indicating the different styles.

The last option is “Wireframe” display. Wireframing is just what the name implies. Objects are depicted with lines at the polygon edges, and nothing else. This X-ray view can be helpful when one object occludes the view of other objects behind it.

It is possible to add edge visibility to viewing modes. This allows for the visualization of all the individual facets of the modeled objects, along with their textures. This is very important when doing advanced modeling and editing the shape of individual facets *Bforartists* features a set of icons in the main toolbar to facilitate easy switching between viewing modes. You can switch by clicking one of a series of small spheres, each drawn to resemble either wireframe, solid, (hidden line), material preview (flat shading), and rendered (preview).

FIGURE 6.6 An object displayed in different shading styles.

NAVIGATION

To navigate the three-dimensional space in any view or mode, you will need to maneuver in several ways. You'll need a way of panning (sliding) the view right, left, up, and down. You'll also need to zoom in and out. In a 3D program, the viewpoint (camera) will be moving through the virtual space. Zooming out may take you from looking at the sofa to seeing the whole set, and then "backing up" further until you're seeing the whole theatre.

To complete the navigation, you need a method to turn the viewpoint. Most of these are "orbit" turns, as in orbiting around a particular object. After selecting an object, the orbit movement causes the viewpoint to move around that object, while it remains centered in the window. A variation is to orbit around the world center, the 0, 0, 0 point in your space. Another variation is to orbit around the center of the viewport or around the cursor. Here, wherever your cursor is or whatever it's pointed at when you begin to orbit, will be the center of the orbit.

The other method of rotation is a "Camera" rotation. Available in some modelers, this allows you to turn the view as if looking through a camera and turning around while remaining in place.

In all 3D programs, these navigation tools are assessed in several ways. Typically, there is an onscreen widget with buttons that can be clicked and dragged. *Bforartists* has such a widget, but like other applications, it also features mouse controls for navigation that are even more useful.

- ORBIT: Pressing the "right mouse button (RMB)" while dragging orbits the view.
- ZOOM: Zoom in and out using the mouse's "Scroll wheel".
- PAN: Pressing the "middle mouse button (MMB)" and dragging pans the view.

If you don't have a three-button mouse, pressing the "scroll wheel" works similarly. If you are using a Mac mouse or, like me, don't like pressing the scroll wheel, change the preferences.

- Edit menu > Preferences > Input tab. Click the "Emulate 3-Button Mouse" box.
  - o Now pressing "Alt" on the keyboard and dragging with the "left mouse button (LMB)" will pan the view.

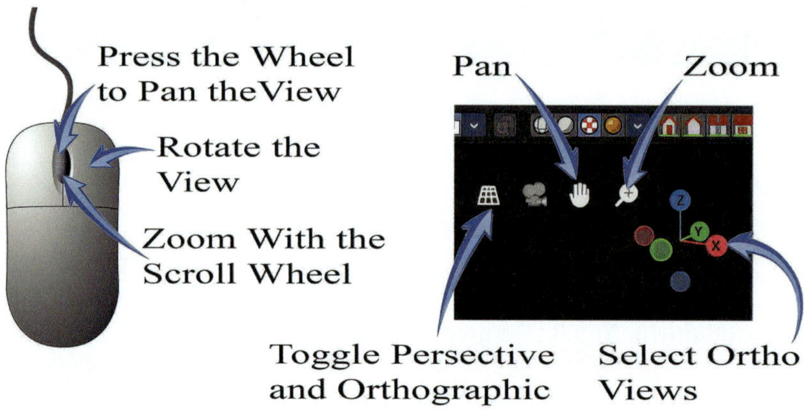

FIGURE 6.7 Viewport navigation, Pan, Rotate, and Zoom.

Also,

- Edit menu > Preferences > Navigation tab. Check the "Orbit Around Selected" box.
  - o Having the view rotate around the selected object is commonly the desirable option, and activating this preference will make it the default behavior.

You will also want to set up your own keyboard shortcuts. Open the program's list of all keyboard shortcuts and key-mouse combinations.

- Edit menu > Preferences > Keymap tab.
- Click the triangle to the left of each keymap in the list to open a dropdown for editing that map.

All of the main movements can be codified with settings such as Z + LMB to pan, X + LMB to zoom, and C + LMB to rotate. (Try these suggestions.) You can also make completely new shortcuts in this tab.

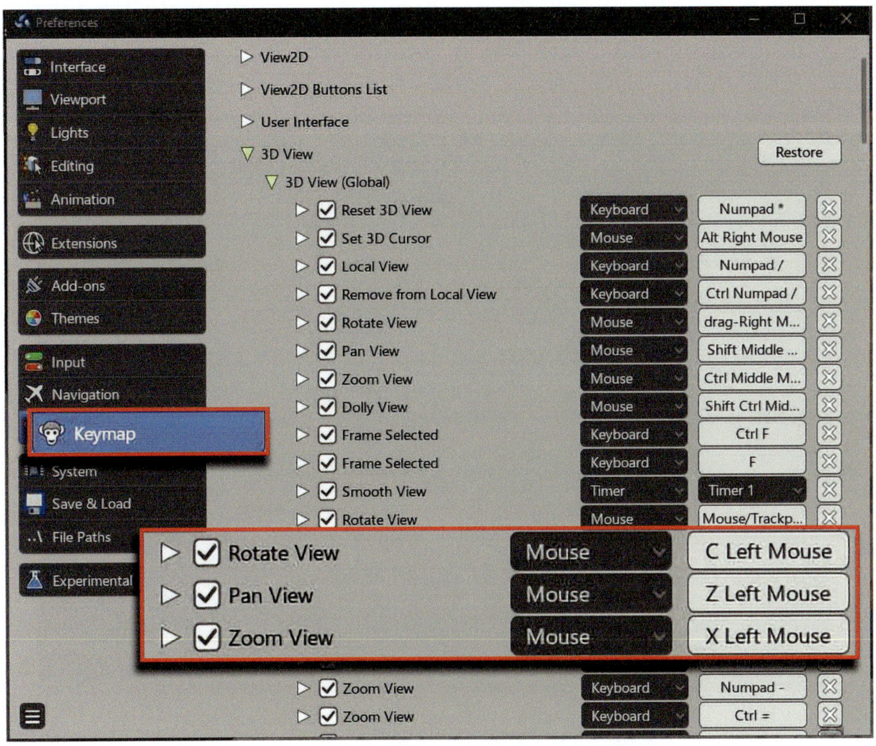

FIGURE 6.8 Setting new navigation shortcuts in Preferences.

3D COORDINATES

After mastering navigation in simulated three-dimensional space using orthographic and perspective views, it becomes clear that a system is essential for locating objects within that environment. The virtual world utilizes a three-axis coordinate system to achieve this. Each object has a center, which determines its location, and every polygon that constitutes the object is positioned using these three-axis coordinates. Additionally, every corner point of each polygon is similarly defined.

The three axes are X, Y, and Z. The x-axis runs side to side, or east to west. On a 2D screen, X moves from right to left, while in our simulated theatre, it goes from stage right to stage left, parallel to the proscenium's plaster line. An object's position is measured along this line with numerical values. Moving left from the center line starts at 0 feet and inches and increases, while moving right decreases the value into negative values. For a proscenium 40 feet wide, the sides are located at x = 20 feet (stage left) and x = -20 feet (stage right).

X and Y are also employed in 2D drawing programs, where X runs left to right, and Y runs top to bottom. Essentially, all windows and icons on your computer screen are located using pixel counts in X and Y coordinates.

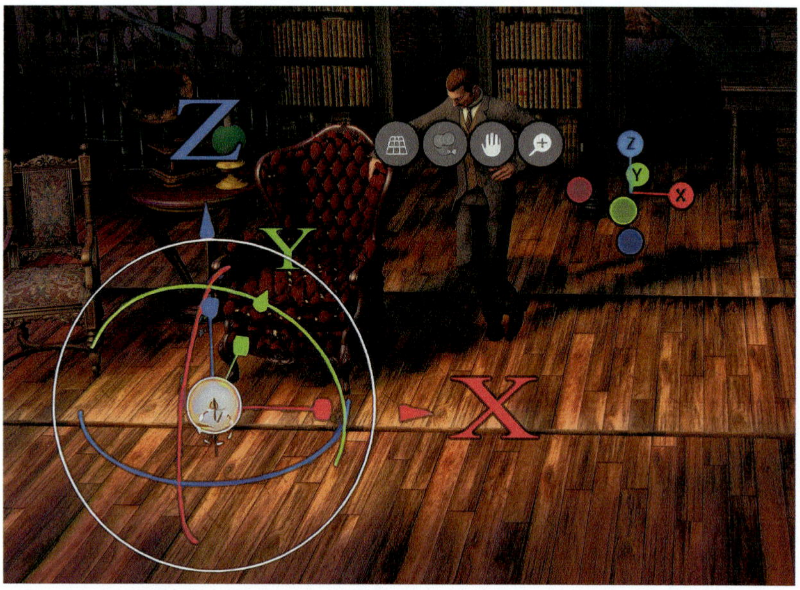

FIGURE 6.9 The X, Y, Z axes and the Viewport widget.

The Y and Z axes may be used differently in different modeling programs. Many (such as *Bforartists*) use a ground plan orientation, making the Y axis parallel to the theatre's center line. Y values increase going upstage and decrease going downstage.

A good location for Y = 0 is the plaster line. Positive (+) values are upstage of the proscenium, and negative (-) values are downstage. So, you can plot the position of an object on the stage floor by using X and Y values. When drafting a ground plan, designers often include measurements that show the location of set props using dimensions from the center line and plaster line, such as three feet stage right and six feet upstage. This is the same principle, using X and Y values rather than stage right, stage left, up, or down stage.

But in dealing with 3D space, we must have a third dimension. The third dimension is the one that goes toward the viewer and away from the viewer. In a ground plan orientation, the third axis, the Z-axis, runs from beneath the stage floor upward into the fly loft. Again, the position of Z = 0 is variable. A typical location would be the level of the stage floor. Positive (+) Z values are upward, increasing into the loft, and negative (-) Z values are downward, decreasing towards the trap room.

Alternately, a few programs, like *Cinema 4D*, start with the front view as the primary view. This is similar to looking at the stage from the audience. In that case, X is still stage right to stage left, but now the Y-axis goes from above the stage to below it, and the Z-axis aligns from up to downstage.

Simply put, different programs use right-to-left in the same way but swap the orientation of the Y-axis and the Z-axis. Practically, this makes little difference to us while we are modeling. Sometimes, when you import an object created using a different Y, Z system, the imported object will import lying on its back or face, improperly positioned by 90°. Most programs have a "Flip Z-Y axis" option to use when importing objects. Even without this correction, turning an object 90° to reposition it correctly is a small matter.

Fortunately, 3D modeling programs share other common interface features. All have a multi-colored widget in the viewport that illustrates the orientation of the X (red), Y (green), and Z (blue) axes. The same colors are also used in the center lines of the viewport reference grids to show the axes orientation.

USER INTERFACES

Some practice is necessary, but you will quickly become adept at maneuvering through 3D space and switching to the most advantageous view. Becoming familiar with the user interface (UI) of 3D modeling programs is key. While the UI differs from one application to another, those differences are mostly cosmetic; functionally, they are quite similar. Tools may have different icons and locations, but they perform the same tasks. UIs are designed to be intuitive, featuring explanatory icons and descriptive names for commands. Most applications also offer tooltips that display brief descriptions when the cursor is hovered over buttons.

The common structure of UIs includes customizable panels, collectively referred to as a workspace or layout. Each workspace contains main menus, a main toolbar, and viewports, which are the windows showing the model in orthographic or perspective views. These viewports often have menus and tabs with commands specific to their properties. In *Bforartists*, they are called editors; in *Cinema 4D*, managers; and in *3ds Max*, panels.

You can customize UIs in all major applications easily. You can close rarely used windows, open frequently used ones, and arrange editors and viewports according to your preferences. Once you establish a workspace that suits your workflow, you can save it as a default for future use.

Most programs provide various workspaces optimized for different workflows, typically represented by tabs. In *Bforartists*, these tabs are located in the Top Bar. Clicking a tab opens a different workspace, and you can find more options by clicking the white plus symbol. Right-clicking a tab lets you customize the tab strip, open and close tabs, and reorder them as desired.

Among the individual panels in the workspace, two are essential: the Outliner, which lists all scene items hierarchically, and the Properties editor, where you can view and edit the properties of selected items.

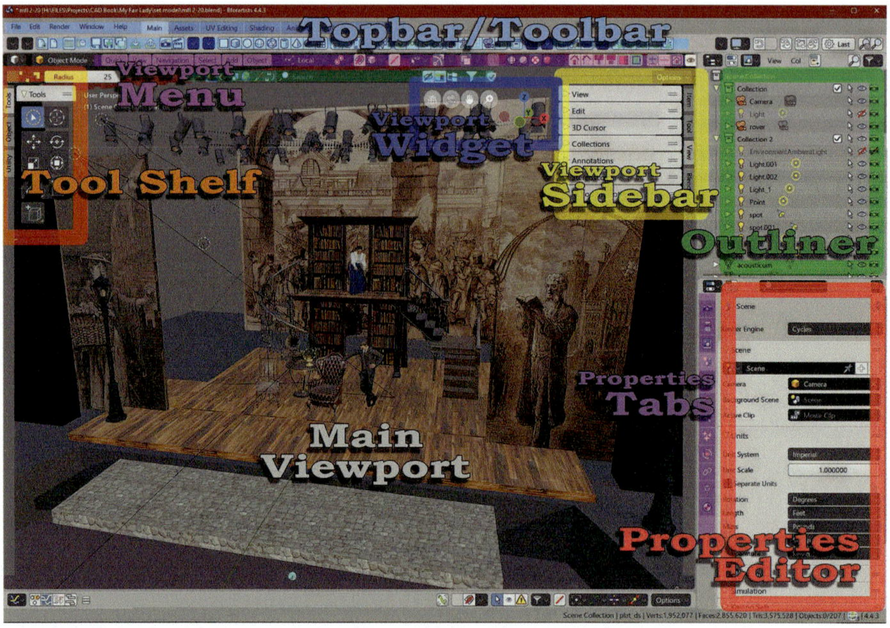

FIGURE 6.10 The *Bforartists* interface, color-coded.

All editors have the same parts, although some may be hidden.

- All have a header. Headers contain menus and toggles. Right-click on an editor's header to check the visibility of its elements. Sometimes, a header will not fit in a small editor window. In that case, the header can be scrolled by dragging while the middle mouse button is pressed.
- Editors also contain panels. A panel is the primary area that contains menus, switches, toggles, dropdowns, editable fields, sliders, and color pickers for adjusting parameters.
- Sidebars are another common feature of editors. For example, the Properties editor features a large sidebar with tabs for all editable parameters. In addition to editing scene elements, most project properties and many program preferences can be set in the Properties editor.
- Editors may also contain tool shelves (small palettes of tool icons).

CUSTOMIZING THE WORKSPACE

There are a few editors in the standard layout that are collapsed by default. The first one is the information window at the top of the screen. It is not terribly interesting to us. At the bottom of the screen, the collapsed editor is the timeline for animation. There is a good chance that you won't need animation anytime soon, so you might want to close it.

The Topbar Toolbar can't contain all of the tools, objects, lights, shapes, lines, and other elements that can be called into use. There simply is not room for them all across the window. So many are hidden until needed. At the far left, marked with downward arrows, are dropdowns for activating groups of assets. At the end of each icon group is another dropdown for activating various subsets.

Edit the Toolbar

Start with only the most useful open and customize the toolbar later as you discover favorite tools and options.

- Primitives – "Open Mesh", "Lights", "Other", and "Empties". Close the rest.
- View – "Align Buttons", "Toggle Orthographic Perspective".
- Navigation – "Frame Selected", "Frame All".
- Overlay – "Wireframe".

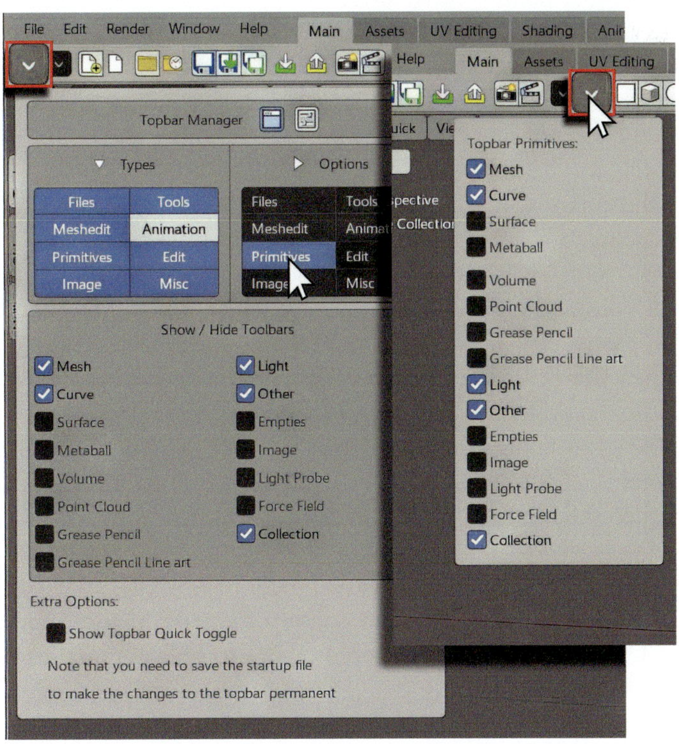

FIGURE 6.11 The Topbar Editor: Settings for the entire toolbar, and Settings for individual groups.

Viewports can be split into two, three, or more views.

- Bring your cursor to either of the top corners of the viewport, and it will turn into a white plus sign.
- Drag it to the side, and it will split the viewport, allowing you to view two different views simultaneously.
- Each view can be controlled separately.

To rejoin them:

- Bring the cursor up to the corner until it becomes the white cross.
- Click and drag the cursor from that view onto another, either horizontally or vertically.

Editor panels can be resized. If you place the cursor over the border of an editor, it will become the familiar two-headed arrow and can be dragged to resize the editor. This is common with many interfaces and programs, from word processors to 2D graphics applications.

You can swap the contents of two editors.

- Move the cursor to the top corner of one editor.
- Press "Ctrl" while dragging it into the target editor.
    - The mouse pointer turns into a Swap icon.
- Release the mouse, and the contents of the two editors will swap positions.

You can also duplicate an editor as a floating window, meaning it is not docked or stuck to the side of the viewport. To do this:

- Move the cursor to the upper corner of an editor so that it turns into the white cross.
- Press the "Shift" key and drag the cursor across the viewport.
    - The editor will detach from the edge where it was attached. That's useful, particularly if you have more than one monitor running.
    - When you float an editor, the original remains behind.
    - Close the original if you only want to keep the copy.
    - When you float an editor, there's no way to re-dock it to an edge. It remains a floating editor. The only way to recover it is to close and then reopen the file.

You can change an editor's type or basic function. Anyone can become a different kind of editor. In the upper right corner of an editor, you'll see the Editor Type icon. That icon may not be visible. That's to reduce visual noise and free up space on the UI.

To show the Editor Type menu:

- "Right-click" on an empty space somewhere in the header.
  - You will see a menu below labeled "Hide Editor Type".
- Check the box to show or hide the Editor Type menu.
- Once visible, click the icon to display a dropdown menu with all types of editors available for you to choose from.

You can collapse or fold menus. That's very handy if you use an editor often but not constantly.

- "Right-click" on an empty space in the header.
- Choose to display the text menu collapsed or expanded.

Tool shelves and their content can also be resized, as can Properties Editor content and the properties sidebar content. Move the cursor over the upper region of a tool shelf, hold down the control key, and click the middle mouse button. The cursor will turn into two white triangles. Drag up or down to resize the content area, or move the mouse over the upper region of the tool shelf and press plus or minus on the number pad.

Customizing the Appearance

You can change the cosmetic aspects of a workspace. Background colors, borders, and separators can all be tailored to your taste, as well as font typefaces, sizes, colors, and styles.

- Edit Menu > Preferences > Themes.

At the top of the panel are several default themes. More can be downloaded from official *Blender* sites or from various users. Below the presets are options to change the appearance of nearly every element in the user interface. Have fun! If you enjoy the interface of some other program, edit the look of the windows, toolbars, menus, and editors in *Bforartists* to resemble it.

Workspaces

You can also make a completely new workspace. Click on the plus sign at the right end of the tab strip to open the Add Workspace menu. Choosing to duplicate the current one will make a new tab. The name will be similar to "My current workspace 0 0 1." To rename the new layout, double-click on the name, and the text becomes editable. Give it a descriptive name. Now you can begin editing the workspace layout and its settings. A workspace is not only a set of editor windows. You can also find some workspace-specific settings in Viewport

Sidebar > Tool tab > Workspace. There, you can activate or deactivate different add-ons and extensions for individual workspaces. These settings will load every time you switch to this workspace.

To delete a workspace, "right-click" on its tab and choose "Delete". You can permanently remove any workspaces that you have created, but **the default workspaces remain in the menus.** Deletion will only make them vanish from the current tabs. These workspaces are protected so that you cannot remove them completely.

When you open a previously saved project, any workspace tabs that were present when you created it will be opened and added to the interface.

Full-featured applications have optional workspaces for different workflows. The main toolbar features tabs that open workspaces for Animation, Shading (textures), Nodes, and another that displays all the assets used in the model. Clicking the white + at the right of the tabs bar opens a dropdown menu with a dozen additional workspaces.

For those already accustomed to working with a particular program, customization allows for a seamless transition to a new one, enabling the workspace to be configured to resemble the familiar one.

Saving Your New Workspace!

After configuring a custom workspace, it needs to be saved.

To save it as the default:

- Edit menu > "Save As Startup File".
    - This will save the current workspace as the new startup and save any changes you have made in other workspaces as well.
    - You can't save new workspaces or the modifications of existing workspaces individually. **The only method is to return to the startup workspace and save it.** Why, you ask? I haven't a clue.

Setting the Scale!

Next, the model's scale and units need to be set. You should be using the correct dimensions from the start. Freestyle modeling, creating shapes that merely "look right," might give you a quick start, but there is a great danger of creating objects that simply will not fit in the simulated theater. To model objects that are the correct size, you need to set the "Scene" properties to the proper measurement units. After setting this property, it should act as the default until changed again, but check it at the start of new projects to be sure.

First, set the preferences to either the Metric or Imperial system. Measurement settings are saved with each individual project, so they are found in:

- Properties panel > Scene tab > Units >
    - Unit System – Select Metric or Imperial.
    - Unit Scale = 1.
    - Length – Select Meters or Feet.

Next, set the base unit. 3D programs don't make calculations based on feet, inches, meters, or miles. They only know "units." The results are displayed in feet, etc., for the user's benefit only. For that to happen, you need to define the meaning of a "unit." While the Scene tab is still open, make sure the Unit Scale is set to 1. But 1 what? To use feet and fractional inches, the "Length" parameter must be set to "Feet." If it is set to inches, a proscenium opening that is 40 feet wide will be displayed as 480 inches. That would require way too much thinking.

Programs like ***Bforartists* and *Cinema 4D* use fractional feet instead of feet and inches.** The imperial system is a mess. Yards have 3 feet, feet have 12 inches, and inches include fractions like 1/4, 1/8, 1/16, or 1/32. The metric system is more precise and easier for computers, as it's based on multiples of 10.

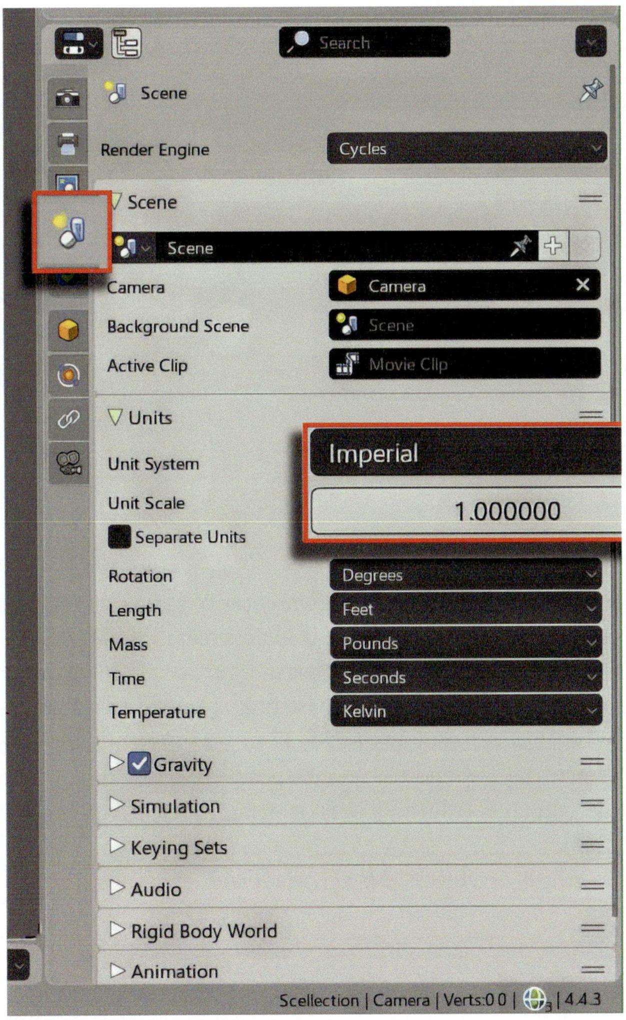

FIGURE 6.12 Selecting units and setting the scale.

Bforartists and *Cinema 4D* avoid the confusion by displaying measurements in feet and decimal feet, like 1.5 feet instead of 1'6". You can check imperial measurements in *Bforartists* by going to the Viewport Sidebar > Item > Transform > Dimensions fields, keeping the Transform tab open for quicker work. In most fields (Location, Rotation, or Dimension) you can input feet and inches, such as 2'9". It will immediately be converted to 2.75', but the result will be the same.

"Decimal feet" requires you to make some conversions, but it is usually enough to remember that 3" =.25, 6" =.5, and 9" =.75. I keep a small sticky note on my computer desktop with a table showing inches to fractions of a foot. Don't worry too much about fractional inches, 1/4", 3/8", etc. Very seldom do you need that level of precision in a virtual stage set.

TABLE 6.2 Imperial inches to decimal feet conversion table.

Inch	Decimal Foot	Fractional Inch	Decimal Foot
1 inch	0.0833	**1/8"**	0.01'
2 inches	0.167	**1/4"**	0.02'
3 inches	0.250	**3/8"**	0.03'
4 inches	0.333	**1/2"**	0.04'
5 inches	0.417	**5/8"**	0.05'
6 inches	0.500	**3/4"**	0.06'
7 inches	0.583	**7/8"**	0.07'
8 inches	0.667	**1"**	0.08'
9 inches	0.750		
10 inches	0.833		
11 inches	0.917		
12 inches	1.000		

When importing and exporting files, awareness of scale is crucial. For instance, a piece of furniture from an online source is likely created in the metric system. If it's 2 meters tall, it will show up as only 2 feet in your scene. To correct this, multiply by 3.28 if your base unit is feet. If your base unit is inches, that same 2-meter object will appear as 2 inches tall; multiply by 39.37 to get the right size. For objects based in centimeters, use 0.0328 and 0.3937, respectively. Rounding off these numbers won't harm the outcome. Adjusting scale is straightforward in:

- Properties editor > Objects tab > Transform.

Or

- Viewport > Item tag > Transform > Change the scale value of 1 to 3.28 (or whatever).
    - o If you type feet–inches (with the words feet or inches) into a property field, it will be converted to a decimal automatically.

7 3D Starting with Primitives

CREATING A NEW MODEL

When beginning the process of designing models in any 3D application, primitives are a natural starting point. The fundamental three-dimensional geometric shapes that we have been familiar with since elementary school are referred to as primitive shapes. These fundamental geometric shapes include planes, boxes, spheres, cylinders, cones, and pyramids. Some modeling programs expand this to include the donut shape (torus), and hollow pipes.

FIGURE 7.1 Scenographer Rana Esfandiary's design for *The Curious Incident of the Dog in the Night-Time* used primitive shapes to create the dramatic space and a projection surface.

With just primitives, you can model nearly anything. For instance, a stage flat is essentially a tall, thin cube. A set of steps is just a stack of cubes, each one taller than the last. Even a doorframe is an example of a simple post-and-lintel structure. Most furniture, such as desks and chairs, can be broken down into basic geometric shapes. A more organic or curvilinear

DOI: 10.4324/9781003571742-7

form, such as an armchair, can be simplified to cylinders, hemispheres, and a few cubes. Even complex objects, like human faces, start from a sphere that's manipulated into shape.

Think of children's wooden building blocks. When a child plays with them, they'll first stack them. But the second thing that they're going to do is to stand up two blocks and put a third block across the top. They will have reinvented post-and-lintel architecture, hearkening back to the ancient Egyptians or Persians. Essentially, they made a proscenium arch. Add a stage floor and outer walls, and you have a theater.

Make a Stage Floor

Start simple.

- Click the "Plane" object icon in the Topbar toolbar.
- Or, Viewport menu Add > Mesh > "Plane".

A 2' x 2' plane will be created at the world center (0,0,0).

Resize it by:

- Drag Scale handles (the small colored boxes).

Or, a faster method,

- Viewport sidebar > Item > Transform > Dimensions, enter 60' for X and Y.

Moving Objects

Next, reposition the stage floor. Where should the model's center, or X, Y = 0, 0, be? At the forward edge of the floor? In the center of the theatre? **Traditionally, 0, 0 is at the point where the theatre's center line intersects the plaster line.** The plaster line runs right to left at the upstage edge of the proscenium arch. (Everything in front of that is beautiful plaster leaves and cupids for the audience to gaze at. Everything behind the line is crappy bricks and exposed beams that the actors and stagehands are forced to look at.) Dragging one arrow at a time guarantees movement straight to the side or upstage and downstage. Using the viewport grid as a guide, slide the floor up or down stage until it matches the ground plan of your theatre.

- Position the floor plane.
  - Viewport Tool Shelf > "Move" tool. Drag the floor's origin widget.

Option:

- Select the plane.
- Viewport sidebar > "Item" tab. Enter new position values.
  - Using imperial measurements, you can enter feet and inches (5'6"), or decimal feet (5.5').
  - If you enter dimensions in feet and inches, they will appear as decimal feet. (kind of a pain) Here is where it's handy to know some conversions or keep a note open on your desktop with a list of basic inches and decimal equivalents, particularly if you want to use fractions of inches.

IMPORTANT! BEFORE MOVING ON . . .

Apply Any Transformations!

Bforartists has a function not found in other modeling programs. After transforming or modifying an object, changes need to be APPLIED in order to make them permanent. For example, a 2' square cube scaled up to 20' will still act like a 2' cube until the applying changes. Future scaling will be based on 2' rather than 20', it will rotate like a 2' cube, etc. This odd feature facilitates some advanced editing and animation workflows but is a nuisance for basic modeling until you become accustomed to it.

- Select the object.
- Viewport "Object" menu > "Apply".
- Select "Location", "Scale", "Rotation", "Rotation and Scale", or "All Transforms".

Optionally:

- Use the Toolshelf > Object tab > "Apply" dropdown.

Or:

- Main Topbar > "Apply" buttons. (If the buttons are not visible, activate them by clicking the Topbar edit dropdowns until you find the option.)

MAKE A PROSCENIUM: START WITH CUBES

With the stage floor the correct size and position, start working in elevation by adding a cube. Once more, clicking the cube icon in the main toolbar or the

Viewport Add menu will place one at the global center. This will be one of the side walls of the proscenium (abutments). Name it something like "proscenium rt." The idea is to use a name that is not too long but is suggestive of the object's position or function. Abbreviations are acceptable if they will not be confused with anything else later on.

The proscenium for *My Fair Lady* is 22 feet tall. Select the object and change the Z dimension in the Viewport Item tag to 22'. How deep is the proscenium arch? 2'? Set the Y to that dimension. Next is the width of this abutment. This could depend on the amount of wing space in your theatre or the width that is visible to the audience. *My Fair Lady* will be using a slip-stage to move set props on and off stage. It is important to match the wing space of the model to the actual dimensions of the theater. So, type in that measurement, X = 12'.

For the first side,

- Click the "Cube" icon in the toolbar at the top of the viewport.
- Or, Viewport header menu: Add > Mesh > "Cube".
- Name it.
- Resize it. 20' tall, 10' wide, 2' deep. Or your choice.

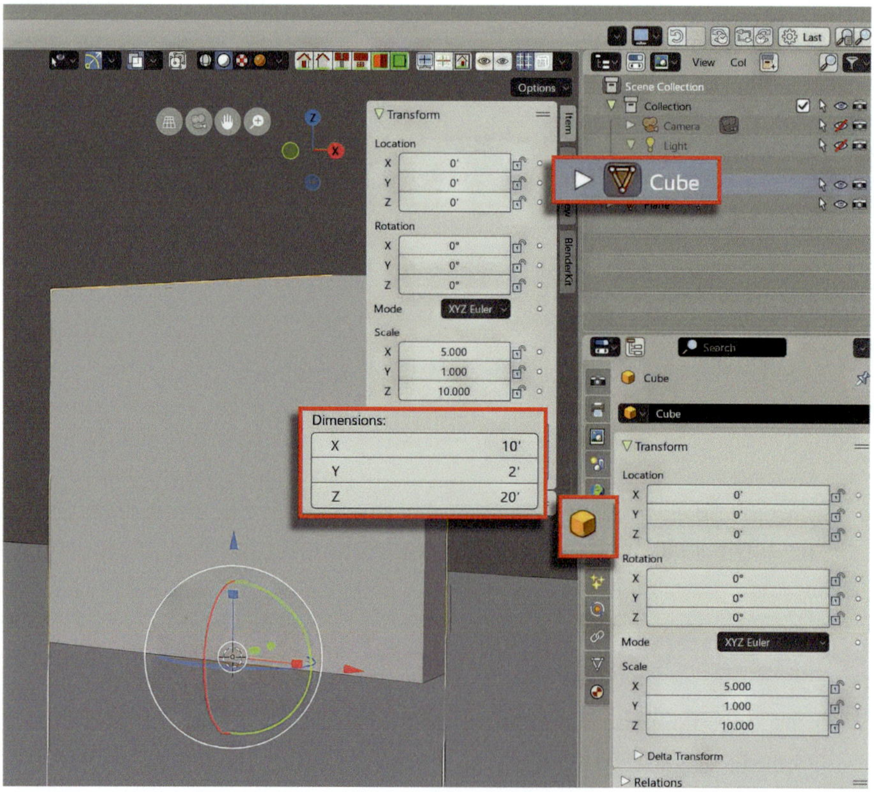

FIGURE 7.2 The proscenium abutment and its properties in the Item tag.

- Select the "Move" tool in the Viewport Tool Shelf and move the object to one side and upwards until it rests on the floor.

At this point, it becomes clear that arranging objects can present a problem. The origin of this side of the proscenium is located at its center, but proper positioning is from the theatre's centerline to the inside face. As it stands, the location of that inside face must be calculated using the object's center with every placement. So does the distance from the center to the floor. Doing this calculation every time an object is moved is incredibly tedious. So, of course, there is a better way. To measure the width of a real proscenium, we use a tape measure to determine the distance from the theatre's center line to the onstage faces of the arch. We can use the same method in a simulated theatre if the origin point of the abutment is moved to its onstage face. Moving an object's origin point is a simple procedure.

Moving an Object's Origin (Pivot) Point

- Select the "Move" tool.
- Open "Options" at the top of the viewport sidebar.
- **Check the box under "Affect Only" that reads "Origins".**
    - Now, moving the Origin widget will move only the origin while the object remains stationary. A good place for the origin is the upstage, centerstage, or bottom corner.
- Move the Origin to that corner with the Move tool.
- Uncheck the "Affect Only Origins" box.

The placement won't be perfect, but by zooming closer to the corner, it will be within a fraction of an inch. **Using two orthographic views will make the placement of the origin precise.**

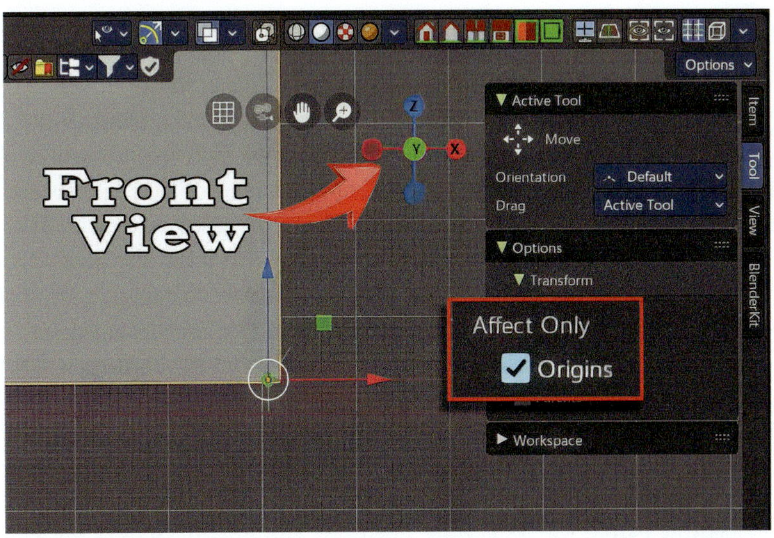

FIGURE 7.3 Activating the "Affect Origin" setting and moving the origin of the object.

A FASTER, MUCH COOLER OPTION

- Turn on "Snapping". This is the "Magnet" icon at the center of the Viewport toolbar.
- With the dropdown next to the Magnet, set the Snapping target to "Vertex". Now, tools will tend to jump to the nearest vertex in the viewport.
- Select the "3D Cursor" tool from the Tool Shelf.
- **While moving the cursor past the desired corner, click on it**, placing the 3D Cursor.
    - This may take a bit of practice.
- Open the "Set Origin" options in the Object tab of the Tool Shelf.
- Click on "Origin to 3D cursor". The name is self-explanatory.
    - **The object's origin will jump to the point you have selected!**
- Deactivate the "3D Cursor" tool by selecting the "Tweak" tool in the Tool Shelf.
    - You might want to deactivate "Snapping" as well, but remember it. It can be very handy at times.

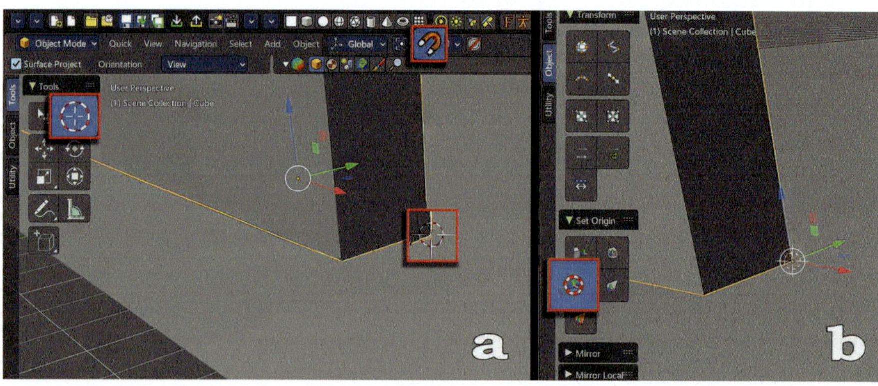

FIGURE 7.4 Using the 3D cursor and moving the origin to it.

Whichever option is used to move the origin, it can now be positioned with ease and precision. If the proscenium opening is 40 feet, this abutment should be moved 20" stage right. Rather than simply moving objects by eye, it can be done with greater precision by first using the "Move" tool to slide it a short distance in the correct direction. This little trick will reveal the axis that needs to be edited and whether the value should be a positive or negative number. The changed value will be visible in the "Item" tag of the Viewport sidebar and in the Last Operation panel. Either can be easily adjusted to the correct distance.

- Enter -17'6" inches in the X coordinate of the object.
    - The abutment will be placed with its upstage corner at the proper distance from centerstage.
    - Minus values for stage right positions and positive values for stage left.

- 0 in Y moves the origin to the plaster line.
- Set Z to 0, and the object will rest on the stage floor.

Cinema 4D and *3ds Max* employ other methods for moving pivot points. In either program, an editor can be opened that is dedicated to the task. Setting the "up" axis to -100% moves the point to the lowest extent of the object. Setting X from -100% to 100% moves the point sideways from one edge to the other, and similar settings for the remaining axis move it front to back.

Moving an object's origin is useful in other ways. For example, if the origin is moved to the bottom of a human figure or a tree, using the scale tool will grow or shrink the object from the base up rather than from the middle outward. A pivot can also be moved outside the object, so several set pieces can all pivot around the same point, perhaps the center of a turntable.

The stage right abutment of the proscenium is now the correct shape, size, and location. It is time to make the stage left abutment. You could repeat the steps that went into the right abutment, but doing so would break one of the cardinal rules of model making.

NEVER MAKE AN OBJECT TWICE.

Instead, duplicate the existing abutment. You can do this with the tried-and-true copy-paste method or use a key combination.

- **Shift + D to make a duplicate.**

Or,

- Right-click > "Duplicate". Works in either the viewport or the Outliner.

Notice that a new icon has appeared in the Outliner. **Rename it to avoid confusion with its original.** In the viewport, the two pieces occupy the same space, making them hard to tell apart.

- Make sure the new object is selected in the Outliner and move it to the side.

It could be positioned with the same method that was used previously, except that the origin point is now on the wrong side for the opposite abutment. Rather than repeat the steps of moving the origin, simply flip the entire object, left to right. Like most object manipulators, the mirror command is found in two locations.

- Use Viewport Tool Shelf > Object tab > "Mirror".

Or,

- Viewport Object menu > "Mirror".

Or,

- Object Context menu, Right-click > "Mirror".
- To mirror left to right, select the yellow X (axis) symbol.

After performing the Mirror operation, the object's scale property will show a negative number in the axis that was flipped. This can be used in any program as a quick way to mirror objects. Simply change the scale value of the relevant axis from positive to negative (or vice versa).

Notice that when the new object was mirrored, a value of -1 appeared in the X scale field. This can be used in any program as a quick way to mirror objects. Simply change the scale value of the relevant axis from positive to negative (or vice versa). Reversing the X value in this way flips it left to right, changing the Y value flips it front to back, and the Z value flips it top to bottom.

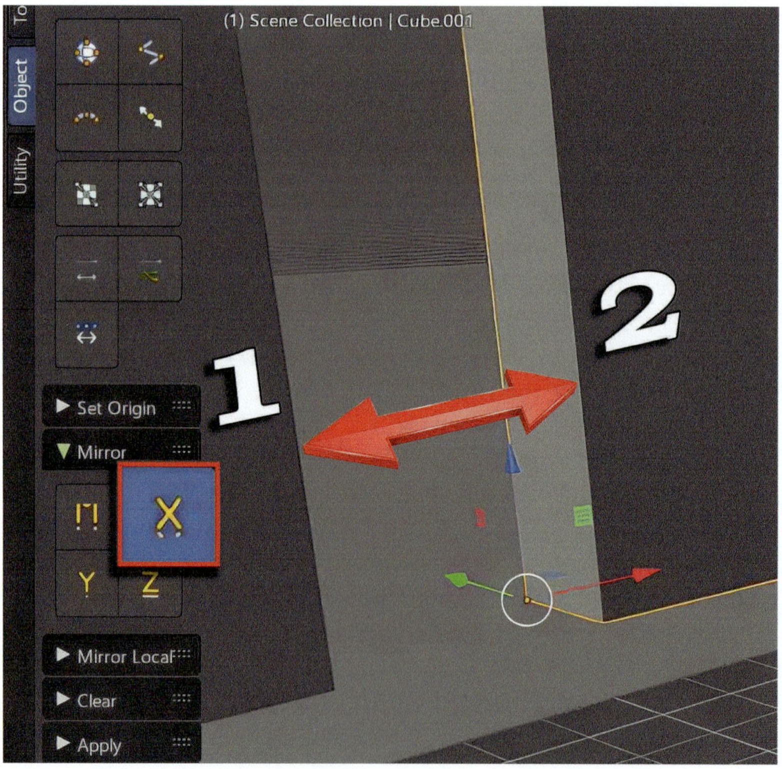

FIGURE 7.5 Make a mirror duplicate of the object.

Place the duplicate accurately on the other side of the arch.

- Viewport right-sidebar > Object tab > Transform.
- Enter 20' for the X value.

Since the duplicate has only been moved sideways along the X axis, the two should still be correctly aligned up and downstage. If not, enter 0' in the Y coordinate for both.

The Top of the Arch

For the lintel of the proscenium, make a new cube rather than just another copy.

- Create a cube.
- Give it a name. Proscenium header?
- Resize it to be as deep as the abutments and wide enough to span them.

The total length of a 40' wide opening and 12' wide abutments on either side is 64'. Change the width of the new cube to that dimension. Continue using the depth of 2'. The height of the lintel may depend on what is needed to provide an attractive frame for the scene, or it may be determined by the height of any flying scenery in your design. *My Fair Lady* won't be using any fly space. Making it 8' tall should be good.

- Move it to the proper position for the top of a proscenium.

Because it hasn't yet been moved, it is still centered in the scene and shouldn't need to be moved right or left. Move it upward to the point that it is barely overlapping the tops of the abutments. Does it need to move upstage or down? In the theater that produced the show, the top of the proscenium is hidden by an acousticum, an acoustic reflector, that protrudes from the front of the arch at a 30° angle.

- Select the "Rotate" tool from the Viewport Tool Shelf and tip the header forward 30°.
- Move it to a position so that it intersects the two abutments correctly.

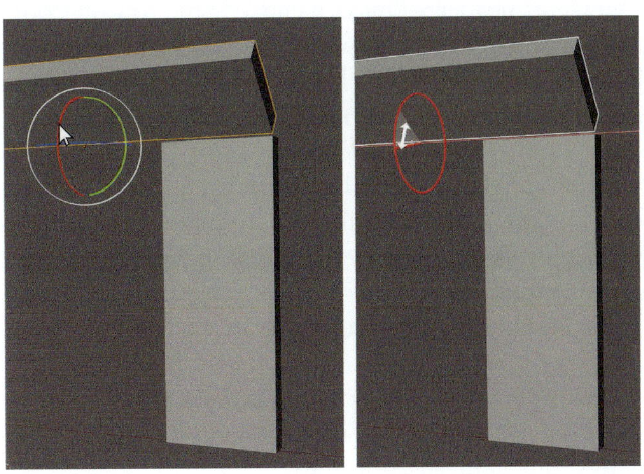

FIGURE 7.6 Move the lintel to the top of the arch. Angling it forward recreates the actual theatre.

Professional modeling practices would say that we should angle the tops of the abutments so that no elements overlap. But that's a waste of time. This isn't the model-making business; it's the stage design business, and time is precious. Modern computers are perfectly capable of sorting the position of overlapping objects and rendering them correctly. You can accept the changed angle of the lintel or return it to its original position by clicking Edit menu > "Undo" (Ctrl + Z).

- Apply any changes to the objects.
- Save the project.

ORGANIZING THE PROJECT

The project now has four items in the Outliner. For good organization, ease, and convenience, organize them into groups. Grouping objects makes it much easier to locate and identify them in the future. Subsequent modifications can be made to entire groups rather than one object at a time. Objects can be joined into a single object, but doing so would make future editing or adding textures much harder. Instead, put them into temporary groups. In *Bforartists*, groups are called collections. In the Outliner, collections have a unique icon. Beneath it, the icons of all the collected elements appear in a hierarchical list. Objects in a collection remain independent. Each can be translated with "Move", "Rotate", and "Scale" without affecting the others. A collection is not an object and therefore has no coordinates and cannot be translated in any way.

Use "Shift + Click" in the viewport to select multiple objects. In the Outliner, you could use the standard "Ctrl + Click" to select multiple object icons one at a time, or "Shift + Click" on the first and last items of a list to select them all.

- Select the three parts of the proscenium.
- "Right-click" in the viewport to open the Object Context menu.
- Click on "Send to Collection".
  - Or, Viewport header > Object menu > "Send to Collection".
  - A pop-up panel will appear with a list of existing collections to send the objects to, and a plus symbol that will create a new collection.
- Name it something like "Proscenium".

Elements can be added to a collection by dragging their icons onto the collection icon while holding down the Shift key. To remove elements from a collection, drag their icons out of the collection's list to a different collection further up the hierarchy of the Outliner.

Another option is to make a new, empty collection and add elements to it.

- Click on the button at the top of the Outliner with the "Collection+" icon.
  - Or, Viewport header Object menu > Collection > "Create New Collection".
- Name it and Shift-Drag elements into it.

Another very effective method of organizing objects is to arrange them into parent-child groups.

- Select the icon of an abutment and drag it over the icon of the lintel while pressing the Shift key. You can see that the abutment becomes a sub-item in the hierarchy of the lintel.
- Do the same with the other abutment. The two abutments are now considered the children of the parent, the lintel.

In parent-child groups, if the parent is transformed, the children follow along, but the children can still be transformed independently without affecting the parent or other children.

- Select the lintel and move it in some direction. The obedient children follow along.
- Select one of the children and move it. The wise parent allows the children to venture out on their own without constant oversight.
    - The same holds true for rotating and scaling.

To translate a parent without affecting its children, you must remove the children from the group by "Shift" + dragging them over a Collection icon higher in the hierarchy. Then the parent can be transformed before the children are returned to its custody.

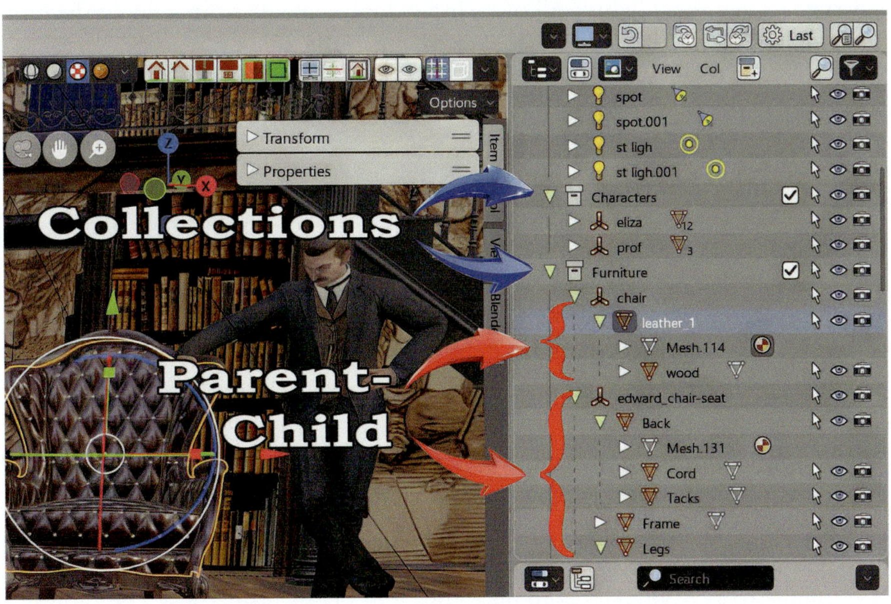

FIGURE 7.7 Collections and Parent-child groups organize the many objects in the Outliner by forming groups that can be opened or closed.

There is a compromise between collections and parents. Like other objects, "Empty" objects have coordinates but are invisible in the viewport.

- Add an "Empty" object to a scene with one of the Viewport Header Add menu > Add Empty > "Axis", "Cube", "Sphere", or "Cone" options.
  - Or, add the "Empty" objects to the Topbar with the Topbar Primitives dropdown, then select one of the Empty objects.

There are eight different Empty objects to choose from. Plain Axes are basic points with the same X, Y, Z gizmos as other elements. When an Empty object is made a parent of other elements, like any parent object, it can be used to move, rotate, and scale the entire group. In *Cinema 4D*, these elements are called Null objects and can be found in the palette with all other primitives. In *3ds Max*, they are called Dummy objects and are found in the Default menus, Create > Helpers > Dummy, or Create panel > (Helpers) > Standard > Object Type rollout > Dummy.

For another layer of organization, collections can be grouped together into larger collections. Similarly, parents can have children who can also have children, each of those grandchildren can have children, etc. Organization can also include parent-child groups inside collections, or collections inside other collections, or collections inside empty objects, inside children, inside other children, inside third cousins, inside, inside, make it STOP!

In addition to organizing elements by their function or location, there is another major advantage to using groups. A group can be opened and closed by clicking the triangle symbol in front of its icon in the Outliner. This makes it possible to temporarily hide all of its individual elements from view in the Outliner, making it much easier to navigate through the project.

ADDING SCENIC ELEMENTS

The next step is to add scenery to the rough theater. Scenic elements for My Fair Lady can be added while exploring the remaining primitive shapes. The columns that support the high platform are basically cylinders.

- Add a cylinder from the "Primitives" in the Toolbar.
  - Or Viewport header > Add menu > Mesh > "Cylinder".

When you add an object from the Viewport menu, the Last Operation panel will pop up. When adding objects using the Toolbar Primitives, it won't pop up, but the key command "F6" will bring it up. You will see that there are some new parameters in the panel. Each geometric shape has a few properties that are unique to it. Cylinders contain radius and depth properties. The radius of a cylinder is recognizable. The depth property might be better described as the object's height.

- Adjust Last Operation panel > Set the radius to 4" and the depth to 7'.

AN OBJECT'S STRUCTURE: VERTICES, EDGES, AND FACES

You can also set the number of vertex points (vertices) that divide the curved surface. Each vertex is the end of an edge or sectioning line. The edges describe the facets (polygons or polys) that make up the outer surface of the cylinder.

The more polygons that divide the surface, the smoother the cylinder will appear. Remember the analogy of the sphere and the mirror ball? Curved surfaces are not really curved. They are an assemblage of flat surfaces. Why not set the number of vertices and polys to 1,000 or 10,000? The problem with huge numbers of polygons is that they place an enormous computing load on the processors. When the view of the scene is rotated, zoomed, or panned, or objects are being moved, the computer needs to recalculate continuously. Smooth, fluid movement in the viewport requires that it refresh itself at least 30 times per second. Furthermore, when scenes are burdened with hundreds of thousands or millions of polygons, generating finished renderings happens very slowly. This can be a major concern when rendering animation clips that contain hundreds or thousands of frames. Also, overburdened scenes do not function effectively when loaded into 3D model viewing or VR applications. For these programs to provide a smooth viewing experience, real-time rendering, with textures and lighting, should not drop below 30 frames per second, and 60 frames per second is preferred.

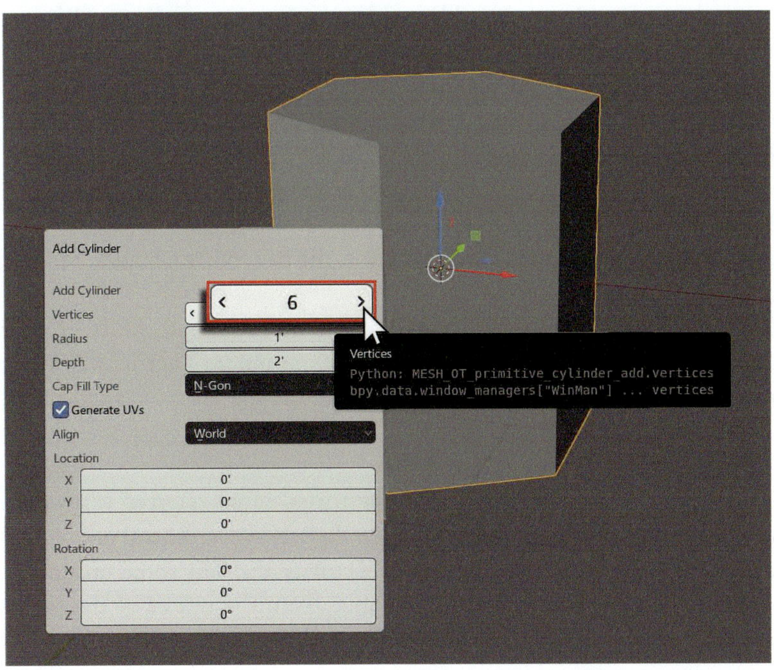

FIGURE 7.8 Changing the number of vertices of a cylinder in the Adjust Last Operation panel.

Try to find a compromise. Set the number of vertices high enough that objects appear as smooth as you want, while using no more polygons than necessary. Luckily, programs recognize surfaces that are meant to be evenly curved and use calculations to smooth them during rendering.

The Rest of the 3D Shapes

- Make another cylinder and explore its unique properties. With some manipulation of those properties, many other shapes are possible.
    - Set the number of vertices to 8 to create a new primitive, an octagon.
    - 6 makes a hexagon.
    - 5 vertices will make a pentagon. Yes, like the building.
    - 4 will give you a cube. We have other ways of doing that, so forget it.
    - A setting of 3 will give you a trigon prism, or 3D triangle. This is also the shape of a Greek periaktoi, the ancient scenic device comprised of three painted surfaces. This simple rotating machine, which presents one of its three sides when needed, is still in common use after over 2,000 years.

Now, drop a cone into the scene. It also has some additional parameters in the Last Operation panel. There are now two radii, one for the circle at the base of the cone and another for the tip. Editing that number will give us a standard cone or a truncated cone. Truncated cones could be used as lampshades or a skirt in a cubist-style costume. They could be stacked one upon another to form furniture legs. Again, the depth property determines the height.

Notice that **cones have an additional property named Rings.** Rings divide the cone with horizontal or lateral vertices. This is extremely important when modifiers are added to bend the cone, squish it or skew it to the side. Dividing shapes with vertices that run horizontally gives them the flexibility needed to make those modifications operate.

- Make a cone.
    - Experiment with the vertices count, the two types of radii, and the number of rings.
- Make a variety of cones, truncated cones, and pyramids of different sizes.
- Add another cone to the scene and edit its number of vertices. Four vertices make a four-sided cone, A pyramid, perhaps the Great Pyramid of Khufu. Three sides form a triangular pyramid. Five, a pentagonal one.

The last primitive on the toolbar is the torus, often referred to as the donut shape. (Bagel?) It can be described as a circle orbiting a central axis or as a cylinder bent 360 degrees, forming a ring. A torus also has some unique editable properties. The major radius is the distance from the center of the torus to its outside edge, and the minor radius is the radius of the orbiting cylinder. The torus also has two editable properties for the number of vertices. The major vertices set the number of cylindrical segments used to complete the orbit. Once

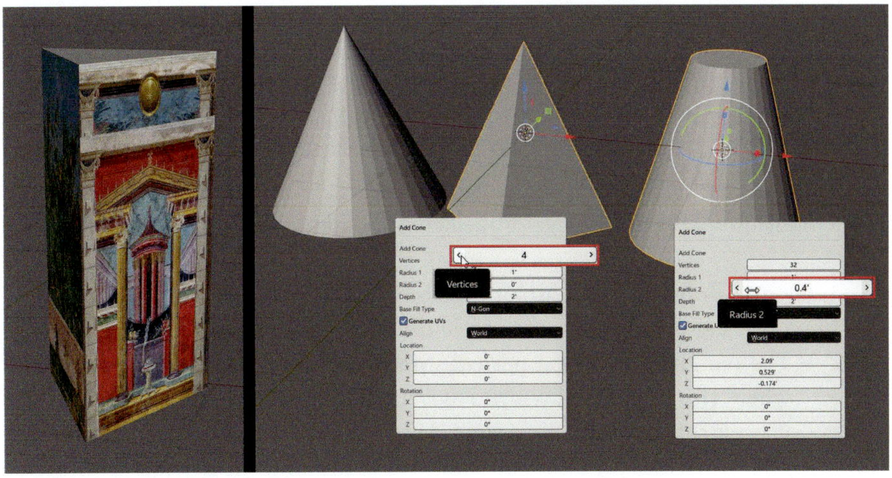

FIGURE 7.9 A Greek periaktoi, cones, truncated cones, and pyramids.

again, this value can be used to make new object types. You can make a square Taurus, a hexagonal Taurus, or a triangular Taurus. Reducing the number of Minor Vertices will make shapes that resemble a spindle or a flying saucer. Perhaps a discus? Making the minor radius larger than the major radius results in some truly odd creatures.

- Make a torus.
  - Have fun with the properties in the Last Operation panel.

Combining Shapes

- Put a few of your creations into the scene.
- Use the basic translators, Move, Rotate, and Scale the objects in different combinations.
- Change an object's origin orientation from Global to Local as part of these combinations.

The legs of the middle platform of the *My Fair Lady* set are tapered. A truncated cone will work well. A flattened sphere will serve as a Doric (sort of) capital.

CREATING PRIMITIVES INTERACTIVELY

Selecting basic objects from a pallet of primitives is a standard practice in most 3D applications. However, there is another very interesting method used by *3ds Max*, which is available as an option in *Bforartists*.

- In the viewport Tool Shelf > tools tab, there is an icon of a greenish cube. Hover the cursor over it, and the tooltip reads "Add Cube".

- Press and hold that button to open the palette of Interactive Create options. They are:
  - "Add Cone", "Add Cylinder", "Add UV Sphere", and "Add Ico-sphere". The same objects that are in the toolbar.
- Click on "Add Cube".

The cursor now appears as a grid-like symbol with an X in the middle.

- Click and drag this new cursor across the floor plane in your model, drawing a rectangle, as you would in 2D drawing or drafting programs.
  - The rectangle will be a perfect square if you drag the cursor to a point where the height and width have equal dimensions.
  - It is extremely difficult to drag a symmetrical shape by eye, so the program provides an aid. The same aid is found in nearly all 2D drawing programs. **Press the Shift key while dragging the cursor, and it will snap to coordinates that result in a perfectly symmetrical shape.**
- When the rectangle is the correct size for the cube you wish to make, stop and release the mouse button.
- Immediately move the cursor upwards or downwards, and the rectangle will extrude along the Z axis until you click the mouse button again.

This method of creation enables you to create a cube of the correct size and in the proper position, without needing to move and scale it in the scene or edit its properties in a panel.

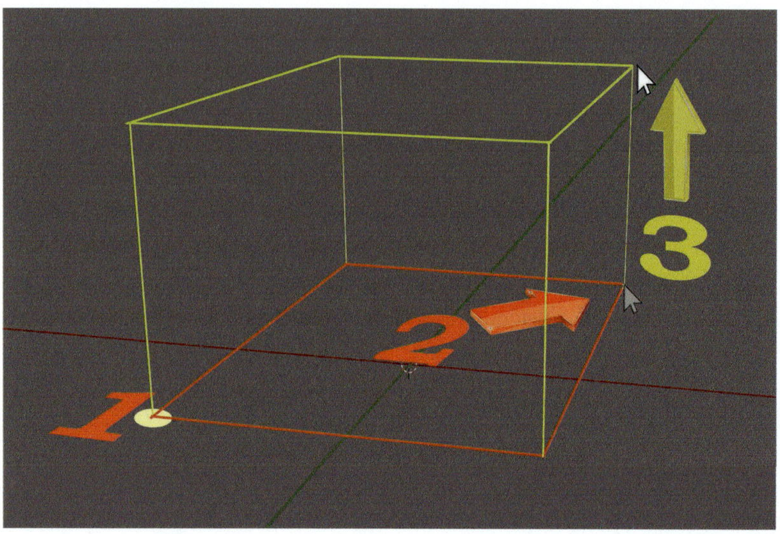

FIGURE 7.10 Click and drag, then move-click to create and resize an object simultaneously.

As always, when you create a new object, the Last Operation panel appears, allowing you to adjust its dimensions and position. The rotation and number of vertices can also be assigned, properties that cannot be determined when using interactive creation.

FIRST MODIFICATIONS

Primitive objects are merely the start. The next step is to tweak and customize them to meet your design requirements. Modeling programs provide numerous tools and possibilities for modifying basic shapes and increasing levels of sophistication. Before using sophisticated tools, start the customization process with readily available tools.

- Begin by scaling them one axis at a time. A sphere can be flattened or elongated. A cone can be made narrow or wide.
- Try combining the principal translations. Rotate an object using an interesting combination of axes, then adjust the scales and see what happens.
- **Try switching back and forth between global coordinates and local coordinates before you make these translations.** Sometimes this makes little difference, and other times a great deal.

Next, experiment with combining objects. Consider mash-ups like a cone emerging from a sphere or a cube expanding through a torus and colliding with a truncated cone. Do not worry about things overlapping. Z-buffering is the process of determining which surfaces should be at the front, and contemporary computers can handle it with ease. Click all the buttons and alter all the properties. See if you can break the program.

8 Modifiers and Deformers

Using primitives is always a good way to start the modeling process. By utilizing only basic geometric shapes, you create something that closely resembles white models used in traditional modeling practices. These primitive objects serve to quickly establish a model without the complexities and details associated with a finished, painted version. The primary goal is to convey sufficient information to initiate the collaborative process among team members.

A white model is designed to help ascertain the general shape and overall volume of the scenic objects being considered. By arranging these approximate elements within a stage model, you can visually demonstrate the relationships between different objects and how they collectively define the acting space. This visual arrangement facilitates discussions and idea exchanges, allowing everyone involved to understand how the components interact within the given space.

If the modeling process requires more detail or if it feels like the project is advancing to a more refined phase, it's time to transition to a more finished model. At this stage, you might begin incorporating more advanced techniques, textures, and materials to create a more detailed representation of the envisioned outcome. It's time to move on to a more finished model.

Obviously, not all shapes that we want to use on stage are made of straight lines. Many shapes in the real world exhibit more eccentric characteristics. These forms curve, twist, and bend, reflecting the complexity of the natural world. It is often stated that in nature, there are no perfectly straight lines; everything embodies some degree of curvature. When creating scenic models, it's essential to incorporate this natural characteristic whenever it is relevant to the design. The next step in the modeling process involves adding modifiers that grant objects properties, allowing them to transform into more eccentric or complex variations of their original shapes.

All reputable modeling programs are equipped with a variety of modifiers intended for this purpose. While each program may define these functions slightly differently and categorize them in unique ways, they all encompass the

DOI: 10.4324/9781003571742-8

FIGURE 8.1 Rough drafts, White models, Traditional, and Digital.

Top model: *La Maschera ou les nuits de Venise*: maquettes construites de l'acte III, par Philippe Chaperon. Bibliothèque nationale de France.

same foundational modifiers necessary for creative modeling. For example, *Cinema 4D* employs pull-down menus accompanied by 3D icons that visually represent the types of deformations being applied to the objects. On the other hand, *3ds Max* utilizes text buttons within a dedicated Modifier List panel. This panel serves as a convenient preset collection of commonly used modifiers for quick access. Users can click the "More" button to unveil an extensive menu showcasing all available modifiers, which can also be added to the preset panel for enhanced workflow efficiency. Importantly, in both of these programs, primitive shapes must first be set to "Make Editable" before any modifiers can be applied to them.

Deformers and modifiers are functions that can be assigned to individual objects. Each of these modifiers possesses variable properties that dictate how strong their effects will be, as well as the direction in which those effects will apply. After selecting an object, the appropriate modifier is applied, and initial property values are set simultaneously. Afterward, these values can be adjusted and fine-tuned according to the specific requirements of the project, allowing for precise control over the final shape of the model. Understanding and manipulating these properties is essential for creating dynamic and visually interesting shapes that resemble the forms found in the real world.

SUBDIVIDING OBJECTS

Objects must be prepared for modification prior to undergoing shape modification. A cube with a basic twist deformer is shown here. The twist appears to be very elementary.

Its maximum twisting radius is restricted, and it twists without creating curves or breaking lines. The cube object is a solid block, which explains why there is little variation, and all the lines are straight. Liken it to the game/puzzle Rubik's Cube. Even though a Rubik's Cube only has three segments on each face, it can twist further and more gracefully than this block. Imagine a solid cylinder or a straight pipe. While a solid pipe cannot be bent, the neck of a gooseneck lamp can. This is a result of the gooseneck's division into dozens of tiny cylinders and some flexibility at every joint.

For deformers to work on an object as they should, that object must be divided into multiple segments. Like a Rubik's cube, the polygons of each face are then divided into multiple, smaller polygons. This is done easily using a subdivision modifier, a modifier that must be applied before you apply other modifiers. Notice how this cube, with four segments per axis, has been twisted.

A subdivision of 4 is a modest amount, but it produces a large improvement. The more an object is subdivided, the smoother it will appear. The illustration shows the same cube, now with a Subdivide modifier and the same twist. Each face has been divided into 16 segments, and now the twist is smooth, curved, and unlimited. Some objects allow for the addition of polygons or segments during their creation. Others do not. If you know that you are going to apply modifiers that will change the object shape, **plan ahead** and add multiple segments in the first step of creation. Typically, this is achieved by using the Last Operation panel. Remember, after you have moved on from the original creation, you can't reopen the Last Operation panel. **Plan ahead.**

There are several methods that all programs use to subdivide objects. These methods fall into two categories: non-destructive and destructive. Non-destructive subdivision divides the object into segments and the faces into smaller polygons, but it does so in a very unobtrusive manner. It is the quicker and easier of the two methods, allowing you to add deformers to the objects successfully. Bending and twisting will achieve the correct results. However, the

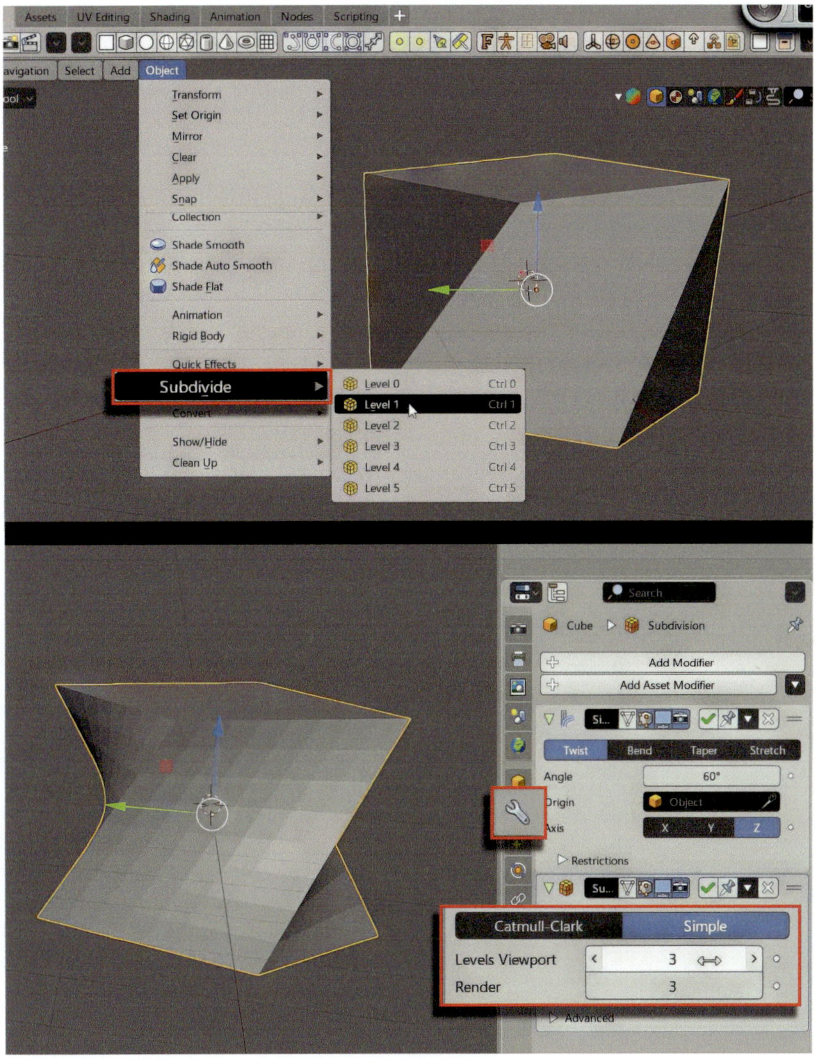

FIGURE 8.2 A cube with the twist deformer applied. The same twist after subdividing the cube.

smaller polygons of the subdivided faces cannot be selected individually and modified, which is important for more advanced modeling.

Non-destructive subdivision is done using a function common in all modeling programs, the Subdivision Surface modifier. This modifier is commonly used to smooth objects. An object with chunky surfaces will be smoothed by subdividing the lumps. Remember the comparison of the sphere and the mirror ball? Imagine a ball made of only 12 mirrors and another in which the curved surface is made with 200 smaller mirrors.

NON-DESTRUCTIVE SUBDIVISION

The My Fair Lady set needs wooden timbers to frame the wall sections. They will make good subjects for modification.

- Make a cube 8” x 8” and 7’-0” tall. Name it. (Timber?)
- Select it to be subdivided.
- Properties editor > Modifier tab (the Wrench icon).
- Click on “Add Modifier”.
- Choose “Subdivision Surface” in the Generator column.
    - Optionally, select the timber.
    - Viewport Object menu > “Subdivide”.
    - Select a number of divisions.

The cube in the viewport will dramatically change shape, and a wrench icon will appear behind it in the Outliner. The Properties Panel will now show the properties of the Subdivision.

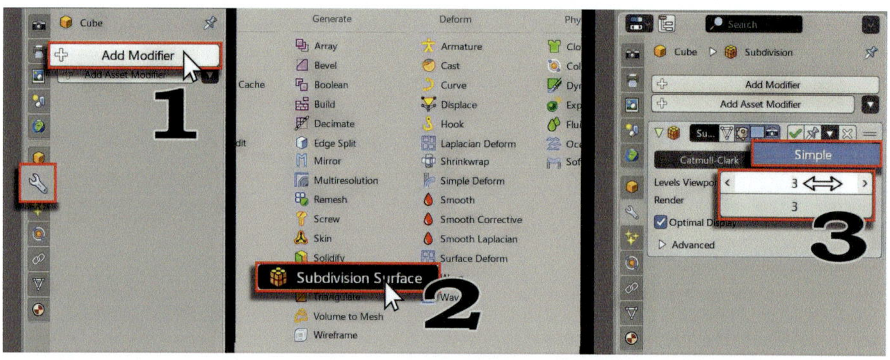

FIGURE 8.3 a) The Modifier Menu. b) Properties of the Subdivision modifier.

The first property option in that panel is the choice of Catmull-Clark or Simple. Catmull-Clark is a method used to smooth objects. Using this option will reduce the sharp edges and give the object a rounded profile. The Simple option retains the object’s original shape while subdividing the object, making it suitable for effective modifications.

- Properties editor > Modifier tab > Select “Simple”.
- Set the subdivision Level to 4.
    - Increase the numbers to enhance the smoothness when rendering the scene.
    - Decrease the numbers if the program begins slowing down.

Levels of subdivision are the number of times the object’s faces have been divided by two. On a cube, Level 1 gives each face 4 polygons (2 wide x 2 tall). Level 2 splits each of those, or 16 (4 x 4). Level 3 = 32, Level 4 = 64. These are the increasing powers of 2 that appear in many other aspects of computing. The quality of images, videos, and sound files depends on their bit depths, 2, 4, 16, 32, etc. The RAM memory in computers is 8, 16, or 32 gigabytes.

Destructive Subdivision

The second method of subdivision is the destructive method. With this, the faces of an object are divided into smaller polys, each of which can be individually moved, rotated, scaled, deleted, and more. This is not necessary for the modifiers in this chapter, but the ability to manipulate the individual polygons of an object is the root of advanced modeling.

To perform destructive subdivision:

- Make another timber cube. Select it.
- Switch the workspace from Object to Edit mode. Use the dropdown switch at the top left of the viewport (shortcut 2).
- Right-click on the object > Select "Subdivide".
  - As usual, the Last Operation panel will appear in the viewport.
  - The Number of Cuts property is not the same as a Subdivision Level. The number of Cuts determines the actual number of vertices to be applied to the object.
- Enter a moderate number such as 5. This will make a 6 x 6 grid of equally sized polygons on all faces.

FIGURE 8.4 a) The Edit Context menu. b) Last Operation panel. c) Divided cube.

- Return to Object mode (shortcut 1).
  - In this mode, the vertices have disappeared. They are visible in Edit mode, allowing individual polys, edges, or vertices to be selected and modified.

To make the subdivisions visible in Object mode:

- Overlays menu (above the viewport) > check the "Wireframe" box.
  - Now the individual polys of every object in the scene will appear.

The color and contrast of the lines can be edited.

- Edit menu > Preferences > Themes tab > "Wire".
- Uncheck the "Overlay Wire" option to view the scene with a closer resemblance to the final render.

ADDING MODIFIERS

There are a large number of modifiers in every 3D modeling program. Many of these modifiers are task-specific. They may be particularly suited to animation or other specialized workflows. For now, concentrate on modifiers that relate to modeling. There are three main categories of modifiers.

First are the Deformers that alter the shape of an object to make it more specific to its purpose.

The second are the Generators. Generators do not simply move polygons into new configurations; they add new polygons to an object in order to create a distinctly altered shape.

The third category is the Modifiers. These are the most exotic and are not often used in a scenic design workflow.

The various 3D programs categorize tasks differently or rename the categories slightly, but they are generally the same.

Deformers are the most commonly used modifiers and are typically the most useful in efficiently making a scenic model. They are also easy to deploy and control. In *Bforartists*, most modifiers are located in the Properties panel > Modifiers tab.

A Basic Modifier

- Select an object.
- Select the Modifier tab, marked by the small wrench symbol.
  - o If a Subdivide modifier has been applied to the object, it will already be in the list (stack) and have a sub-panel in the main panel.
- Click the "+Add Modifier" button at the top of the panel.
  - o The Modifier menu will open.

This menu lists many modifiers separated into five categories: Normals, Edit, Generate, Deform, and Physics.

- Select the "Simple Deform" modifier in the 3rd Deform column.
  - o Simple Deform will appear as a sub-panel in the object's Properties panel.
  - o In the Outliner panel, the object's icon is now followed by a Wrench (modifier) icon. Clicking on that "Wrench" icon will reopen the modifier's Properties panel so that parameters can be edited.

BEND

The Simple Deform offers several basic deformers. The second in the list is Bend.

- Select "Bend", the second option.
  - o In the Viewport, the effect on the object should be immediately apparent. A new set of editable parameters will appear in the Properties panel.
  - o The Angle property determines how much the object bends.
  - o The X, Y, and Z buttons determine the basic direction of the bend.
  - o The Limit sliders determine how much of the object bends.
- Experiment with these. Try scaling the object to different proportions and note the effect of the bend modifier.

The effect of a modifier on an object is based on the object's origin point. The radius of a bend or twist is centered on that point. **If the origin point is moved within the object, it will result in entirely different bending effects.**

- Select the Move tool.
- Viewport sidebar Tools > Affect Only > Select "Origins".

- Move the origin point without moving the object. Move it inside the object and outside as well.
  - o Where would the origin be positioned to bend a tall, thin cube into an arch? Try it.

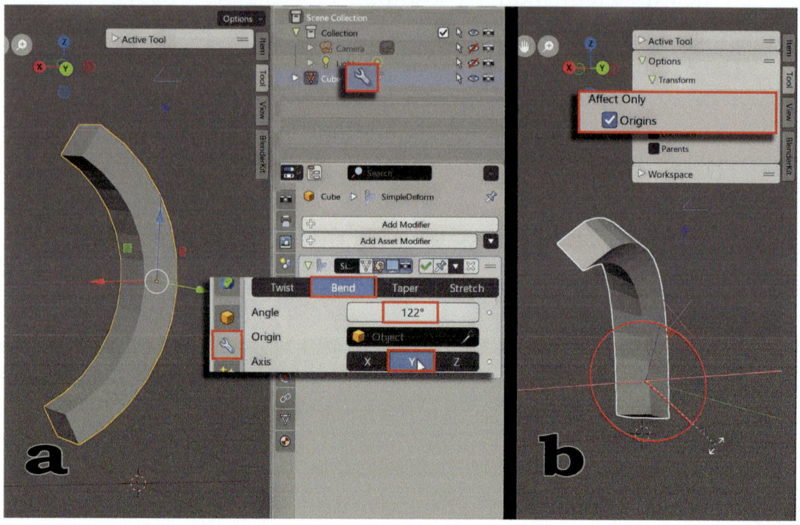

FIGURE 8.5 a) Adding Bend to a cube. b) Changing the axis.

Next,

- Select the Rotate tool.
- Rotate the object's origin for dramatic changes in the Bend deformer.

With rotation, the object can be made to bend at angles between the major axes. Imagine creating a tree branch. Branches are not limited to the three global axes. They bend in any direction they want.

- Select the Scale tool.

If the Affect Only > "Origin" box is still checked, the Scale tool will be changing the size of the origin, not the object. In other programs, this is not possible, but in *Bforartists*, it is. Experiment with changing the scale of the origin and the scale of the object.

TWIST

Now, everybody, do the twist. The spiral staircase, stage right, needs an interesting center post.

- Make a new cube, 6" x 6" x 7'-0" and subdivide it.

- +Add Modifier > "Simple Deform".
- Select the first button, "Twist".
  - The new sub-panel has the same options as the Bend deformer. Try everything. Move the origin point all over. Change the origin's rotation and scale the object. This should produce some completely unrecognizable shapes.

TAPER

- Make a new cube and subdivide it.
- +Add Modifier > "Simple Deform".
- Select "Taper".
  - The new sub-panel has familiar options, but instead of Angle, there is Factor. Just like Angle, the Factor property determines the extent of the modifier's effect on the object. Once more, try everything.
- Adjust Restrictions parameters to taper only side to side or front and back.
- Move the origin point all over. Change the origin's rotation and scale the object. This should produce some nearly unrecognizable shapes.

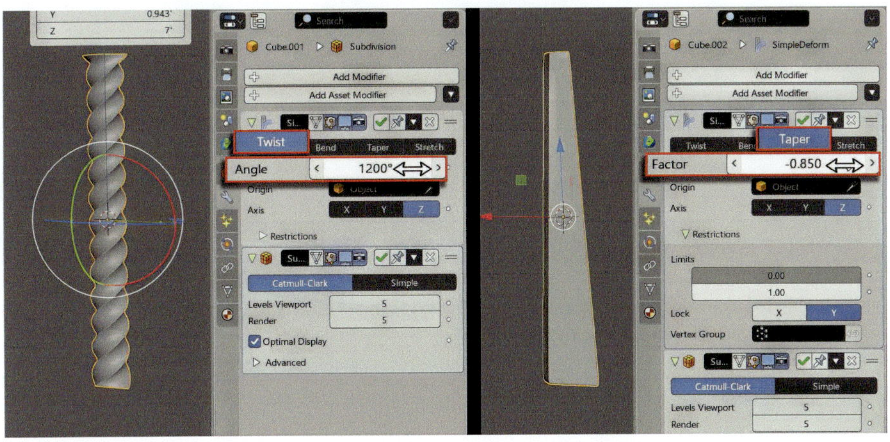

FIGURE 8.6 a) Twisting the stair post. b) Tapering the wall timbers.

Taper and the other transformations can be used overtly or more subtly. Tapering scenic elements such as walls and columns to make them slightly wider at the base can give them the visual impression of weight. Manipulating bends and tapers can contribute to the illusion of age or dilapidation.

Get Creative, Stack Modifiers

Try applying one modifier on top of another modifier.

- Apply a bend deformer and set the properties to make the modification obvious.
- Add another deformer by clicking the "+Add Modifier" button again and selecting another "Simple Deform" modifier.

- o Another sub-panel will appear in the Properties panel, below the first, Bend sub-panel.
- o As more modifiers are applied to an object, the line of sub-panels continues to grow. Each is applied to the object in the order of this list.

The list can be reordered by moving sub-panels up or down:

- Click on the dotted rows icon at the far right of a sub-panel's header and drag it to a new position. It is surprising how much difference can be made by changing the sequence of even two simple deformers.

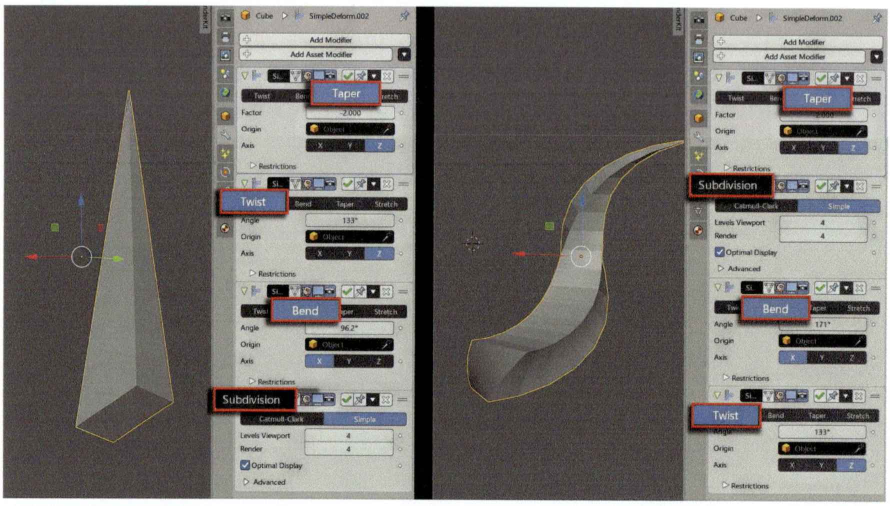

FIGURE 8.7 Changing the stack order: a) Taper, Bend, Subdivide, and Twist. b) Taper, Subdivide, Twist, and Taper.

The header of a modifier sub-panel contains a button to collapse it to only the header. More buttons toggle the modifier in the viewport and in the final render, and the last button deletes the modifier entirely.

Make Modification Permanent, APPLY

The button with a green checkmark icon in the header is important. This "Apply Modifier to Selected" button integrates the modifier with the object. When clicked, the sub-panel disappears, and that modifier can no longer be edited. The object is now permanently in its present shape. This may be necessary for any later editing of the object. Without it, later modifications may act on the object's initial shape, not its current form. To avoid this confusion, make the modifications permanent by applying them before editing. The same function is performed in *Cinema 4D* using the context menu command "Current State to Object". In *3ds Max*, open the Collapse utility, select "Surfaces" options, and click the "Collapse Selected" button.

MODIFIERS IN THE EDIT MODE

There are several more deformers that are standard across 3D programs. In other programs, they are included in the menus and lists of the usual deformers. But in *Bforartists*, they have been added to the tools in Edit mode. Typical of most operations in that mode, they function better when working on an object that has been subdivided.

In any program, objects are edited by manipulating vertices (a vertex is the point found at every intersection of edges), edges (the lines that separate individual polygons), or faces (a common term for those polys). To modify the entire object, select the faces icon.

In the Object Tab

SHEAR

- Create a cone.
- Switch to Edit mode (shortcut "2").
  - In this mode, the Viewport Tool Shelf will have a different set of options.
- Select the "Object" tab of the Tool shelf.

With the cone still selected:

- Click on the "Shear" function.
  - As the cursor draws away from the tool shelf, the cone will lean to one side. Try moving the cursor up and down, right and left.
- Click when the angle appears to be correct.
- The Last Operation panel will again appear, and the angle and axis of shear can be adjusted.

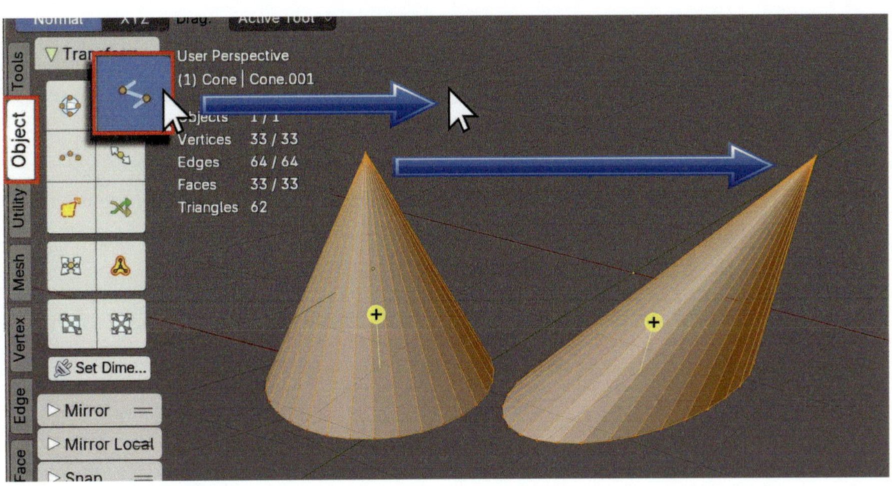

FIGURE 8.8 The Object tab b) Shear applied.

TO SPHERE

Another available function is To Sphere. This modifier causes the object to expand and become rounded as if it had a run-in with an air hose. It may continue to swell until it becomes a complete sphere, provided the object has been sufficiently subdivided.

The other functions under the Object tab are intended for use primarily when some, but not all, polygons of an object are selected and being edited. Bed, Push-Pull, and Shrink Fatten differ from similar-sounding simple deformers because of this distinction.

In the Tools tab

Opening the Tools tab in the Tool Shelf presents a few more options. Notably, the Bevel tool is valuable for rounding the hard edges of objects. The perfectly straight, angled edges of computer-generated objects can give them an artificial appearance that often contradicts the mood and atmosphere needed in a scene. Easing some edges, even a small amount, can make a model appear more natural and less "CGI." Beveling is an example of a tool that is selected and then applied directly to an element with a click-and-drag motion to perform the deformation.

BEVEL

- Create a cube.
- In Edit mode, Tool Shelf > Tools tab > select "Bevel".
- Click-and-drag on the object to bevel all edges equally.
    - The longer the drag, the wider the bevels become.
    - The last Operation panel will present many parameter settings.

Edges

- Click the "Edges" icon that appears in the Viewport toolbar when in Edit mode.
- Select "Edges" in the Effect Only dropdown, below the icon.
    - Increasing the number of Segments changes a flat, one-cut bevel to a rounded edge.
- Click and drag a single edge to bevel it.
    - The further you drag, the wider the bevel becomes.

Faces

- Click the "Faces" icon.
- Select "Edges" or "Vertices" in the Effect Only dropdown, below the icon.

  - Edges will bevel both the face's edges and vertices. Selecting Vertices only bevels the corners.
- Click and drag a single face to bevel it.

Vertices

- Click the "Vertices" icon to bevel (Yes) vertices.
- Select "Vertices" in the Effect Only dropdown, below the icon.
  - Increasing the number of Segments changes a flat, one-cut bevel to a rounded edge.
- Click and drag a single vertex to bevel it.

After a beveling operation, the Adjust Last Operation panel will appear, giving you the opportunity to fine-tune the bevels. In addition to the basic Affects, Width, and Segments properties, additional properties can be used to customize the edit.

- Profile Type:
  - Superellipse = a simple bevel.
  - Custom makes it possible to add an elaborate profile.
- Profile Shape changes the sharpness of the curve and can convert the curve from an outward to an inward bevel (a quarter curve to a quarter cove).
- Mitre options alter the way beveled edges meet.
- Width Type changes the way that the bevel width is calculated. Try them all to see how each might be used in a project.

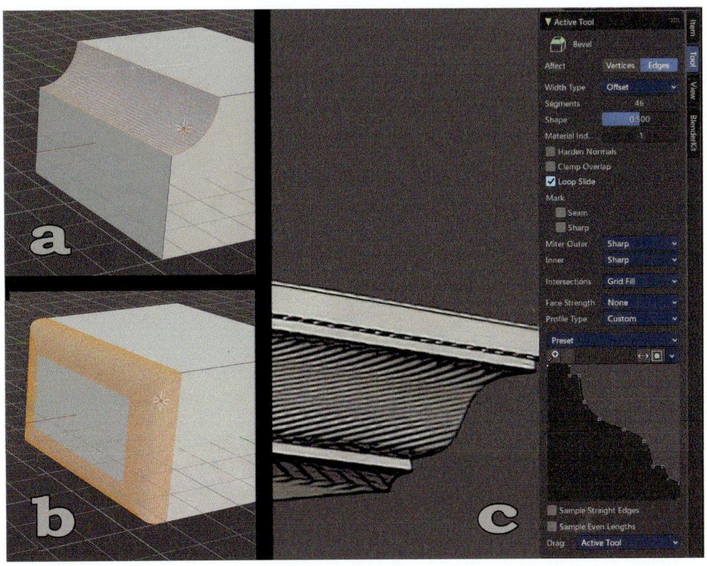

FIGURE 8.9 a) Beveled edge. b) a beveled face. c) The Upper platform for *My Fair Lady* is beveled in edit mode using a preset that resembles a traditional cornice molding.

SHEAR

The Shear tool at the bottom of the Tool Shelf is a variation that has a distinct advantage over the Shear deformer of the Object tab. When this tool is selected, the object's origin widget changes to include multi-colored tags on each axis. Clicking and dragging these tags will shear the object with greater control over the direction and amount.

TO SPHERE

Click-and-hold the "Shear" tool button to reveal the To Sphere tool button. This variation does not noticeably differ from the deformer with the same name in the Object tab when applied to a whole object. Its value is in deforming selected groups of polys, edges, or vertices.

9 Generators and Splines

FIGURE 9.1 Complex architectural elements are made by applying Generators to basic primitives.

DOI: 10.4324/9781003571742-9

The next method that can be applied to creating scenic models is a combination of creating objects and modifying them. These are the modifiers found in the Generate column of the add modifier menu, the Generators. Generate modifiers differ from the deformers described earlier because they don't rely on moving or manipulating the polygons of objects. They create entirely new surfaces and polygons to transform the existing object into the desired new shape. In many cases, generator modifiers can be used to create entirely new objects, rather than simply modifying existing ones.

ARRAYS

The most basic generators are those that work on mesh elements or the types of three-dimensional objects we have used so far. The first of these is the array modifier. As the name suggests, arrays are multiple duplicates of objects in an organized pattern. They can be invaluable at times when repeating the Shift + D, duplicate operation, or cut-and-paste operations would be too slow or labor-intensive. When you add an array, you can make 100 copies of an object with just a few clicks. They also have added power in that the organization of arrays can be manipulated in 3D space. Arrays can be rectangular or circular and defined incrementally so that each copy is a set distance away from the original or the preceding copy. This is a perfect way to make a staircase in which a single step can be arrayed to generate an entire staircase. each step a set distance above and behind the one that came before it.

Similarly, you can make the balusters that go along with the staircase. You could even group each step and its adjoining balusters together. Making an array of that group would result in a staircase that could be easily adjusted by changing a single parameter.

There are two straight staircases for the stage left platform for *My Fair Lady*. Making arrays should do the trick nicely.

A Simple Array

IMPORTANT!

- Apply any transformations in the object's scale or rotation.

Those transformations must be applied to the object before going further. If they aren't, the program will build the array based on the original dimensions of the object, not its current ones. Applying changes to an object is quite easy.

- Select the object either in the viewport or in the outliner.
- Viewport header Object menu > Apply > "Scale" (or "Rotation").
  - Or, Topbar icons.
  - Or Toolshelf > Objects tab > "Apply".

Next,

- Select Properties panel > Modifier tab > Add modifier.
  - "Array" will be in the center column in the familiar menu that appears. The Generate modifiers are grouped together and are a lavender color.
- Select "Array", and a properties sub-palette will appear.

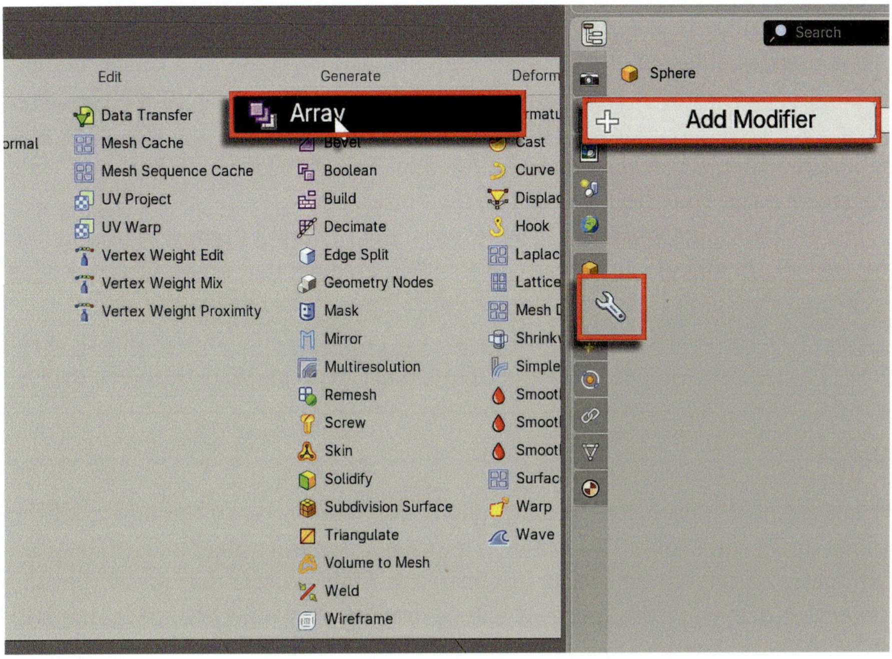

FIGURE 9.2 The Modifier menu and the Array properties.

The first parameter that needs to be set is Fit Type. How would you like to incorporate this array into your scene, and how many copies should there be?

Fixed Count

The first option is Fixed Count. If there needs to be 10 steps in a staircase, enter that number, and the size of the array will be determined by the spacing between each step.

Fit Length

The next option is Fit Length. If the space for the array has been determined, enter that dimension. The number of objects and the space between them can then be adjusted to achieve a proper fit. For example, if a staircase needs to go from the stage floor up to a platform 7 feet high, and the ground plan shows its length, use that dimension. Afterward, adjust the number of steps and the amount of each rise until the total is 7'. Or, for making a picket fence, use the length of the fence and then adjust the number and spacing of the pickets.

Fit Curve

The next is Fit Curve, which will make sense after the brief discussion on creating a curve on the screen. In that case, the array will follow the path of the curve.

Offsets

The spacing of objects in the array is set with the next parameters.

Relative Offset is one option. Remember that it works by using scale factors of the original object, rather than its real dimensions. It can be a quick method to align copies without calculations. To make a staircase from a simple cube, move each step 1 (cube's depth) back and 1 (cube's height) up. All steps will be just touching those above and below. This only works correctly if any scale transformations have been applied to the object.

The next option, Constant Offset, is generally preferred because it uses actual dimensions. In making a staircase, enter 8" in Z to get that amount of rise with each step. One foot for X or Y moves each step that distance to the side.

Object Offset uses the distance between the original and a second object to set the interval between copies. This is used in special situations such as circular arrays.

Merge

When the next parameter, Merge, is activated, all objects in the array will be joined into a single object rather than a group of separate objects. The Distance parameter sets the tolerance for the merging. Only objects that are within the dimension that you have specified will be merged. Any objects outside that will be set aside as separate objects.

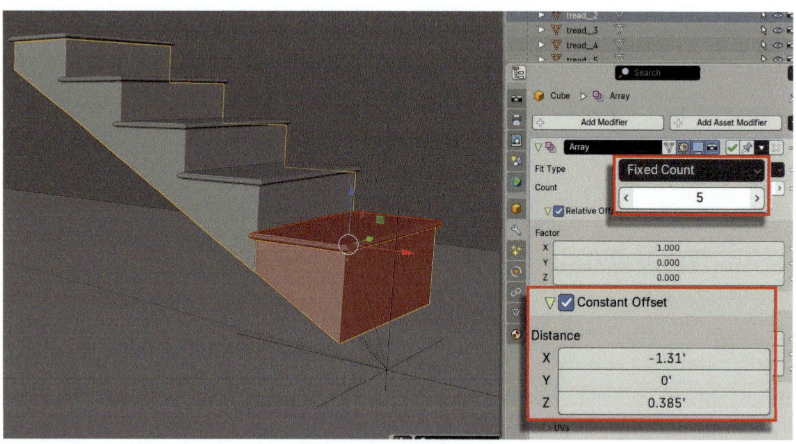

FIGURE 9.3 A basic array creates the stage-right stairs for *My Fair Lady*.

Circular Arrays

There are times when you want to make multiple copies of an object in an organized pattern, but that pattern is not a straight line. The simplest form of this is to duplicate in a circle, which is called a circular or radial array. There are several ways to create radial arrays in *Bforartists*. Let's concentrate on two of the most straightforward methods. All programs have options for making circular arrays. In *Cinema 4D*, the Array modifier panel offers options for creating square or circular arrays. Select one and set the values for the number of copies and the size of the array.

In *Bforartists*, the quickest method is often found in Edit mode. You may have noticed a tool in Edit mode with the enticing name of Spin tool. This is a very cool tool. Using the 3D cursor as a center point, it can extrude circles into hemispheres, toruses, or complex pipes, or spin squares into whole or partial cylinders.

Use the Spin tool for a Simple Array

Making circular arrays is another major function of the Spin tool. First, note that the 3D cursor will be positioned at the center of the array. When you start a new model, the 3D cursor is located at the global center, 0, 0, 0. It can later be changed to another position, but it's best to start there. If the 3D cursor has moved off center, you can recenter it with:

- Viewport menu, View > Center Cursor and "Frame All".
    - Or, right-click > Snap > "Cursor to Origin".
    - Or simply, "Shift + C".
- Next, make a sphere.
- Move it back from the global center. The distance will be the radius of the array.
- Tap the "2" key to switch to Edit mode.
- Select the "Spin" tool in the Tool shelf.
    - A blue arc Gizmo appears in the workspace, centered on the 3D cursor.
- Drag on one end of the arc, and you will make copies, spaced around the 3D cursor.
    - The last operation panel will open. The Steps value is the number of copies that you want to have in your array. Degrees are how far around the 360° circle the array will extend.
    - You also have options to move the center point to a different location or rotate the array using X, Y, and Z values. Simple.
    - After the initial creation, the array is a single object and can be moved, scaled, and rotated like any object.

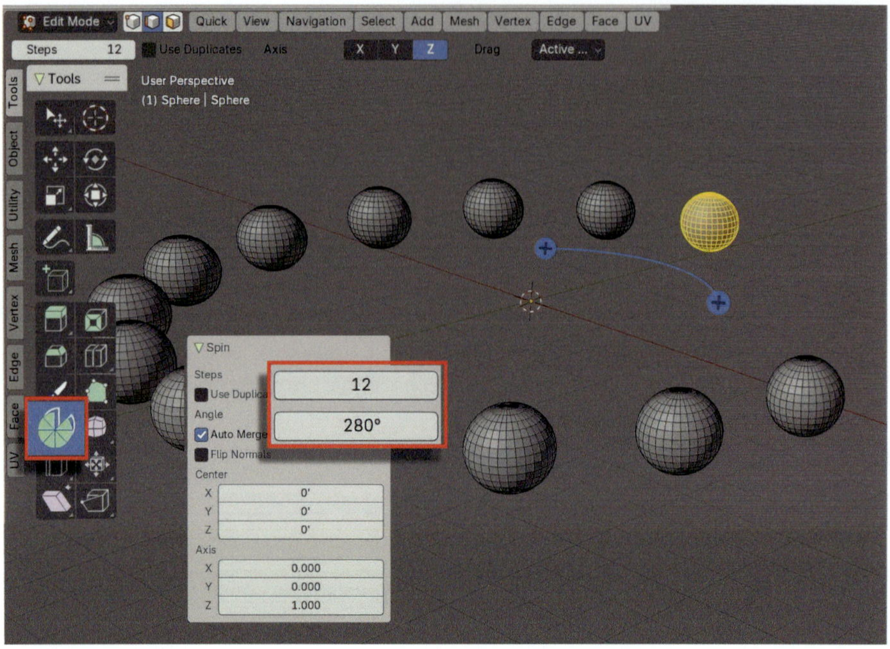

FIGURE 9.4 The Spin tool quickly spaces objects in a circular pattern.

Use the Array Modifier for Complex Variations

That was pretty cool, but it can be even cooler. What if you want the circular array to do tricks? For that, return to using the Array modifier. There are a few steps to this, and it will go smoother if the 3D cursor is used as the center of the array.

- Center the cursor.
- Make a cube (or whatever).
- Move it back from the cursor a distance equal to the radius of the desired array.
  - The cube's origin point is going to be the pivot point of the array, so it needs to move to the 3D cursor. Piece of cake.
- Tool shelf > Object tag, Select "Object origin to 3D Cursor".
  - Or, right-click > "Set Origin to 3D cursor".
  - The cube's pivot point will jump to the Cursor at 0, 0, 0.
- Add the Array modifier to the cube.

Here comes the tricky bit.

- Add an Empty object to the scene.
- Add menu > Empty > (pick one) (or Shift + A).
  - It can be any sort of empty object, try "Plain Axes".

Next:

- Array's Properties panel > Clear the "Relative Offset" box and check "Object Offset".
  - This means that the relationship between the cube and some other object will be used as the spacing between each copy.
- Pull down in the Object Offset text box and set the new empty object as the offset.
  - The little eyedropper in the textbox can also be used to select the empty object manually.

With everything set up, it's time for a bit of math. Sorry, it can't be helped. Luckily, all operating systems come with built-in calculators. Rotating the empty object sets the interval between copies. For 10 copies, spaced around 360°, the spacing is 36°. Making eight copies around a 180°, half-circle means 22.5° spacing, and so forth.

- Rotate the empty object by the calculated amount to equal one space. At least one copy will be made.
- In the array modifier, set the Count value for the total number of copies.

Now the fun begins!

Move the entire circular array by selecting both the empty object and the original object and using the move tool.

- Like a standard array, the X and Y offsets in the properties panel control the spacing between copies.
- The Z offset still controls the distance that each copy is to rise above the previous one. However, in a circular array, X and Y are not typically used, and changing the Z offset results in a spiral.
- Increase the number of objects, and the array will spiral up and up.
- Change the radius of the array by moving the empty object, the offset of the array, closer or farther from the object.
- Moving the empty object up or down on the Z axis will also cause the array to spiral.
- The spiral of objects can even be tapered by changing the scale values of the empty object.
  - This might be used to make a tornado or a wormhole.
- Transformations of the original object will be repeated in all the copies.
- Rotating the empty object on the X or Y axes will cause the objects in the array to spin increasingly with every copy.
- By experimenting with the parameters of the empty object, the array, and the original object, you can create all kinds of formations and special effects.

When you get an array that is to your liking, **apply the modifier and any transformations to the initial object to set it permanently. SAVE THE PROJECT.**

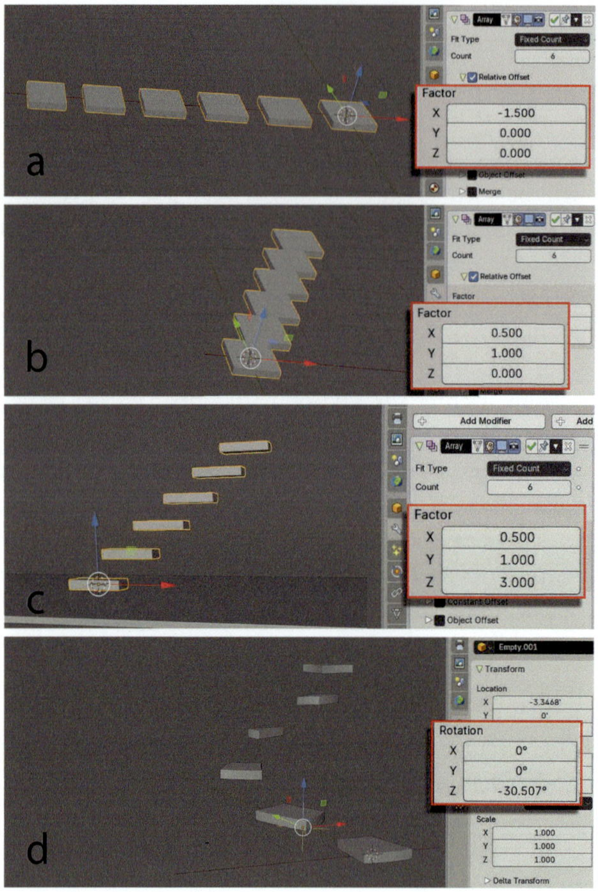

FIGURE 9.5 A few variations of circular arrays. a) Changing offsets. b) Z offsets. c) Transform of the original object. d) A change in rotation is added cumulatively to each object in the array.

A Spiral Staircase

One practical application of a spiral array is the aptly named staircase, difficult to sketch, draft, and construct in a traditional model. It provides a good subject for reviewing the technique.

First, a single step is needed. Each step is essentially a long triangle prism. A flattened cube with a taper modifier would work well. A cylinder with only three vertices is even quicker.

In a spiral staircase, the inner third of each step is too narrow to be used, so each must not be less than 4' long. As the center of a step should be as wide as a standard stair, the outside edge will be 1'-6" to 2' wide.

- Make a sphere.
- Create a three-sided cylinder measuring 4' by 20" (item tab in the viewport sidebar). **NAME IT.**

- Move its origin to the point that will become the center of the staircase.
- With vertex snapping turned on, drag and drop the 3D cursor tool onto a vertex point, then:
- Object > Set Origin > "Origin to 3D Cursor".
- Move the step to the global center (in the Properties panel or the Item sidebar, enter 0, 0, 0).

Be sure to **apply all transformations to the step** (Object > Apply).

- Move the 3D cursor to the center.
- Object > Snap > "Cursor to Global Center".
- Make an Empty object.
- Select the step and add an Array modifier.
- Uncheck "Relative Offset".
- Check "Object Offset".
- Select the Empty object.
- Almost there. Rotate the Empty object until the step and copy overlap just a bit.
- Check the constant Offset.
- Set the height between steps.
  - Spiral stairs tend to be steep, so the Z offset could be 9 or 10 inches.
  - Make as many copies as necessary to reach the desired height.
  - If the number of steps or the amount of rotation needs adjusting, change the Z offset or the rotation of the empty object.

BEVEL

Another Generate modifier that gets a lot of use is Bevel. The Bevel Generate modifier is different than the Bevel tool in the Edit mode because the Bevel Generate modifier is non-destructive. It bevels the sharp edges of objects without making new editable polygons. It is similar to the subdivision modifier because it divides faces into polygons that cannot be selected separately. The Bevel modifier is best used when all the edges of an object need to be rounded. To bevel only selected edges, switching to Edit mode and using the Bevel tool is better.

- Select an object.
- Modifiers tab > Add Modifier > select "Bevel".
- The first bevel options determine what is to be beveled.
  - "Vertices" only affect the corners.
  - "Edges" puts a bevel on both edges and vertices. This is a more all-over general bevel effect.

Selecting a Width Type option determines the method used to measure the size or amount of the bevel.

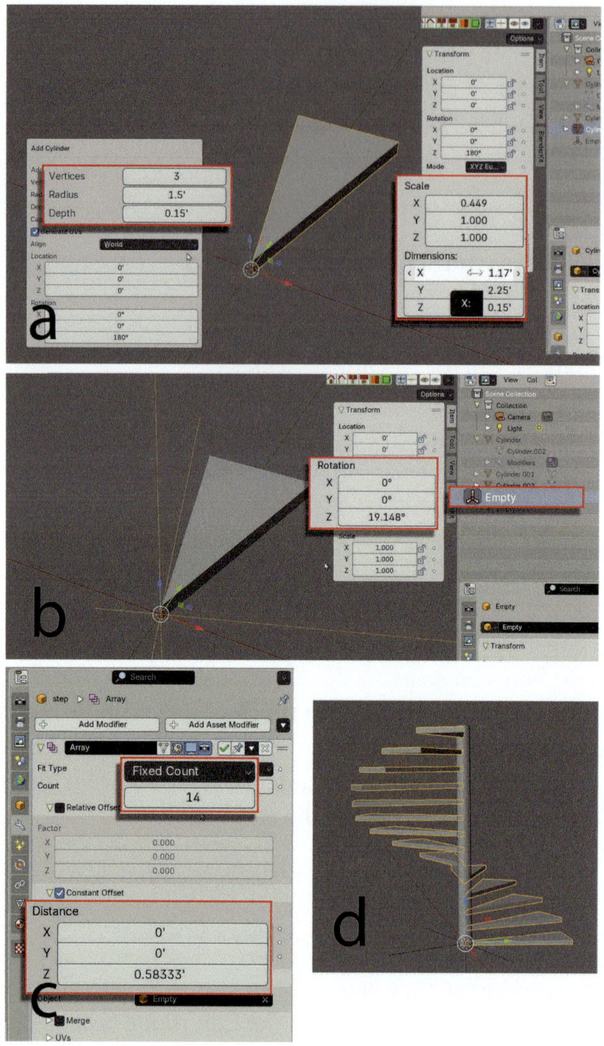

FIGURE 9.6 Simple spiral stairs. a) The first step. b) The Empty object. c) The Modifier settings. d) The staircase.

Offset

The first method is Offset, which is simply the measurement from the original edge to the start of the new bevel on a face. Drag the cursor across the Amount field to alter the value, or click inside the field and enter a new dimension manually.

Width

The next is Width. This is the dimension from the start of the bevel on one face to that on the adjoining face. To bevel an edge with a simple, flat, 1” wide bevel, enter 1”.

Depth

The third method is Depth. Depth is the perpendicular distance from the new bevel face to the original edge. Enter the desired distance into the amount field.

Percent

The Percent method is similar to offset, but the value is interpreted as a percentage of the adjoining faces, rather than just a simple distance. This can be useful because the beveling extends further into large faces than smaller ones. Flat bevels are not necessarily 45°, and rounded bevels are not quarter circles, but quarter ellipses.

Absolute

This may be the most useful of the options. The Absolute method applies the bevel equally to each face being beveled, regardless of their sizes.

The value entered into the **Segments** field determines the number of new faces being added in each bevel. One segment equals a simple, flat bevel. As the number increases, the bevel will become rounder.

The Limit parameter sets a limit on where a bevel is applied to the mesh. Only edges whose adjacent faces form an angle smaller than the defined threshold will be beveled. None means no limit, and all edges will be beveled. This is primarily used on objects that are more complex than the primary shapes. When making an armchair, we might want the sharp edges of the frame to be beveled, but not the subtle wrinkles in the upholstery.

The Profile subpanel has methods to fine-tune the shape of the bevel. None will have an effect if the number of segments is below 2.

Super Ellipse

The Super Ellipse method is the most straightforward means to describe the shape of the rounded beveled edge. A value close to 0 bends the rounding inward, making a concave bevel. Carpenters call this a "quarter-cove" and may use a router with bits of that name to cut the shape into wood. The value towards 1 bends the curve outward, creating a convex bevel, which is familiar to carpenters as a "quarter-round."

Custom

Using the Custom method, you can create a bevel that is more elaborate than a simple curve, or you can select a preset profile from the Preset drop-down. Complex bevels make messy corners when used in object-level modifiers. The geometry can't be resolved where three edges meet. For this reason, custom profiles are primarily used when the Bevel tool is applied to only one edge or one face of an object.

- In the Profile editor, left-click on the profile line to make new points.
- Move them to positions that will create the desired silhouette.
- Click the buttons at the bottom of the window to designate points as on a curve or at a corner.
- There are additional buttons to zoom in and out in the window.
- Use the drop-down in the upper-right corner to reset the view to the default or reset the profile.

The Geometry section of the panel contains Miter options, which define the shape of the beveled corners or vertices. Leave the Miter type as Sharp and the Intersections as Cut Off.

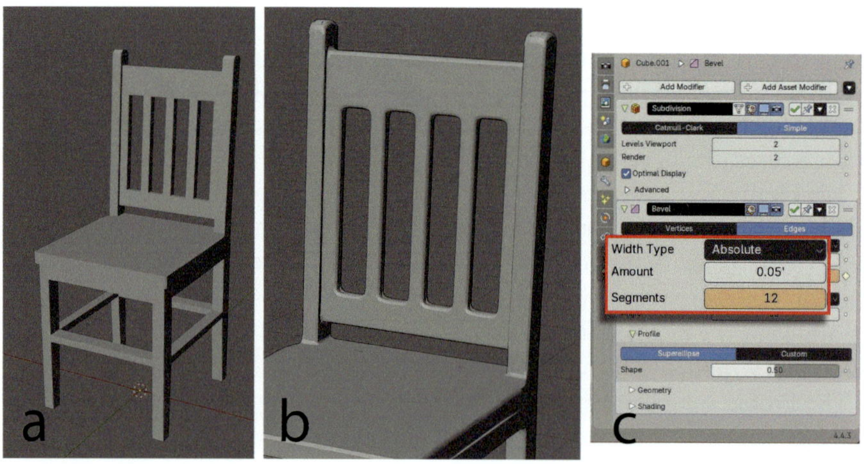

FIGURE 9.7 a) A simple chair made of cubes. b) A bevel modifier makes it appear more natural and cohesive. c) The settings for the modifier.

BOOLEANS

The Boolean generator can help create very interesting shapes. It is also a lot of fun to use. Booleans are logical operators that we use all the time but may not be aware of. Boolean operators in other contexts are words such as and, not, or, and the combinations, but not that, and/or. When using a web search engine, Boolean operators are very useful. Entering a word surrounded by quotation marks means that a specific word must appear in the search results.

Other words are optional, but not that one. And, when the word NOT or a minus sign immediately precedes a word, it means the results can have combinations of the other words, but it can never show that one. Using AND between words means the two must be linked. OR signals a search for one word or the other.

Booleans are used to combine objects and create new objects by combining them. A Boolean modifier can be a bit tricky to use, and the resulting objects often require some adjustments during the process.

- Select the first object to be combined.
- Properties panel > Modifiers tab > Add Modifier > "Boolean".

The main options set the type of combination.

Intersect

Intersect produces a new object that retains only the section that is common to both of the component objects. Anything that is part of only one object is left out.

Union

Union welds two objects together. It is more efficient than simply joining the objects because any unnecessary polygons hidden inside the combination are removed.

Difference

The Difference boolean is used to subtract the geometry of one object from the geometry of another. This can be used for cutting holes in walls to create openings, such as doorways, windows, or proscenium arches.

The Object field is used to identify the second object in the combination.

- Enter the name of the second object into the Object field.
    - Or use the eyedropper to select it in the Viewport or the Outliner.

The Solver Options allow you to fine-tune the Boolean operation.

- If the Solver is set to Fast, Overlap Threshold can be used to exclude small polygons from the operation.
- If Exact is selected, then the Hole Tolerant option can be used to combine objects that already have holes in them.

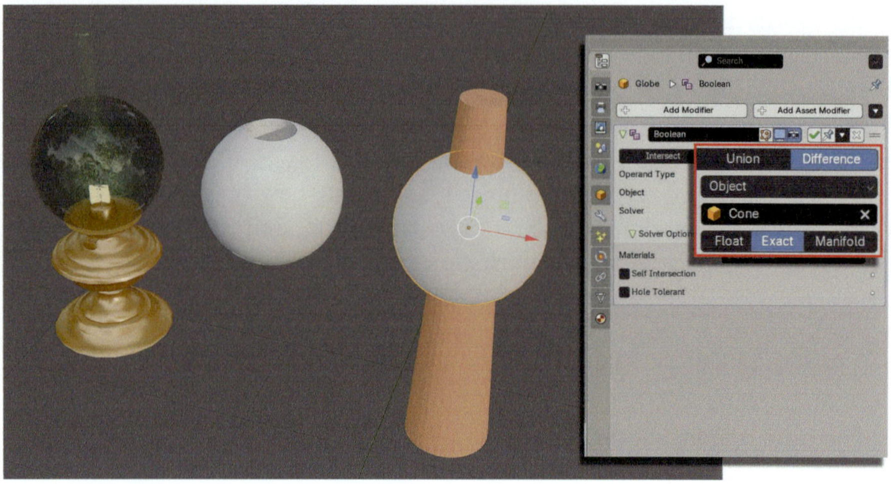

FIGURE 9.8 The Difference Boolean is the type used most often.

DECIMATE

The Decimate generator is more of an anti-generator. Rather than creating new polygons, it is used to reduce the number of polygons. Its function is to take a highly detailed object and remove extra polygons that are not absolutely needed to describe the shape. This can be useful if your model becomes overburdened with objects made of too many polygons.

If the computer bogs down when running a particular project, the objects in the scene that are heaviest in the number of polygons can be reduced or "decimated." Objects imported from other models or online sources are often extremely over-modeled with thousands, hundreds of thousands, or even millions of polygons. This can slow down a modeling project in a hurry. It is often a good idea to open such a resource as a separate model, decimate it, save it, and then import it into your project.

- Select the object.
- Add the Decimate modifier.
- In its properties, choose the mode that you want to use to decimate.

Collapse

Collapse is the most generally effective option. It merges vertices, taking into account the overall shape of the mesh. The Ratio is roughly equivalent to the percentage of the original polygons in the object. 1 (100%) means not altered, and the lower the value, the stronger the reduction and the fewer the polygons. The number of remaining polys appears at the bottom of the panel. Please note

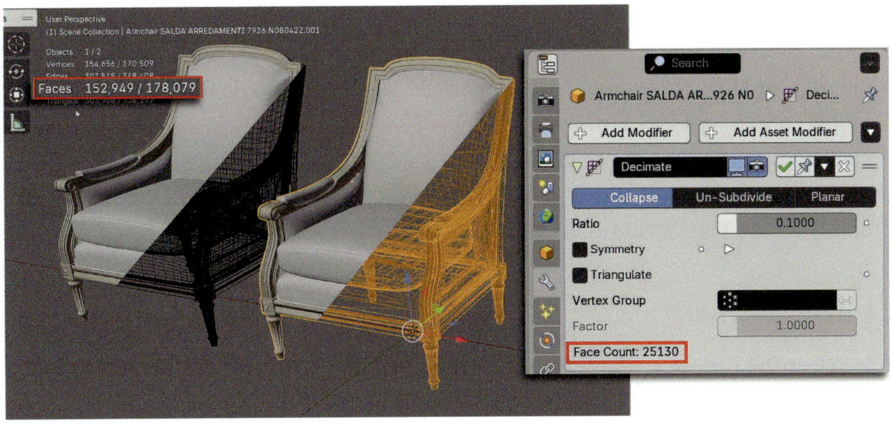

FIGURE 9.9 The Decimate modifier is essential when importing overly complex models such as this chair. Note that the face count has been reduced from 152,949 to 25,130.

that the number of remaining faces may be slightly inaccurate because triangles are used in the calculation of the ratio. If the mesh contains quads or four-sided polygons, the number of remaining faces will be larger than expected. Watch the object's appearance in the viewport and judge when the polygon reduction has gone too far. For imported objects with tens of thousands of polys, the ratio may go as low as .1 (10%) before you notice a real difference. Checking the Triangulate box forces the program to calculate a quad as two triangles. Symmetry maintains symmetry on a single axis so that decimation of the polygons on one side of the axis will be the same as that on the other. If you plan to perform other operations in the future that require symmetrical construction, Triangulate should be used frequently.

Subdivide

This algorithm tries to unify divided faces. It will take a flat plane that is divided into many smaller faces and connect them all together, thereby losing no detail in the model, but losing the number of polygon iterations. Picture the Subdivide modifier working in reverse. Two iterations are the same as one subdivision operation, so you'll usually want to use even numbers.

Planar

This algorithm reduces details by unionizing adjacent faces that are below an angle limit. If two faces are only a couple of degrees from being in the same plane, they can be joined into a single face. Planar can be used as a type of smoothing device. If the object has more than one material, the Material option prevents decimation from occurring along the border where the materials meet.

EXTRUDING

There is another Generate operation that is not grouped with the Generate modifiers in the add modifier menu because it does not affect an entire object, only specific polygons. This is the Extrude operation. The extrude operation is performed only in Edit mode. The extrude tool is in the Tool shelf > Tool tab. Holding down the button discloses several tool variations.

Extrude Individual

- Select the object with faces to be extruded.
- Switch to Edit mode.
- Tool shelf > Tools > Select "Extrude Individual".
- Select a single face of the object.
  - Once selected, a blue line extending perpendicularly from the face (its normal) and a yellow handle with a + sign will appear.
  - Drag the plus sign yellow handle along the blue line, and the extrusion will grow outward. Drag it the other direction along the blue line, and the extrusion will grow inward.
  - Avoiding the handle and dragging the face allows you to extrude in any direction.
  - As an extrusion grows, new polygons are generated, forming the sides of this new appendage.

Extrude Region

- Used mainly for extruding edges and vertices. You can make objects without distorting the original with this tool.

Extrude Along Normals

- Useful when working with faces that have been twisted in odd ways.

Extrude Manifold

- If your extrusion collides with another part of the object, the colliding portions stop, and the rest continues on. Very Sweet!

Extrude to Cursor

- This tool is wild. Selected faces, edges, or vertices extrude to the spot of a mouse click. Hard to control but wicked fun!

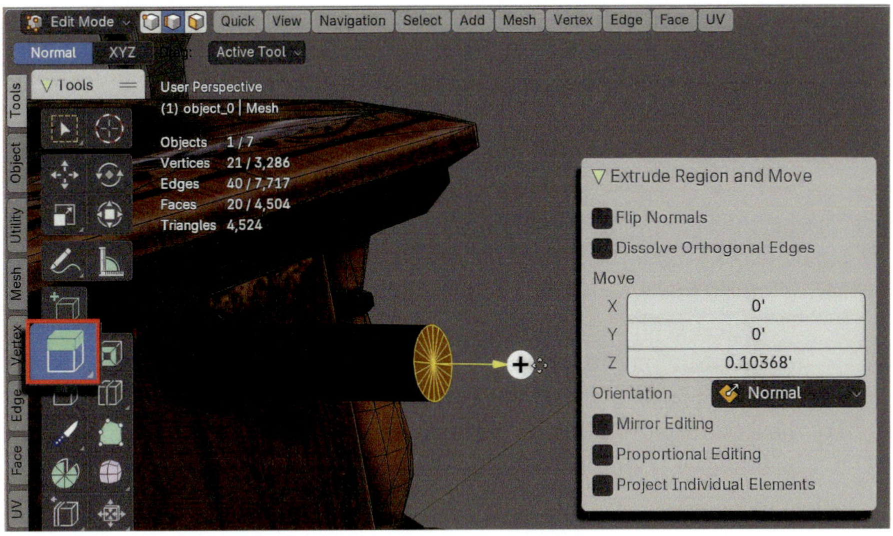

FIGURE 9.10 Extrude handles make it easy to extrude single faces or groups.

EDITING FACES

In Edit mode, individual polygons, edges, and vertices can be selected and transformed. This is the basis of sculpting. Any shape can be created with sculpting. A sphere can be manipulated to become a human head, and a cylinder can become an airplane. Moreover, any shape can be edited with the same techniques. The features of a figure's face, even its expression, can be altered. However, this way of manipulating objects can be extremely time-consuming. Be certain that editing objects at this level will pay off in the final renders and presentation, and are worth the time spent. Again, our objective is the final production, not the design sketches.

Whether time-consuming or not, it is worth taking the time to become familiar with the basics of editing.

- Make a sphere.
- Switch to Edit mode.
    - In *3DS Max*, go to the modifier panel and add the Edit Mesh modifier, or right-click on the object and select "Edit Mesh".
    - In *Cinema 4D*, select the object and click the "Make Editable" button, right-click the object and select that command, or tap the "C" key. Next, pick an element to edit by clicking the face, edge, or vertex button.
    - These buttons are common to all modeling programs.

- Tool shelf > Move tool.
- Select a face (polygon) on the sphere.
- Use the familiar Move widget to move the face along any axis.

In the middle of the Viewport toolbar is the **Transform Orientation pulldown.**

- Change the orientation from Global (standard X, Y, and Z) to Normal (perpendicular to the surface of the polygon).
- Move another face.
  - The effect is much the same, but on a curved or irregular surface, moving a face along its normal will help maintain its relationship to the greater object.
- Try the Rotate and Scale tools on selected faces and edges.
  - Rotating or scaling a vertex has no effect as it represents a single point in 3D space.

LATHE OPERATIONS

Lathing is an important operation that functions much like a Generate modifier. In other programs, it is lumped with operations such as extrude. Making an object with a Lathe modifier works as the name implies. Using a lathe, a carpenter uses special chisels called gouges to carve a shape, such as a chair leg, out of a rapidly turning piece of wood. In 3D modeling, an object is created by spinning a profile shape or outline around an axis. Spinning a circle makes a sphere, and spinning a square makes a cylinder. Those primitive shapes are easily made with direct methods, but more complex profiles can be used to make objects like vases, columns, or baseball bats.

Unlike other Generate modifiers, a Lathe operation works best on a two-dimensional shape, not a 3D object. In particular, an outline, which is called a "Curve" in *Bforartists* and a "spline" in other modeling programs. So, before using the Lathe, some practice in making curves is needed.

Bézier Curves

Bézier curves were first introduced in Adobe Illustrator and are used in most drawing and drafting programs, such as *Vectorworks*.

- Start a new scene.
- Set the measurement units to imperial.
- Add menu > Curve > "Bézier".
  - By default, the very simple curve will appear flat on the floor (X, Y) plane.
- Switch to Edit mode.
  - Note that the Tool shelf has a different set of tools when working on curves. Also, the options for editing a vertex, edge, or face have

disappeared because curves consist only of vertex points. The simple curve has only two points, one at each end. Because it is a Bézier curve, each point has two control handles. These handles control the size and shape of the curve that passes through the point.

- Select a vertex's control handle and move it around the point, closer to it and further from it.
  - o You will quickly get the hang of changing the curve's shape, making it larger or diminishing it to a sharp angle.

Convert A Curve Point to A Corner Point

- Right-click > Set Handle Type > "Vector".

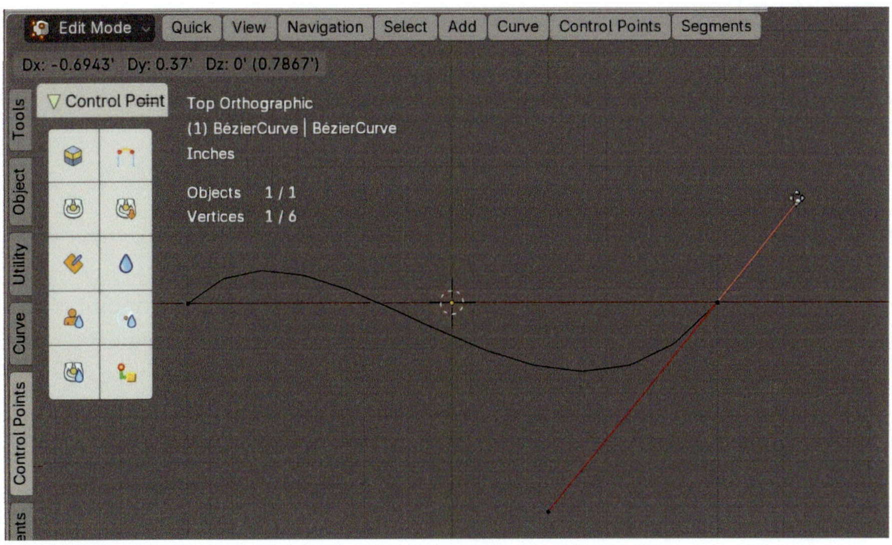

FIGURE 9.11 a) Editing a simple curve. b) Extruding a complex curve.

Complex Curves

To make a complex shape, you will need to add more vertices. There are several methods to accomplish this.

- Make a Bézier curve.
- Select a vertex at one end of the curve.
- Select the Extrude Curve tool on the Tool shelf.
- Drag the new yellow handle on the endpoint's controller.
  - o A copy will be extruded along the orientation of the controllers.
- Alternately, left-click in a different location.
  - o A copy of the endpoint will jump to that spot. As a copy, the control handles will have the same orientation.

- Another option is to tap the "S" key.
  - A new endpoint will follow the cursor until it is set with a left-click.

The Extrude to Cursor tool quickly adds points to a curve.

- Select the tool.
- Click around the desired profile.
  - The control handles on each new point will be roughly oriented to form a smooth curve from the previous point. They will need to be adjusted afterward.
- Alternatively, Ctrl + Right-Click is equivalent to using the Extrude to Cursor tool.

The Curve Pen

For more complete control, using the Curve Pen tool is similar to the method for making splines in most other graphic programs.

- Select an endpoint.
- Select the "Curve Pen" tool.
- Click a new location for a new endpoint.
- Click and drag will pull out the point's bézier handles.
  - This turns the corner point into a point on a curve. If an endpoint is not pre-selected, the Pen will start a new, disconnected curve segment.
- Click on a curve between two vertices and drag it into a new shape.
  - These are only a few of the many gee-whiz tricks that the curve pen can do.

Joining Curve Segments

Any curves can be joined, regardless of how they were made.

- Select menu > All or keystroke "A".
- Right-click > "Make Segment".

To keep only the new segments:

- Select the vertices in the original curve.
- Click "Delete".
  - A small dialog box will appear asking if you want to delete the vertex or the segment that connects them. In this case, it makes no difference.

Adding Vertices

To add a vertex between two existing points:

- Select two adjoining points.
- Right-Click > "Subdivide".
    - Or, Segments menu > "Subdivide".
    - Or, Tool shelf > Segment tab > "Subdivide".

Convert the Curve to a Mesh

A curve can be lathed, but to make it easier to model with the object, give it materials, etc., it should be converted to a mesh object before proceeding.

- Object mode Object menu > Convert > "Mesh".

Lathing the Curve

The *My Fair Lady* set needs some columns to support the high platform. The bases and capitals of these columns could be made by stacking cylinders and applying bevel modifiers to each, but that sounds like a lot of work.

For this, it would be better to use one half of a profile spun 360° rather than an entire profile spun 180°. A half-profile is easier, faster, and better allows for later adjustments. A curve spun 360° is sure to be symmetrical, but using 180° may produce a shape with sides that don't match.

This is a simple profile. Several vertices were converted to corner vertices. There are small horizontal segments at each end that will partially close the ends of the capital, just in case it doesn't align perfectly with the column or the platform. This profile is lying flat on the ground. No matter, it can be turned upright later.

- Go back to Object mode.
- Property panel > Modifier tab > Add Modifier.
- Select the "Screw" modifier. (There is no lathe modifier; there should be.)

When the Screw modifier is added, the curve becomes a strange pancake because it was spinning around the Z, upright, axis.

- Change the spin axis to Y.
    - It is almost right, but the radius is a bit off.

The curve spins around its origin point. So, the distance between the curve and that pivot point is the radius of the capital. It is changed by moving the origin.

- Select the Move tool.
- Viewport sidebar > Tool tab > Options > Transform > "Affect Only".
- Check the "Origin" box.
- Move the origin closer or further from the curve.
    - The radius of capital changes!

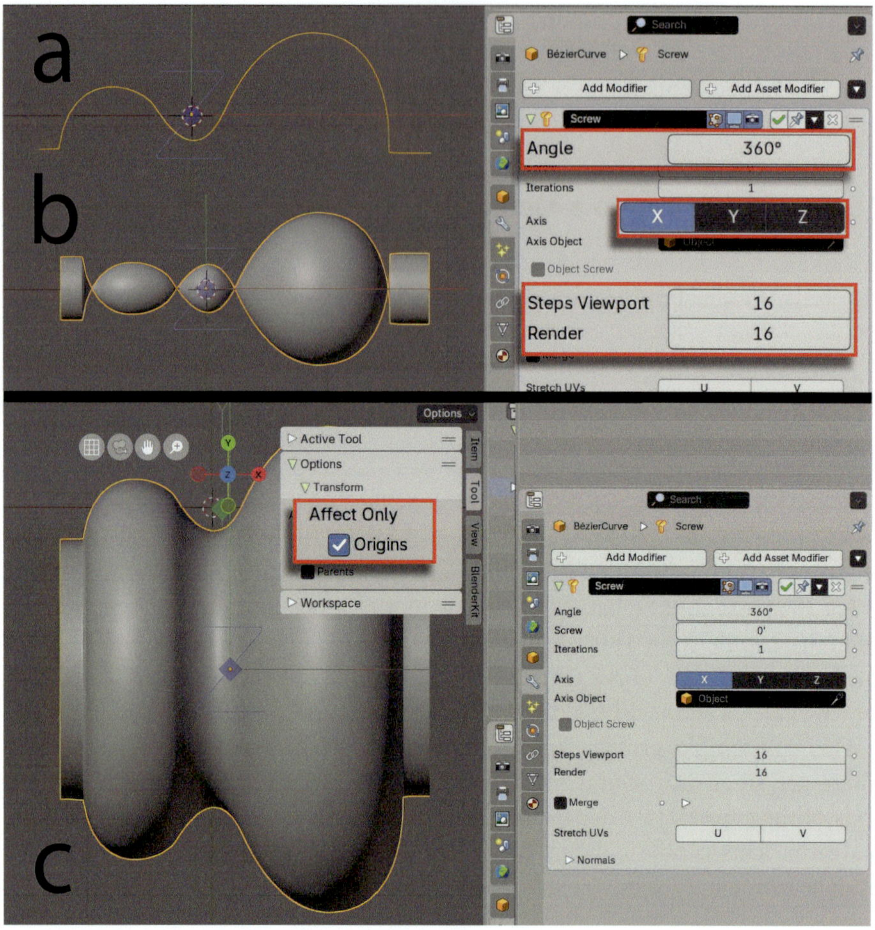

FIGURE 9.12 a) A profile for making a simple turned capital. b) Turning the shape with the Screw modifier. c) Expand the shape by moving the origin further from the profile.

It's looking pretty good.
To permanently set the new shape:

- **Click the green, apply, checkmark in the modifier properties panel.**

The Screw Modifier's Special Talent

The Screw modifier gets its name because, in addition to doing ordinary lathing, it can be used to make cool, spiraling shapes like screws and bolts or even graceful Bernini columns. (Put lots of those in your scenic designs: the people in the scenic shop will love you!)

- Make a Bézier curve.
- Edit mode > make some wild shape with the spin axis along one side.
  - A square that has a point sticking out on the side opposite the turning axis will become a bolt.

- A simple semicircle will turn out to be a Solomonic column or Barley-twist. (Get it? "Turn out to be . . .? Turn out . . .").

- Object mode: Object menu > Convert > "Mesh".
- Add a Screw modifier.
- Change the axis of rotation.
- Increase the Screw value to make the rotations offset and form a spiral.
- Increase the Iterations value to raise the number of rotations.

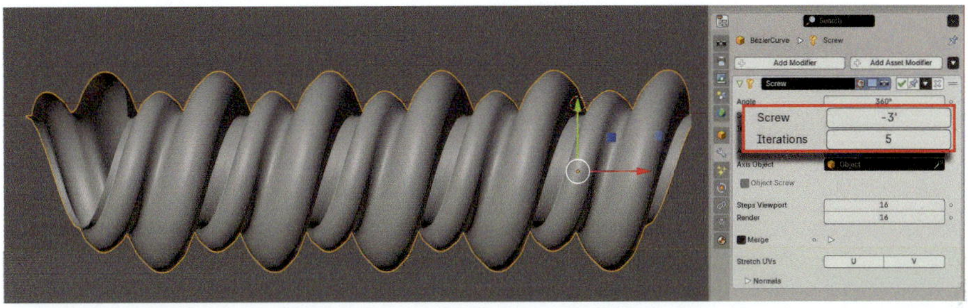

FIGURE 9.13 Changing only the Screw and the Iteration values converts the simple shape.

Pretty fun, yes?

10 Importing Objects

FIGURE 10.1 A vast amount of usable content is readily available for your projects.

When modeling a scene, start with elements that are unique to your design. For more common items, such as set props, furniture, hand props, or well-known architectural features like doors and windows, it's efficient to source them online. Typically, these found items are well-made, detailed, and complete, saving you time on the tedious aspects of modeling. Given the tight timelines of designing a show, outsourcing these specific set pieces makes a lot of sense.

The great availability of online objects allows you to choose from numerous options without sacrificing quality. Other modelers have invested time in creating these assets, often resulting in better quality than you could achieve yourself. Furthermore, these objects often come with appropriately fitted materials, also offering a significant time advantage. You can easily modify these materials to

DOI: 10.4324/9781003571742-10

match your color palette or completely change the look, such as transforming a shiny new door into an old, distressed one with a different texture.

Imported objects can be used whole or segmented. You can adapt a single step from a staircase or extract elements like clocks and chandeliers from larger scenes. With some creativity, an armchair can be stretched into a sofa, or parts can be repurposed, such as using a framed picture as a tabletop. This approach to adapting objects mirrors inventive stagecraft, transforming seemingly unrelated items into innovative designs, such as creating Macbeth's crown from a lampshade, glass beads, a doily, and plenty of hot glue.

FIGURE 10.2 A Georgian table serves well as the raised platform, stage left.

SOURCES

There are thousands of great pieces available online, many of which you can acquire for free or at very affordable prices, often around $5. By importing a set of Winsor furniture for your production of *1776* instead of making it, you can save both time and money while meeting your deadline. Plus, all downloaded assets can be reused whenever needed.

The number of sources is growing, including renowned institutions such as the Louvre, the Smithsonian Institution's Open Access program, and the Minneapolis Institute of Art. You can also find extensive 3D assets from the British Museum, the National Gallery of Denmark, NASA, and other notable institutions. Be sure to download a model of the 4-Cyclopropyl-7,8-difluoro-5–[4-(trifluoromethoxy)phenyl]sulfonyl-1,4-dihydropyrazolo[4,3-c]quinoline molecule from the National Institute of Allergy and Infectious Diseases. Nobody should be without one.

Remember, 3D collection sites come and go. It's often best to search for specific items rather than relying on one or two favorite sites. Start with terms like

"3D model of Victorian armchair" and add "free" to see those options first. By adding "-Free3D" (with the minus sign), you can avoid results from sites like Free3D.com, as their models are typically not free.

The image search of your favorite engine can yield valuable results. Familiarize yourself with various collections to determine which ones are free, affordable, or expensive. Some sites may require registration, which is not unreasonable, but be sure to opt out of newsletters. Avoid sites that charge for membership fees; payment should only be for content.

Bforartists users have access to valuable resources unavailable to others. Being a branch of *Blender* software, it can directly connect to *Blenderkit*, which offers over 14,000 models, 15,000 materials, and more. Registration is optional but beneficial for creating wish lists and utilizing cloud storage. It is free to use, and a reasonable pay plan unlocks thousands more assets. The *Blenderkit* add-on integrates easily, adding a toolbar and sidebar for searching and downloading resources directly into your project.

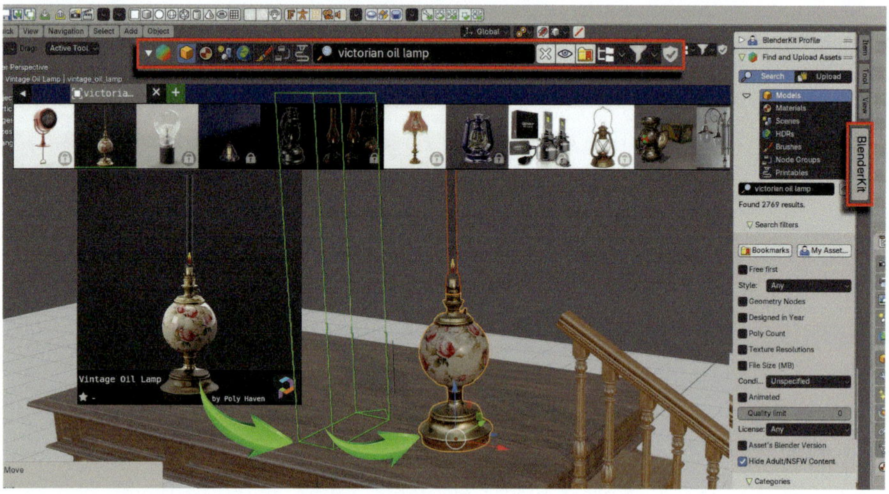

FIGURE 10.3 The Blenderkit tools in the interface.

With the *Blenderkit* add-on, you can also upload an entire scene or individual objects to your account at the *Blenderkit* cloud.

There are a few other sites that deserve mention. One is Sketchfab.com. *Sketchfab* is an online gallery and marketplace for creators of 3D content. It is now owned by the game giant, Epic. Anyone creating interesting 3D objects or scenes can upload them to *Sketchfab*, where visitors can experience them. *Sketchfab* has an enormous number of users, most of whom have uploaded not one, but a collection of objects and scenes. Many are available for free download or at a price set by the user. *Sketchfab* is the host site for many of the collections of the great museums and institutes mentioned earlier.

One very useful option for collaboration is to upload your scenic design model to *Sketchfab*. After limiting it to private viewing, you can share the address with other members of the production team, who can then visit the site and view your model in 3D. They can rotate it and see it from all angles. They can zoom in and out, even walk through it in a virtual reality mode. A user equipped with a VR headset, such as a Meta Quest or Vive XR, can enjoy the full immersive experience.

FIGURE 10.4 *Sketchfab* displays your scenes in 3D and can present them as virtual reality (VR) walkthroughs. These can then serve as a means of collaboration or an interactive online portfolio.

There are also many websites dedicated to hosting models for use in 3D printing. These sites offer models that are downloadable in the STL format, which is native to 3D printers. This format is a bit unusual, but it can easily be uploaded into most 3D modeling programs. Printer hobbyists have largely contributed the models at these sites, so they have unusual objects you won't find anywhere else.

The quality of STL models varies from pretty good to really lousy. Designed for 3D printing, most of the objects are single meshes, so they may require a bit of extra work to get them to look good in your scene. For example, a chair will be made with its frame and cushions as one piece, rather than separate objects. In such a case, you will need to do a bit of extra work to make the chair cushion one color and the chair frame another. However, since many of the objects at these sites are items like statues, it usually works out okay. Additionally, since they are intended to be realized in a 3D printer, many objects lack texture files, so you'll need to do a little extra work to apply the wood grain or leather surface to the object.

As you download and utilize models in your projects, create a library for future use. Preserve any significant modifications that work well and keep everything organized with descriptive file names. It's also helpful to make quick renderings of objects and save them in the respective folders or in a new catalog folder. This will save time later, preventing unnecessary downloads of objects you already have. Remember, you can also open old projects and copy objects for new ones – NEVER MAKE ANYTHING TWICE.

Avoid cluttering your hard drive with unused files, and don't save two nearly identical items. Let the internet be your library; bookmark sites with good collections and use long, descriptive names for easy future reference.

For 3D modeling, certain file formats are essential for sharing objects. *Bforartists* saves in *Blender's* "blend" format but supports all common file formats you'll encounter. The ones you'll see most are:

- **.fbx (Filmbox):** FBX is popular because it compresses models, textures, and animations into a single file. Its high compression makes sharing and storing easy.
- **.obj (Wavefront):** OBJ is another widely used format. While typically larger than FBX due to less compression (resulting in fewer errors), OBJ files come as.zip files with texture and MTL files, which detail the material coverage on the object.
- **.stl (Stereolithography):** The go-to format for 3D printers, there are countless STL downloadable models meant for printing, but also useful for scenic purposes. Almost all 3D programs can import/export STL files.
- **.glb, .gltf (glTF 2.0):** These formats are growing in popularity for gaming due to their reduced materials and high compression. Nearly all 3D modeling software can now import them.
- **.3ds (3ds Max):** One of the oldest formats, originally from Autodesk's *3DStudio*, it's handy when other formats fail. However, it adheres to antiquated MS-DOS standards, which limit file names to 8.3 characters. 3DS files often serve as backups.
- **.max (3ds Max):** Widely used globally, many downloadable files are only available in MAX. While this can indicate quality, converting MAX files without *3ds Max* is tricky; you'll become the go-to person if you can do it.
- **.dae (Collada):** Developed by *Autodesk* for file sharing since the MAX and other Autodesk formats are proprietary. Its popularity is on the decline.
- **.skp (SketchUp):** *SketchUp* has a unique workflow and gained traction when it was free. Most programs can import SKP files, but post-import work can be tedious due to many sub-objects. It's often better to export it to a friendlier format like OBJ or DAE after opening it in *SketchUp*.

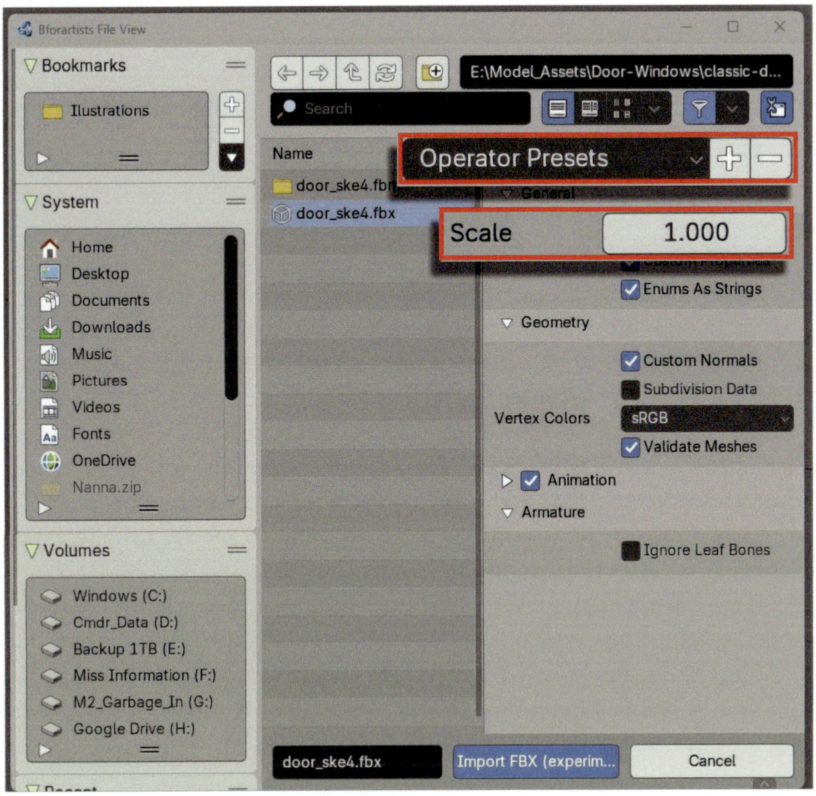

FIGURE 10.5 The Import panel of *Bforartists*.

IMPORTING A MODEL

You can import downloaded models directly into an open project. Still, it is often a good idea to open a new, blank project and import the model into that, so that your scene will be protected while you make modifications. This will also allow you to work on the new objects without any existing objects being in the way. When ready, a simple cut-and-paste will transfer the model back into your project.

Preparing a Model for Import

The *My Fair Lady* set could use some period armchairs. They should be readily available, so no time needs to be wasted in making them. A good candidate, downloaded from *downloadfree3d.com*.

- The model is downloaded.
- Unzip the downloaded file.

- Search the folder for additional zip files and unzip them.
- Move all the model files and textures to the topmost folder so the program can easily locate all the necessary parts.
- Start a new scene. File menu > "New".
  - Remember to set the Scene Units to match your project.

Next,

- File menu > "Import".
- The chair is an .obj file. Select it in the file explorer.
  - If the needed format is not visible, there may be an add-on for it.
  - Go to Edit > Preferences > Add-ons tab and activate the missing format.

This will have opened *Bforartists'* file explorer window, which includes the Operator Presets panel. This helps filter objects for proper orientation and size. Stick with the defaults; they work for 90% of imports, and it's usually easier to make corrections after the import.

In the Transform panel, you'll find a scale multiplier. Since most creators use the metric system, imported objects can often be 10 or 100 times too big or small. Adjust the scale value to 0.001, 01, 10, or 100 to get the right size. If you're using imperial measurements, *Bforartists* will try to convert, but inaccuracies are common.

Rotation

Different modeling programs use various axes for the "up" direction, so models might arrive flipped. To fix this, simply rotate the X axis by +90 ° or -90°. You can adjust the rotation during import if you anticipate issues, but it's not worth the hassle to re-import for minor tweaks.

For instance, importing the chair's OBJ file may show it lying face down and measuring 4,208 feet tall! That's messed up!

Adjusting the Model

BEFORE MAKING ANY CHANGES, ORGANIZE THE MODEL.

Consolidate the group if the model is made of several objects, such as a chair with separate cushions and pillows.

- NAME THE OBJECTS
- You can select all the objects and then scale and rotate them together.
- Or join them into a single object with: Object menu > "Join" (Ctrl + J).
- A better option is to group them as parent-children. Select the smaller objects and shift-drag them onto a main object.
- Or select them all and Object > Parent > "Object" (Ctrl + P > Object). Then rotate and scale the parent. The child objects will all be affected at the same time.

The chair is rotated nearly upright with the Rotate tool, and then the Transform > Rotation value is adjusted to 90° to fix the orientation.

Now, to correct the size of the chair . . . Dividing by 1000 moves the decimal point three places to the left and is worth a try. Entering .001 in as the X, Y, and Z Scale values makes the chair 4.2' tall or 4'-3"ish. Looks about right.

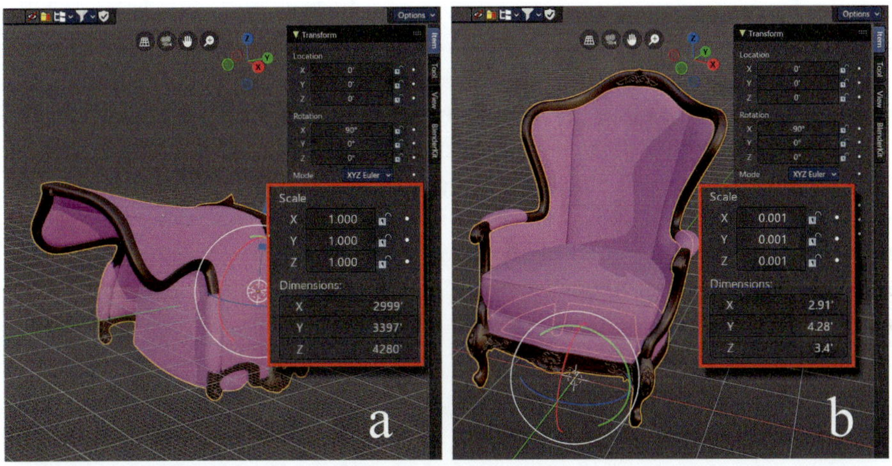

FIGURE 10.6 a) The Item panels. b) The imported object is rotated and scaled.

AGAIN, REMEMBER TO APPLY CHANGES TO THE OBJECT AFTER A TRANSFORMING PROCEDURE.

It is always a good idea to compare objects to a human figure. Scenic models, renderings, and lighting storyboards should all include a performer to set the scale and capture a moment. Character models can be found at nearly every site with downloadable 3D models. Sometimes, a simple human-sized cube or cylinder can also be used for a quick check.

Here's a model of Dr. Watson from *rigmodels.com*. My favorite on-screen Watson is actor Martin Freeman, but he is only 5'-7", a bit short to use for measurement comparisons. But since this Watson will become Professor Higgins, he can be made 6'. After setting his height, he can be trotted around the set, helping to establish the size of furniture, doors, stairs, and whatever.

No matter which method you use to scale the imported object, REMEMBER TO APPLY ANY MODIFICATIONS BEFORE MOVING ON.

MATERIALS

In the Viewport toolbar, SWITCH THE VIEWPORT SHADING TO MATERIAL PREVIEW. By default, the viewport doesn't show materials.

Changing the colors and materials of the imported model is quick and easy and has a big payoff in visibly changing the model to fit the design. The downloaded armchair file included two textures. These ordinary graphic files can be opened in any graphics program and edited for brightness, contrast, hue, etcetera.

Another option is to substitute a completely different texture. Typically, textures for 3D models are seamless. They can be repeated next to each other like wallpaper with no seams showing. Downloadable texture files and materials are even more numerous than 3D models. Search the web for "seamless dragon hide texture" or "(free) PBR material dragon hide." (More about super cool PBR Materials later.)

Download a texture from *3Dtexture.me* and place it in the chair model's folder. (A luxurious tufted leather texture.)

A quick check reveals that it is 4,096 x 4,096 pixels. Yikes! That's ridiculous, so change it to 1,024 pix with a simple image editing utility.

Select an object that uses the cloth texture.

Open the "Materials" tag of the Properties panel. (The circle with red and yellow quarters) Next, open the Surface > "Base Color" property with the small triangle/arrow icon, to reveal the name of the cloth texture file.

When the folder icon is clicked, an Explorer window opens. Locate the new texture file.

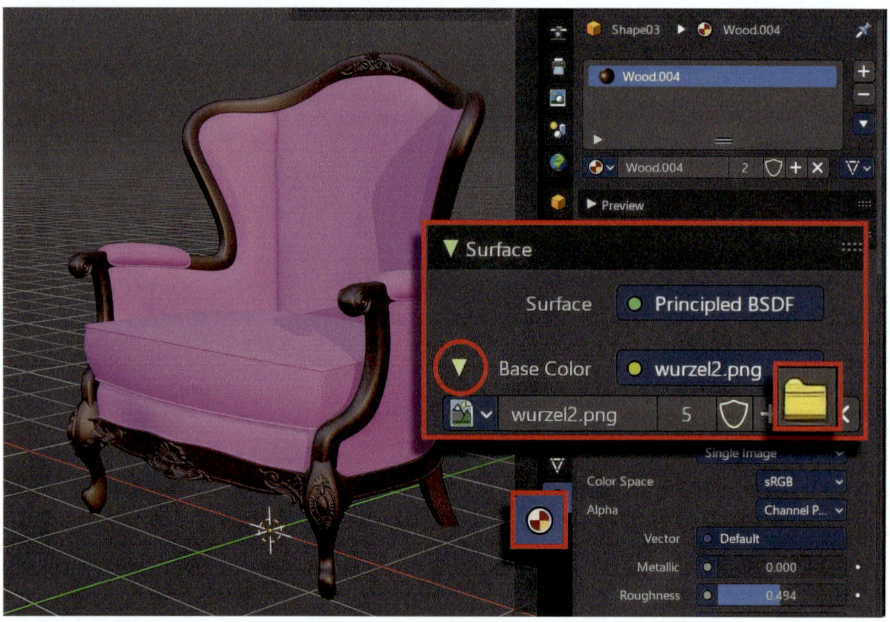

FIGURE 10.7 Changing a Base color texture in the Material tab of the Properties panel.

Texture Mapping

The new leather texture doesn't look quite right. In some places, the tuffs are the correct size, while in others, they appear too small. This means that the UV mapping needs to be adjusted. UV mapping is the scheme that dictates how the materials are arranged on the surfaces of a model. UV mapping will be discussed in greater detail later. For now, these are the basic steps for correcting texture organization in *Bforartists*.

The seat cushion appears to be the one in need of adjustment and is selected. If the existing leather texture is adjusted, the change will affect all other leather objects. That won't help, so its texture is deleted, and it gets a new one.

- In the list at the top of the Material tab, the texture is selected and deleted with the "X" button.
- A new blank material is added by clicking "New Material".
- It gets a distinct name, like "Leather 2".
- In the Surface property, the leather texture is opened with the Base Color > Folder icon, just as before.
- The Vector menu is opened, and Mapping is selected.
- A new Vector parameter has appeared. It is opened, and "UV" is selected.
- **With that, transform controls for the UVs of the texture have appeared.**
- The Scale is adjusted .5 for X, Y, and Z looks right. The front of the cushion looks odd. Moving the texture 4" in Location's Y vector aligns the tufts better.

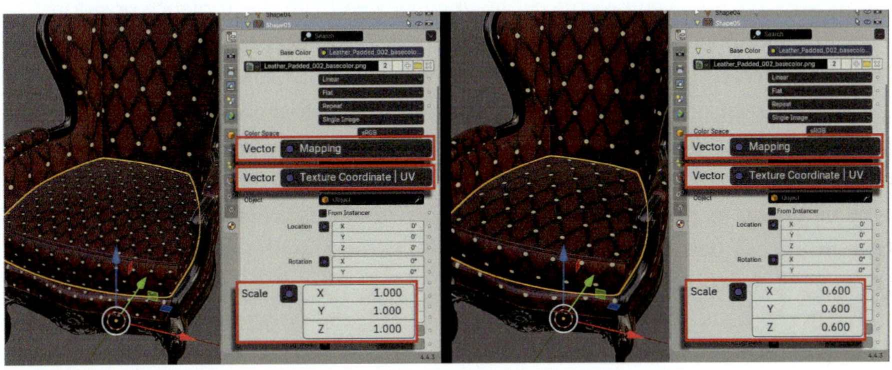

FIGURE 10.8 a) The tufts in the new leather texture on the seat don't match those on the back. b) The basic mapping controls in the Material tab look like this.

More objects need the same adjustment, but doing it from scratch for each one is too much work. They can all use the seat cushion's new material.

- An object is selected.
- In the toolbar of the Material tab, there is a pulldown menu called the Material Browser. With it, the new leather material is selected and applied to the object.

New Material

You may want to use a completely new material, or the object may have come with no materials from the start. Making a new material is not significantly different from editing and repositioning an existing material. The techniques needed for this are described in the next chapter. Skip ahead, then come back.

ADDING MODIFIERS TO MULTIPLE OBJECTS

Join the Objects

Open the Wrench icon and drag the modifier icon to the second object. A pop-up will appear. Choose Copy to Object.

Optionally, after adding a modifier to one object, select all the objects to be modified. Be sure to select the modified object last. Then Ctrl + C > Modifier. This technique can copy all sorts of properties from one object to another.

EDIT MODE MODIFIERS

The need may arise to modify specific portions of some objects in the model. Be careful here. Editing specific elements of objects' geometry can use up a great deal of time and can be a black hole that keeps pulling you in. Often, changes of this sort are not evident or even visible in the finished scenic model. When you start making small changes, zooming in for a better view of vectors and edges, changes that seem significant may not even be noticeable when viewed from the audience position.

Switch to Edit mode and select Faces mode. All polygons in the back of the chair are selected using the box selection. But this only selects the polygons that are visible from one angle. The polygons on the opposite side of the chair also need to be selected. This can be done by rotating the viewpoint to different sides of the chair and selecting polygons while holding down the Shift key. But there may be polygons that are hidden from view in places where one material overlaps another. A better option is to toggle X-ray mode with the button in the view controls of the toolbar on the right side.

When the back of the chair is selected again, the polygons on all sides have been selected.

To shorten the back of the chair, the first option is to use the usual scale tool. However, when using this scale tool with the origin of the selected polygons in the center, the selected area is shrunk on both sides, top, and bottom. This creates a strange distortion at the edge where the selected polygons are connected to the unselected.

One way to address this problem is to move the origin point of the selected polygons to the bottom and then use the Scale tool. Or, better yet, Bforartists has a tool not found in other 3D programs that is precisely what is needed. In a situation such as this. **In the tool shelf, the small triangle adjacent to the scaling tool opens the Scale box, a transparent box around the selected portions of the object.**

Grab the handles of the scale box and pull, push, move up, down, or to either side. The selected polygons will contract or expand to match the box. The orientation of the scale box mirrors the selected polygons. In this case, angled back at the top. Now, scaling down the selected polygons to shorten the chair's back is a piece of cake.

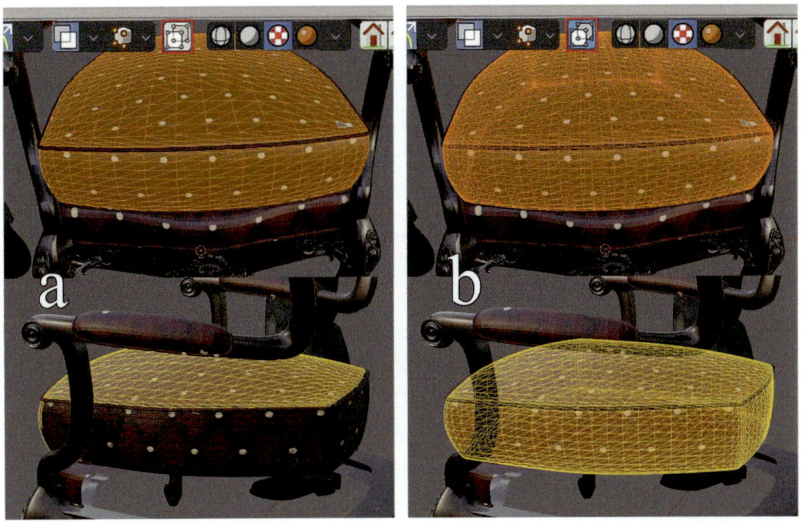

FIGURE 10.9 a) In the standard view, only the front polygons are selected. b) In X-ray view, hidden faces are selected as well.

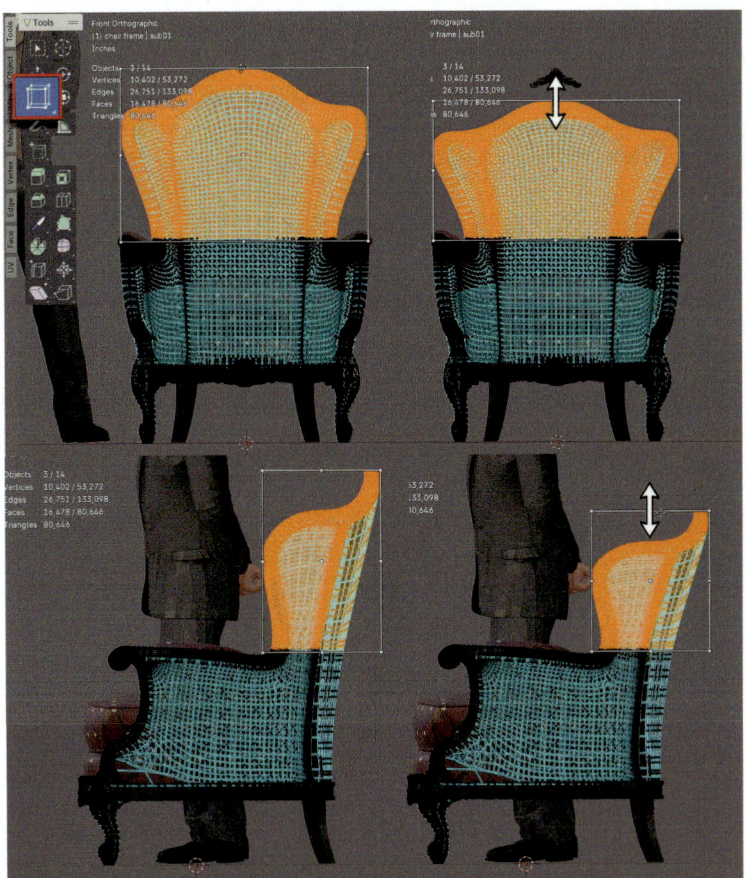

FIGURE 10.10 Using the Scale box, adjustments are made in the right-side view.

CHARACTER MODELS

Adding character models to your project is a blast. Nothing brings your set to life like a few characters enacting a scene. Human figures are crucial for defining the scale of your project and enhancing dramatic lighting effects.

Finding contemporary characters for modern plays is easy; there are tons of models available. You can search for "3D model character old man in a Hawaiian shirt" or "child with a skateboard" and likely find something that fits or helps refine your search.

Finding historical characters for period plays, however, can be trickier. While certain styles, such as those of Roman soldiers, are easy to find, sourcing a toga-wearing Mark Antony is more challenging.

When you do find historical characters, download them! Even if they're not needed for your current project, they might come in handy in the next. If you discover a site with several historical figures, bookmark it with a detailed name for easy access.

Sometimes, you'll want to combine parts of different character models. Don't try to fit clothes over a body. That way leads to madness! Instead, make a Frankenstein. Swap heads, hands, or other parts as needed. When adding elements like coats or hats, scale them correctly and delete any bits of shirt or hair that stick out. If you want to change pants, move the entire lower body. Skin tone and fabric differences can be fixed later.

- Select the figure to be dissected.
- Go into Edit mode (Key2).
- Select the faces to be deleted and hit "Delete".

or

- Select the parts you want to transfer.
- Mesh menu > Sperate > "Selection". The body part becomes a new object.
- Move it to the other character and group them together.

FIGURE 10.11 Building an Eliza character from two different models.

No single model was found for the character of Eliza Doolittle. A simple Victorian skirt model and another containing a shirtwaist were found at Sketchfab.com. The head, hands, and feet were wrested from a model of an elaborately dressed Victorian woman found at *DeviantArt.com*.

Posing a Character

Characters that you download may already be posed dramatically. If so, all is well and good. Don't try to repose a figure by editing groups of polygons. Life is too short!. You will burn hours of your time. Other characters are available in a neutral T-pose or an A-pose. A character in a T-pose stands upright with arms extended straight out, forming a letter T. Characters in A-pose have their arms outstretched but angled down at 45 degrees, mimicking the letter, you guessed it, A.

The key to posing characters is to have them rigged. A rigged character possesses an internal skeleton or armature that can be moved with the usual rotate and move tools. This saves time, and a correctly rigged skeleton uses inverse kinematics, which is a fancy way of saying that the knee bends in the correct manner when you lift the foot off the ground.

Many characters can be downloaded already rigged. This saves effort, and you can begin posing the character immediately. For other cases, nearly all 3D programs have some built-in rigging tools, but there are other tools that are quicker and easier.

The first is a very popular online rigging system, freely available from Adobe Corporation, called *Mixamo*.

- Save the character model as an FBX file.
- Go to *Miximo.com*, log in to your free Adobe account, and upload the file.
- Follow the prompts.
- Download a new, rigged FBX file in a standard T-pose or the original uploaded pose.
- Or, you can choose from a menu of standing and seated poses. Your choice is instantly applied to the figure.
- Download this already posed figure.

AccuRIG

Some third-party software programs can be used for greater control over the creation of rigging. One program that deserves special mention is the free *AccuRIG* from Real Illusion.

For rigging with AccuRIG:

- Import an FBX version of your character. It will make some assumptions about the size and stature for your approval.

The character is given a basic human skeleton rig, which you can custom-fit to your character. It has a great deal more detail than is found in a *Mixamo* rig.

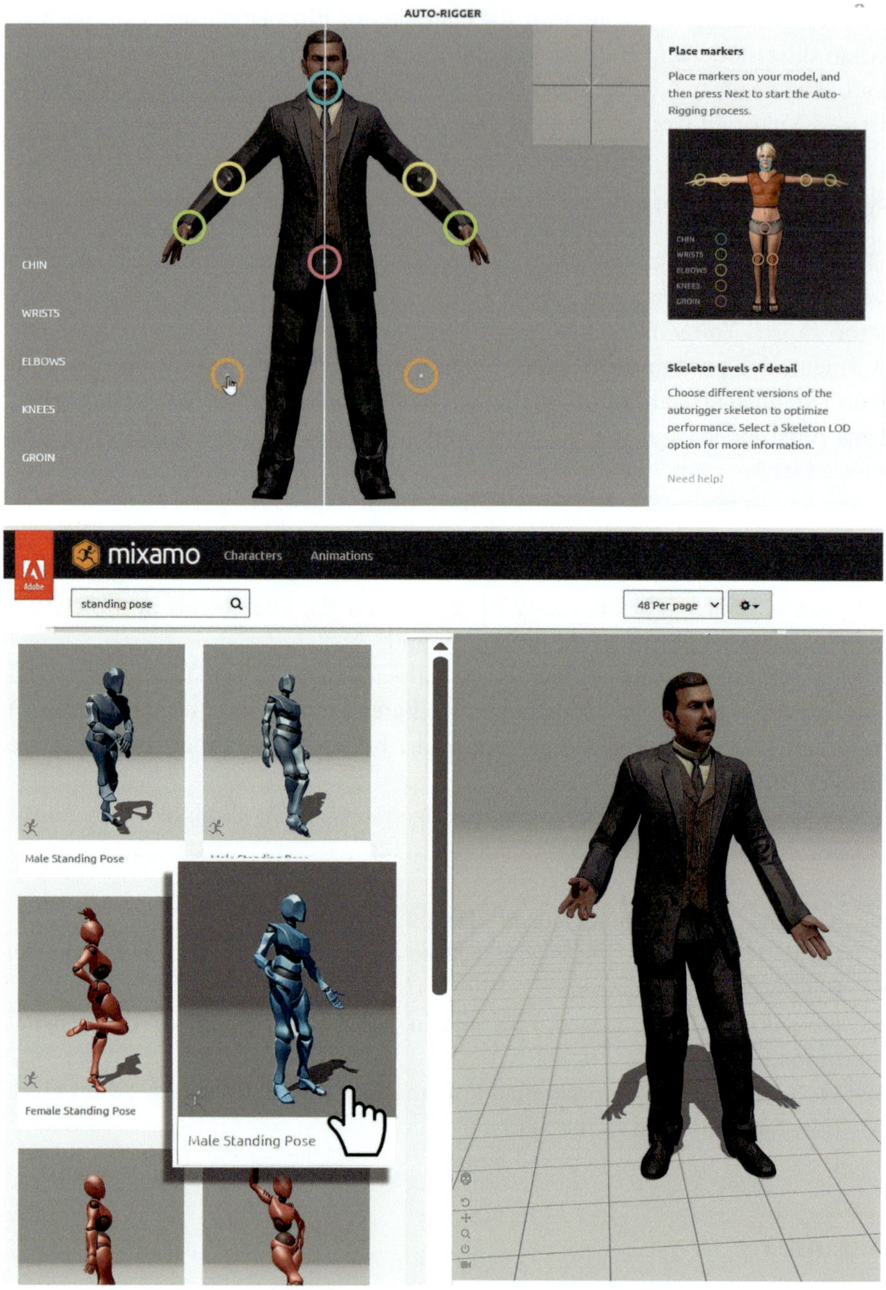

FIGURE 10.12 Professor Higgins is getting rigged in Mixamo.com.

The interface allows you to view the character from all sides, either as a solid or as a wireframe (translucent).

- **Continuously change the view as you place the joints.**
- Select either an A- or T-pose or another from the small menu of preset poses.

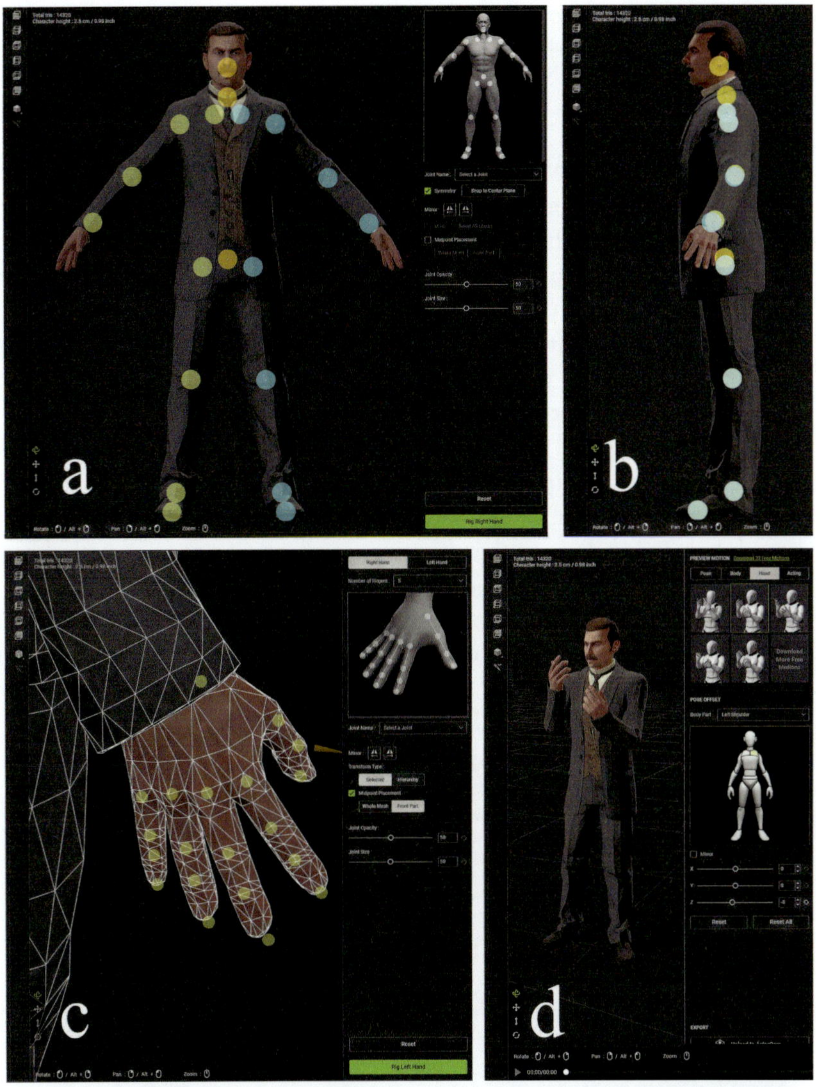

FIGURE 10.13 Rigging a character with *AccuRIG*. a) Placing the major joints. b) The side view is used in conjunction. c) Next, hand and finger joints are placed. d) Simple poses and movements are selected to test the location of the joints.

- Click the Export button to save the fully rigged character.
- Import in your project and pose it with the new rigging.

Optionally, you can upload your rigged character from within *AccuRIG* to your account at the Reallusion ActorCore site and shop from the hundreds of available poses and animations. Some are free, while others cost a few dollars, typically ranging from $3 to $5.

Posing a Rigged Character

The posing process is very straightforward. In *Bforartists*:

- Select the entire figure.
- Open the mode pulldown.
  You will see that, Lo and Behold, there is a new option. It is called Pose mode. Amazing, it's almost as if the program knew you had a poseable figure and would want to put it in a beautiful position. (There are also three new tabs in the Properties panel.)
- Select pose mode. (Shift + 2). In pose mode, you can select only bones without selecting the outer mesh. That operation is very difficult to do in other modes and other 3D programs that don't have this feature.
- Once you have selected a bone, you will notice that the pivot point is already set where a limb's natural joint lies.
- In the Viewport toolbar, change the transformation orientation to local rather than global. This will cause the object's axes of rotation to align with those of a joint's natural rotation and not the arbitrary axes of the 3D model.

Now, the arms and legs will bend as you expect normal human limbs to bend. **Finding some research photos of people standing in approximately the same**

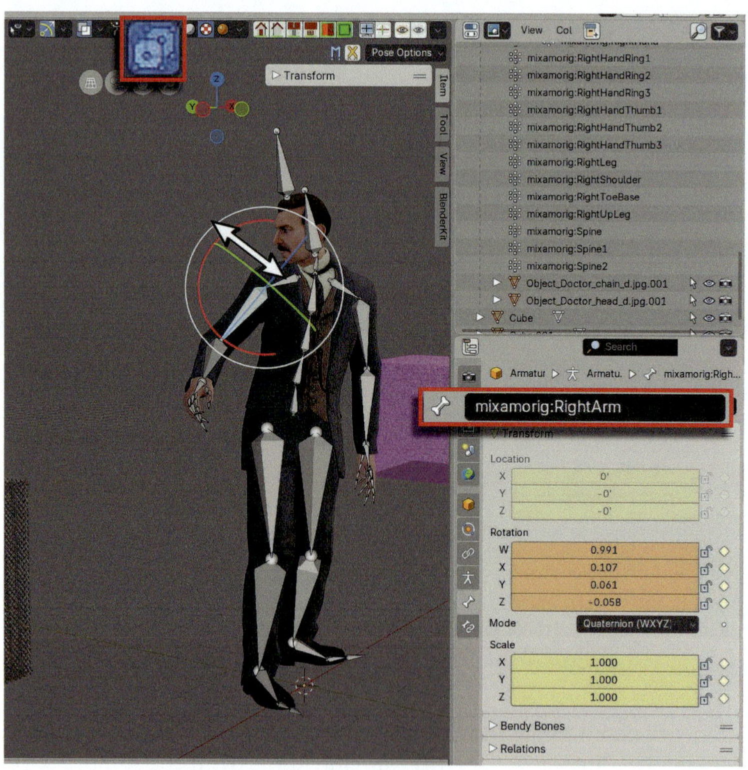

FIGURE 10.14 With the proper settings, each bone can be rotated just like its counterpart in a real person.

attitude you have in mind for your character is a good idea. You don't need to make things up out of whole cloth, but can be inspired and restrained by examples from the real world. **As you pose the character's body parts, rotate the view repeatedly.** Examine the effects of your posing from many different angles. This will help reduce inadvertent body contortions.

Start with the larger parts of the body. This will keep you from having to redo things later. First, adjust the torso, the pelvis, and the lower back. Work your way up the spine to the neck and head and out to the extremities, saving the fingers for last.

Positioning Multiple Bones Simultaneously

When positioning the hands, there are some shortcuts to save time and save your sanity. Typically, default hands appear very stiff, the fingers sticking straight out. To get a more relaxed hand or even a fist,

- Select all the finger joints at once.
- In the viewport toolbar, change the "Transform Pivot Point" to "Individual Origins". (The Transform Orientation is still set to Local.) Individual Origins will cause all the finger joints to move, not as a group, but each on its individual pivot point and axis.
- Select all the finger joints.
- Rotate the control widget, and the hand will open and close, with all fingers working simultaneously, transitioning from a relaxed hand to a fist.

Applying the New Pose

When you have a pose that you were shooting for, you need to make it permanent to prevent unfortunate surprises. (A wrong click or keystroke can make the figure jump back to its original resting state.)

- Save a draft of the figure for safety.
- In Object view, apply all transformations to each object as usual. Object menu > Apply > "All Transformations".
- Each mesh object that is part of the rigged character automatically receives an Armature Modifier in the properties panel, Modifier tab.
- Apply this modifier as you do all modifiers by clicking on the green checkmark icon.
- When you have done that for every part of the figure, it will remain in position.

To completely lock the pose and simplify the model, delete the skeleton.

- Save this draft of the figure.
- Select the armature (only the bones).
- Delete it.

This will result in basic mesh objects, frozen in position and no longer poseable.

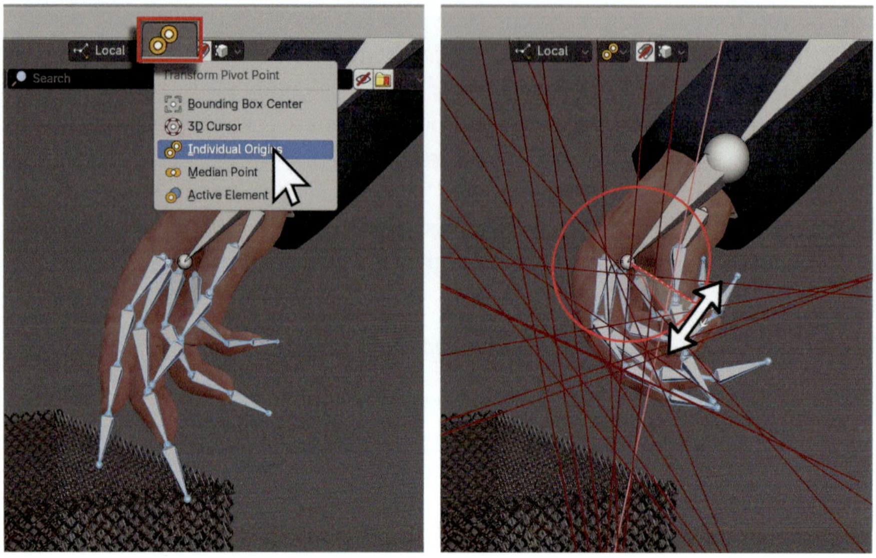

FIGURE 10.15 Multiple bones can be posed simultaneously, each using its individual pivot point or all revolving around a common pivot point.

Character Materials

Just as you modify the scale and shape of an imported character, you may also want to modify the materials that give the character its appearance. You may want to change the color or the texture, or even superimpose new articles of clothing on the basic figure by manipulating the base color and height maps.

Some imported figures have no associated materials. This is particularly true of figures that were designed for 3D printing. In this case, you must decide if it is worth the time required to put materials on the figure or search for another. To add materials to a figure that has none, change to edit mode and select all the faces that would share a material. Then, in the material tab, either select an existing material or create a new one and click the Apply button.

Some figures feature complex composite maps, where a single map encompasses multiple textures. These maps are applied to the character, utilizing complex UV coordinates that ensure the map fits all sections correctly. Professor Higgins has two such maps, one for his body and another for his head.

You can open the map in a decent 2D graphics program and make edits carefully. Use a program that has tools to select areas by color. *Krita*, for example, has two such tools: the Continuous Selection tool and the Select by Color tool. *GIMP* also has a Select by Color tool. Select all the parts of the map that represent the same texture and make changes. Save the edited map in its original format and name. Then, it is a simple matter to refresh the character's materials.

In the composite color map for Eliza's body, the brown skirt sections are selected, and the hue is changed to blue. Her head, hands, and feet were taken from a model with its own maps. The base color texture is edited to give her a fairer skin tone and grey shoes.

FIGURE 10.16 Assigning multiple materials to a single object.

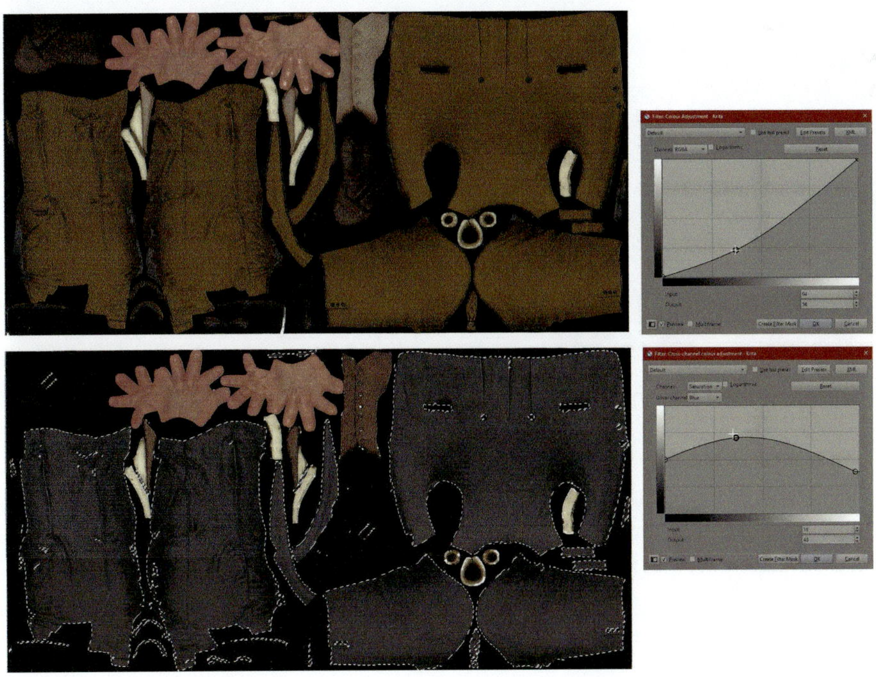

FIGURE 10.17 Select sections of a map that share the same texture, for example, Higgins' suit.

11 Textures, Materials, and Mapping

FIGURE 11.1 Textures and materials create marvelous surfaces when rendered.

One of the key ingredients that gives CGI models the realism, believability, mood, and atmosphere that other forms of sketching can't is the amazing finishes that can be applied to the objects in a scene. These finishes can be photorealistic or totally fantastic. They not only look good by themselves but also give surfaces 3D finishes that make lighting simulations look fantastic.

Even the simplest photo texture can make an object look very good, and that is a good place to start. Later, additional reflective and tactile properties

DOI: 10.4324/9781003571742-11

will be added to make the finishes appear three-dimensional in their own right.

To understand how textures work, it's necessary to start with some definitions. The terminology associated with creating surface finishes on objects in 3D modeling programs is kind of slippery. Terms are used differently by each program. Some terms have different meanings depending on the context in which they're used. Sometimes the terms in a program's manual or available tutorials don't match those seen in the actual program.

So, it is very important that you understand what the role of the materials and textures are, how each element affects the appearance of the object, so that when you encounter them in different programs, no matter what they're called, you'll be able to work effectively.

TEXTURES

The first, most basic term is texture. A texture is simply the more obvious colored pattern that is put on an object. It can be something as simple as a color. It can be a picture or an image file stored on your computer and added to the properties of an object. Very often, it is a texture or surface pattern that is repeated, like wallpaper, as often as needed, to cover the faces of the object.

The most basic example is a single image of texture. Imagine a backdrop for a set. You have a picture of a lovely garden or a gnarly alley, and it is applied to a large plane or the front face of a cube, located upstage in your set. Or it could be a sign for *You're a Good Man, Charlie Brown*. Make a graphic that reads, "PSYCHIATRIC HELP 5¢" and stick it to a plane or cube that is placed over Lucy's booth.

So far, this is very simple. It's a matter of creating or finding a graphic image, saving it with your project, and setting a single parameter to apply it to an object. The *My Fair Lady* set has a painted backdrop and painted wings on stage right and left. The etchings are from Gustav Doré's London and are added to some plane objects.

- Select the backdrop object.
- Properties Panel > Material tag.
- There's no material yet. Click "New".
- Name it.
- Surface > Base Color > Click the small round button.
- Select "Image Texture".
- Click on the Folder icon.
    - The Bforartists' file explorer will open.
- Search for the image and open it.
    - THAT'S IT! If the image needs position or scale adjustments, keep reading.

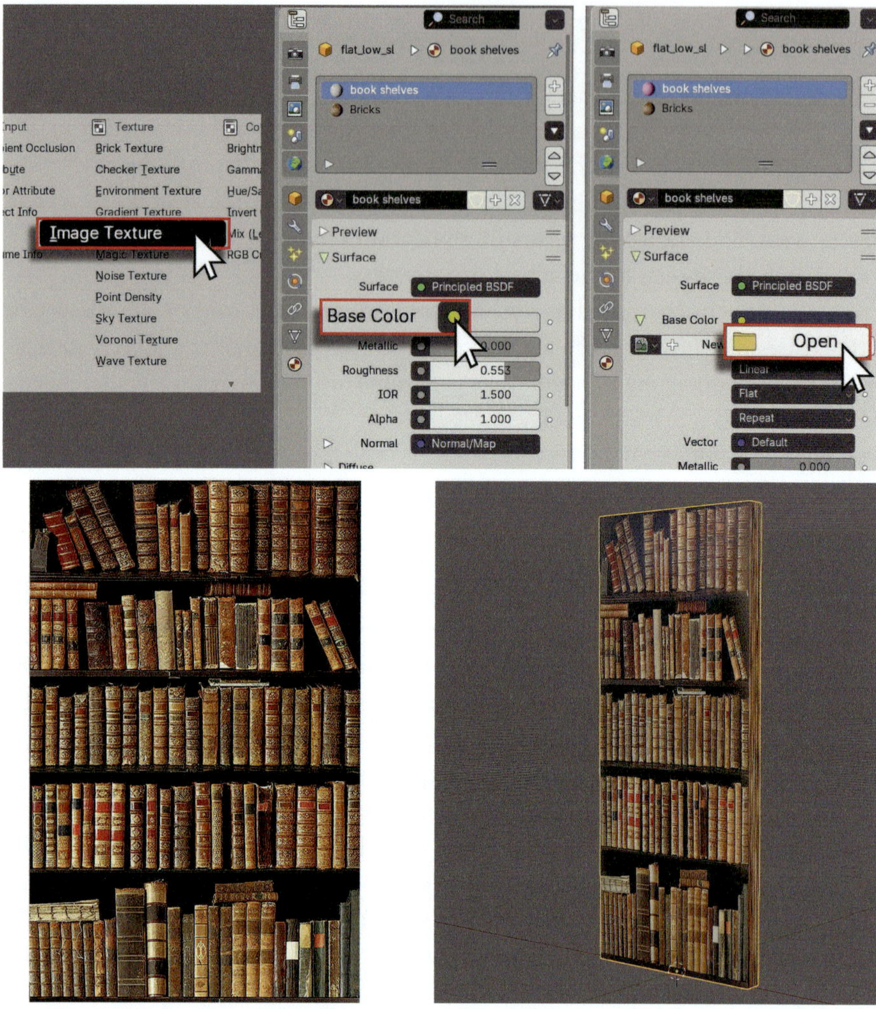

FIGURE 11.2 Applying a single texture in the Material property.

Seamless Textures

The most often used maps are the repeatable textures, those that simulate surfaces such as brick walls, wood floors, or even water. These can be found online almost anywhere. Do a web search for "seamless concrete blocks" or "seamless Roman tiles." Examine the patterns to see if the right edge aligns with the left edge and the top edge aligns with the bottom edge. Of course, the goal is to have a texture that, when placed next to itself in a repeating pattern, has invisible seams, hence the term seamless. With a little bit of experience, at a glance, you'll be able to recognize if a texture is, in fact, seamless. There is an amazing number of downloadable textures online that are labeled seamless, but are not even close.

There are several 2D graphic programs that offer tools for creating seamless textures by painting across the seams and disguising them.

Procedural Textures

Procedural textures are color sets that are made into patterns using various control settings. To create wood grain, start with a medium brown and then add darker brown streaks using control settings to adjust the length, width, spacing, transparency, and other parameters until it begins to resemble wood grain. It has the advantage of not requiring any external files to accompany the original model. Procedural textures are very popular with some people, and most 3D modelers have some procedural texture presets.

FIGURE 11.3 A wood texture made with procedural mapping.

MATERIALS

A collection of textures that define the overall optical properties of an object, such as shininess and reflectivity. Each type of texture map has specific properties that define how light interacts with the surface.

PBR Materials

Physically Based Rendering (PBR) is a method of shading and rendering that provides a more accurate representation of how light interacts with surfaces. It is referred to as Physically Based Rendering (PBR) or Physically Based Shading (PBS).

1. PBR removes the guesswork of authoring surface attributes, such as specularity, since its methodology and algorithms are based on physically accurate formulas. It is therefore easier to create realistic-looking assets.
2. Assets will look accurate in all lighting conditions.
3. PBR provides a workflow for creating consistent artwork, even between different artists.

MAPS

Textures are referred to as maps when they are part of a material. Each texture image defines a specific aspect of a surface, such as color, texture, or shine.

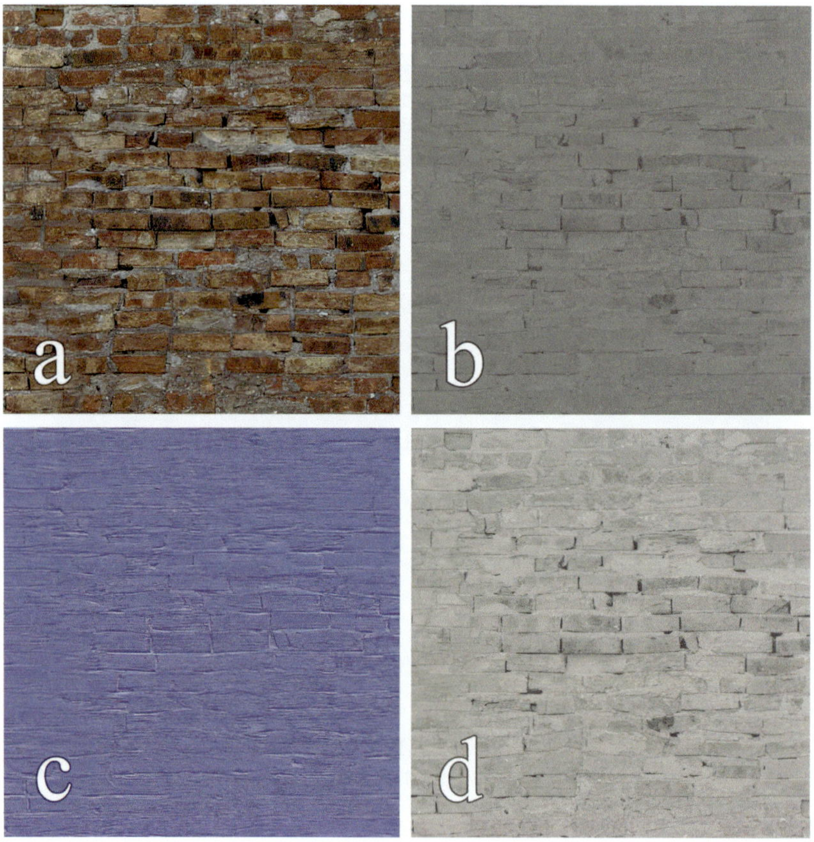

FIGURE 11.4 A set of PBR maps for a brick wall. a) Base color. b) Roughness. c) Normal. d) Displacement.

1. Base color, also referred to as Albedo or Diffuse.

   (Base) Color texture maps are one of the most basic maps used in your model since they define its basic color with no shadows or glare. A color map functions much like a painter's elevation that is given to the paint shop as a guide for the scenic artists. They can be a photograph, a pattern of your invention, or a simple color.
2. Normal.

   Normal maps are distinctive due to their overall purple pastel color.

   In normal maps, RGB values (green, red, and blue) are used to create bumps and cracks in your model to add more depth to the polygon mesh. The R, G, and B dictate the X, Y, and Z axes of the base mesh in three directions to ensure better accuracy. Normal maps don't actually change the base geometry of an object. They simply use complex calculations to fake the dents or bumps with the light effects. The really cool part is that because they use 3D coordinates, the cracks and bumps change depending on the angle of the viewer, just like real cracks and bumps.

   They have a great effect on the final appearance of the material. Sometimes, a character model will have a single color map for the face but will include two normal maps: one for a smooth-faced youth and another for an aged, craggy old codger.
3. Reflectance.

   Reflectance can be a simple setting that determines how shiny an object will appear, but it can also be a more complex arrangement of several sub-maps. Each sub-map defines one of the properties that make up reflectance. Some third-party rendering software categorizes all PBR maps under the reflectance category. That makes some sense, as everything we can see is a result of light reflecting from them.

   The Reflectance Sub-maps.
4. Roughness or Glossiness.

   A roughness or glossiness texture map is a self-explanatory map, so I will explain it. It defines how smooth your model is, depending on how light reflects off it. This map is vital since different objects have different levels of roughness. These maps are typically in grayscale. In Roughness maps, the lighter the color, the rougher the surface. For gloss maps, the lighter, the smoother. If the base color is an old Victorian street lamp, the iron parts would be a lighter gray in the roughness map than the smooth glass parts, colored a very dark gray. A gloss map would be the exact opposite.
5. Specular.

   Specular maps can be grayscale or color. They are assigned to tags labeled Specular Strength and/or Specular Color. Different programs use varying names, but their use is typically easy to determine. This texture map is responsible for the color and amount of light reflected by the object. It is important if you want to create shadows and reflections on non-metallic materials.

6. Metalness.

   Another grayscale map. Black denotes non-metallic, white fully metallic. This one's fairly easy to guess. This texture map defines whether an object is made of metal. Metal reflects light differently from other materials, so it can make a difference to the final look of your object. This map is often left out of workflows for stage designers.

7. Reflection map.

   The most apparent use of reflection maps is to provide the image that is seen on the surface of a highly reflective object. If you put a glass bottle on your set, the reflection map can be used to create the illusion that the missing fourth wall is being reflected in the glass. For an object as reflective as a mirror, it can be used to create a false reflection. Optionally, the scene can be rendered with the mirror showing a true reflection of anything in the model that would be seen from the angle of the camera.

8. Height or Displacement.

   Displacement maps are alien technology. They are so amazing that they defy description, so let me describe them. These grayscale maps instruct the renderer on which parts of the texture should protrude from the surface of the object and which should recede. Lighter shades in the map protrude, and darker shades recede. Not a mere illusion, the renderer will use the information to subdivide the mesh and temporarily **remodel to surface** with exaggerated dimensionality, BUT ONLY WHEN THEY ARE IN SIGHT OF THE CAMERA! How great is that!

   These maps are used to create killer 3D textures, such as cobblestones and roof tiles, but they can also significantly reduce modeling when used to create complete objects, like paneled doors, timber-framed walls, or even entire building facades.

   Because height maps actually modify the geometry of your model, they require the computer to work harder and slow down the rendering process. Height/displacement maps are not used in VR or gaming applications, which need to render scenes 30–60 frames per second.

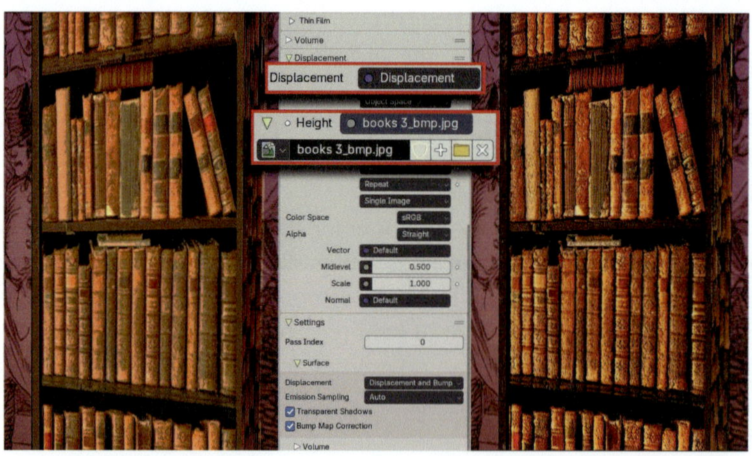

FIGURE 11.5 Fundamental Displacement settings. The books now appear to catch the light on any raised edges.

9. Opacity or Alpha map.

This map is also a lot of fun. This map makes certain parts of your model transparent/translucent. Images that have built-in alphas, such as transparent PNGs, are the easiest to use as alpha maps. Grayscale textures can also be used with a bit more effort. Black is completely transparent, white is totally opaque, and shades of gray are levels of translucency. Adding an alpha map to a material can create realistic metal grates, wooden lattices, and wicker baskets. When rendered, not only can you see through the openings of such a grate, but light shines through, making a fantastic gobo effect.

Alpha maps can make quick and easy versions of objects, such as an iron railing or picket fence. Find a picture of an iron railing and use it as a base color. Then, using an image editor such as *Krita* or *Photoshop*, create a transparent version where the iron bits are opaque and the negative spaces are transparent. This version will have an underlying alpha map and must be saved as a PNG file. When the two textures are combined in a material and applied to an object, it will become transparent/translucent in the appropriate areas. That's it.

Chapter 2 provides in-depth details on creating transparent images using Krita. Similar procedures will do the job in other image editors.

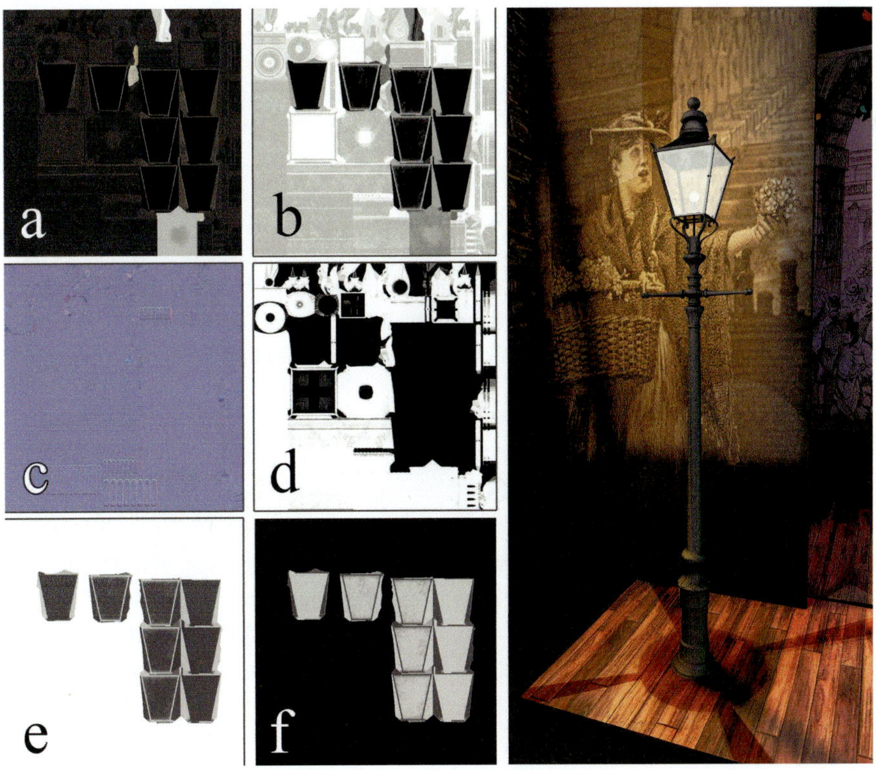

FIGURE 11.6 A combination of many textures creates a material that is very responsive to light. a) Base color. b) Roughness. c) Normal map. d) Metallic. e) Opacity/Alpha. f) Luminance.

10. Emission, Luminance, Glow.

    This map will cause a material to appear to emit light. It can be a simple color or a complete image. There are usually two options. Luminance or emission means the material will act like a light source and illuminate nearby objects. Glow means that, when rendered, the material will appear to be lit from the inside but may not have an effect on other objects.

    Emission and glow can be used to create cool lamp effects or neon signs. A fantastic projection screen effect can be achieved by creating a material with luminance and glow maps and applying it to a plane that represents the screen.

    *HINT. If you put a flame inside a lamp, making its glow will look great, but its luminance may not pass through the glass panes or chimney of the lamp. It won't pass through a lampshade either. But you can add luminance to the glass or the lampshade and get nearly the same effect.
11. Ambient Occlusion, or AO.

    This is a rather fussy map and doesn't produce much of an effect. This is a grayscale map that provides guidance on how ambient light should be distributed in the unlit areas of the scene. The software's render engines can calculate ambient light without the help of the map. Additionally, you may not want to use AO while rendering, as it slows things down and offers little benefit.
12. Bump map.

    Bump maps are similar to displacement maps, but they have a much less dramatic effect. They are not used in PBR rendering. They are used in VR and game programs.

Additional Maps

- Transparency, Transmission, Refraction.

The manner in which light passes through transparent objects correspondingly affects whether an object looks real enough. It is especially important for certain surfaces, such as glass and water, since they affect the speed of light that travels through them.

USING PBR MATERIALS

Building new materials is a relatively straightforward process. All 3D modelers have the same maps and work in a similar manner. Bforartists lacks the drag-and-drop features present in *Cinema 4D* and *3ds Max*. But despite that, it is pretty hard to go wrong. A good way to get a jump on the process is to download complete materials from BlenderKit. Of course, it is usually easier to edit than to build from scratch. If you start with a finished material, you may simply need to change the specific texture files to get what you are after. Alternatively, a downloaded material with multiple maps can act as an instructional tool or roadmap for the material you want, indicating which texture is needed and where to put it. Some of the materials at BlenderKit are quite sophisticated, so it wouldn't hurt to take a look to see the difference between basic materials and those with many components.

To make a New Material

Download a PBR texture pack and unzip it to a convenient location in your project files.

- Download a PBR texture pack and unzip it to a convenient location in your project files.
- Select an object.
- Properties panel > Material tag.
- Click on "New Material".
- A new material pops up in the material library. This is where all materials used in the scene will end up.
- Enter a name for your new material.
- You can change this at any time by double-clicking on the name of the material.

Just below the name of the material is the Preview dropdown. If you open this, you can see a quick rendering of your texture as it progresses.

The "Surface" dropdown holds the majority of properties and textures that will be used in the material. The first dropdown is the Surface type. For basic materials, leave it as "Principled BSDF".

- Select a Base Color using the swatch if that's all you need.

To add a base color texture map:

- Click on the yellow dot next to the label "Base Color" to open the input menu.
- Select "Image Texture".
- Click "Open" in the file selector that appears.
    - The file explorer window will pop up. Find your downloaded textures.
- Open the "base color" texture (diffuse).

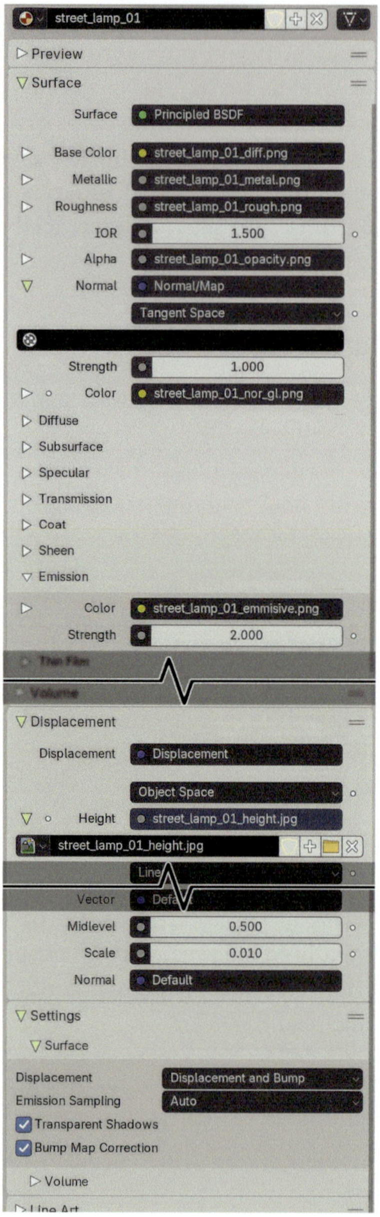

FIGURE 11.7 The main surface properties of the Material tab.

This straightforward procedure for adding image textures is the primary method for filling most of the slots in the material editor. There are two or three texture slots that require an extra step, but otherwise, they operate nearly the same way.

Metallic

Going down the list of texture fields that can be entered, the next is "Metallic". This is a specialized texture that confines metallic shine to specific parts of the material, such as a belt buckle, a doorknob, or a sheriff's badge.

Roughness

Next is "Roughness". The slider is used to set a general roughness quality for the entire material, ranging from 0 to 1, with 1 being the roughest. For a more specific application, use the appropriate map.

- Click on the small gray button next to "Roughness" and load the rough texture map just as you did the Base Color.

Normal

The next property of interest is "Normal". This requires one extra step.

- Click on the lavender dot next to the label "Normal" to open the input menu.
- Select "Normal Map".
  - The usual input options will appear.
- Click on the yellow dot next to the "Color" to open the input menu.
- Continue as you did with the Base Color to open the normal map in the downloaded materials.

Alpha

The default slider is used to add overall transparency to materials without the need for maps.

Alpha maps aren't used often, but the transparency effects are incredibly useful. (and cool) This map may also require one extra step.

For a transparent PNG alpha image, only one step is required:

- Click on the small gray button next to "Alpha" and load the alpha texture map just as you did the base color.

For a grayscale alpha image:

- Click on the gray dot next to the "Alpha" to open the input menu.
- Select "RGB to BW" under the Convert category.
  - The usual input options will appear.
- Click on the yellow dot next to the "Color" to open the input menu.

- Continue as with the Base Color to open the grayscale alpha map in the downloaded materials.
    - The extra step tells the program not to use the image's alpha layer (it doesn't have one) but to convert whatever is in the main color layer to black and white and use that.

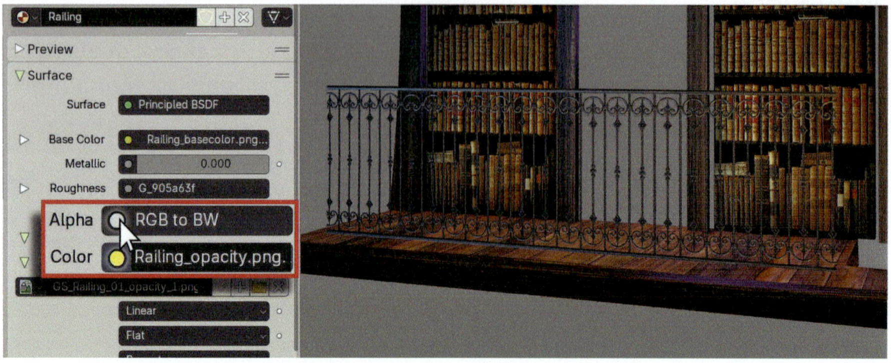

FIGURE 11.8 Alpha mat settings.

Displacement (Height)

Remember, Displacement maps will only work when the Render settings are set to use the Cycles render engine, not EEVE.

The Displacement is in a separate dropdown, a bit lower in the Materials tab. It requires an extra step and a change in the material's settings.

- Settings dropdown > Displacement.
- Select "Displacement and Bump".
- Displacement drop-down > Displacement.
- Select "Displacement" under the "Vector" category.
- Click on the gray dot next to the "Height" to open the input menu.
- Continue as with the Base Color to open the displacement map in the downloaded materials.

MAPPING, OR UV MAPPING

Mapping is the process of applying a material or texture map to the different surfaces of a 3D object. The scheme that is used in applying a material to make a sphere look the best doesn't work when applied to a cylinder, and not at all with a cube.

Complex shapes with very specific maps have complex mapping schemes that assign the material to each of the object's faces individually. An imported character model is a good example of this. This type of mapping is time-consuming and generally doesn't fit a designer's workflow. It's better to stick to basic mapping and leave the mapping of imported models undisturbed. Imported objects can be transformed in most ways without ruining the appearance of their materials. Polygons added to the object won't be part of the mapping and so will not be textured. Often, this can be fixed by simply assigning a color that matches the surrounding material.

All modeling programs perform the same mapping operations, but they all seem to use a different interface. *Bforartists* defaults to a rather complex system designed for precise control. Luckily, there are easier and faster ways to do the job with completely acceptable results.

When applying a wallpaper pattern to the wall of your set, you usually start by placing a single instance of the pattern, which would look very weird. However, to make it truly resemble real wallpaper, you're going to need to repeat that pattern, maybe 10 times horizontally and 15 times vertically. This ensures that the design covers the entire wall area in a reasonable scale. Similarly, if you're using a pattern that mimics wooden planks for your floor, those planks may need to be angled at 45 degrees or 90 degrees, depending on the floor's layout. Achieving this level of detail is not a one-size-fits-all process; you will have to customize the mapping scheme for each object you're working with.

In some applications, mapping is a property that can belong to the object itself, whereas in others, such as Bforartists, it is treated as a property assigned to the material. This distinction can play a crucial role in the workflow. When you apply a mapped material to a second object, the mapping attributes will mirror those of the first object, meaning the wallpaper pattern will repeat the same number of times on the second surface. More often than not, this will not yield the desired results, especially if each object has a different scale or layout. In such cases, you need to repeat the process. Duplicate the material, assign it a new, distinct name, and establish a fresh mapping scheme for it.

Basic Projections

All modeling programs provide a fundamental set of mapping formats as a starting point: cubic, spherical, cylindrical, and flat mappings. When you first assign a material to an object in Bforartists, it makes an educated guess as to which mapping scheme is appropriate based on the object's characteristics. For predominantly angular objects, a cubic mapping is often the default. If the object is more organic and features curves, it may decide to implement spherical mapping, and if the object can be classified as vaguely cylindrical, you will get that style of mapping.

However, it's crucial to remember that Bforartists often guesses wrong, particularly when it comes to complex forms. Therefore, you will frequently need to adjust that foundational mapping scheme to better suit your model. The quickest approach to do this is by switching to edit mode.

- Open edit mode (shortcut "2").
- Viewport menu > UV.
- Select Cubic, Cylinder, or Sphere Projection.

Or,

- Toolshelf > UV tab.
- Select a Projection.

Cylinder and sphere projections will be applied to the object relative to the view in the viewport. The central axis of the mapping will be perpendicular to your angle of view. For example, a spherical projection will place the material so that you are looking directly at the equator, and the poles will be at the top and bottom from your viewpoint. In most cases, this is not the desired mapping. To align the mapping with the global coordinates, switch the viewport to one of the orthographic views: front, back, right, or left. In some cases, top or bottom views will give the desired result.

While basic foundational mapping schemes can effectively cover singular instances of textures, such as signage or decals (think of an iron fence), they generally fall short when you require special texture effects or intricate proportion adjustments.

Mapping Controls

In cases where you need your mapping to be repeated, adjusted in proportion, or set at an angle, you will have to open and use some fine-tuning controls. This will allow for greater flexibility and precision, ensuring that the materials and objects meet the scale and aspect of the set.

- Select the object.
- Material tag > Surface > Vector.
- Click the small circle to open the vector menu.
- Select "Mapping".
    - A new set of property fields will open, including a new "Vector" button.
- (New) Vector > Vector menu > Select "Texture Coordinate | Generated".
    - The material will now have a full set of X, Y, Z controls for Location, Rotation, and Scale.
    - The Scale value not only controls the size of the material, but as a consequence, it also sets the number of times the pattern is repeated across the faces of the object.

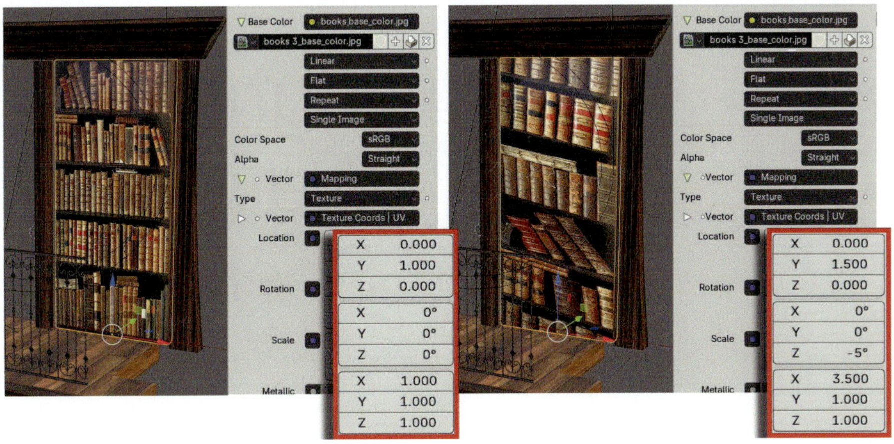

FIGURE 11.9 Vector settings in the Material tab and the material coordinate controls.

12 Lighting the Scene

FIGURE 12.1 Careful, dramatic lighting makes the textures and materials come alive.

Lighting your project is the last step in bringing it all together. Just like in real theater practice, lighting is where the magic happens. When you see a set on stage under work lights, it looks like exactly what it is: a collection of muslin, wood, styrofoam, and scene paint. When viewed on the rack down in the costume shop, costumes look pretty lifeless. Not at all what we had imagined

DOI: 10.4324/9781003571742-12

when designing them. But under stage light, when they are all bathed in unifying colors, quality, and direction, everything comes to life. Even in 1665, Samuel Pepys wrote about the startling differences in his famous diary.

> but my business here was to see the inside of the stage and all the tiring-rooms and machines; and, indeed, it was a sight worthy seeing. But to see their clothes, and the various sorts, and what a mixture of things there was; here a wooden-leg, there a ruff, here a hobbyhorse, there a crown, would make a man split himself to see with laughing; and particularly Lacy's wardrobe, and Shotrell's. But then again, to think how fine they show on the stage by candle-light, and how poor things they are to look now too near hand, is not pleasant at all.
>
> (Pepys, 19 Mar. 1666)

Lighting in the computer model is equally fantastic, and the techniques for setting up lighting in a simulation are very straightforward. At its heart, lighting on the computer works much the same way as it does on the stage. With the proper constraints, virtual lighting will follow the rules and practices of common stagecraft very closely. There are only so many ways to put light on objects. Like real lighting instruments, they can be colored, dimmed, and moved about. They cast shadows. Lights of different colors and from various directions blend with the same results we expect in real life.

On the other hand, virtual lights can break all the rules and do things that their real-life counterparts only wish they could. They don't have to obey the laws of physics, so they can produce remarkable effects. These lighting instruments have unlimited brightness. You can not only turn the dial up to 11, but you can turn it up to 11,000. And, they can go on forever without becoming any dimmer. They are not subject to the inverse square law, which states that light will dim and finally die out over a given distance.

One lighting instrument, a single source, can take the place of an entire color system. It may take two dozen instruments to achieve a blue sidelight wash on stage. But in a computer simulation, one light source can do the whole thing. We can not only bring the sun inside the theater to light a scene, but we can also bring in two or three suns. (Simulating the light on the planet Tatooine?)

Light can go through objects. Suppose a front wash comes into the playing area at 45 degrees, and the proscenium blocks the light to half the stage. You can ignore it. Set the lights to go straight through the proscenium without casting a shadow. In effect, you are directing the lights to go around corners. Neat trick. The lights can be configured to illuminate only one object and nothing else around or behind it. That would be the coolest follow-spot effect of all time. Light the singer as she walks back and forth across the stage with zero overspill. Light nothing and nobody else!

FIGURE 12.2 a) Virtual light at 5000 watts, b) going through walls, c) lighting one object alone.

The trick to drawing the line between the realistic and the fantastic is to identify the final goal before you start and understand the intent of the exercise. In some cases, it's good to stick to the physical laws that we know, and other times, it's so much better to ignore them.

LIGHTING VISUALIZATION

Goal number one: make the rendering of the set look stunning. Remove the modeling project from under the work light, put it on stage, and give it a sexy light cue. When the goal is to sprinkle some magic onto the set, lighting that adheres to physical laws needn't apply. You can do whatever you want to achieve the desired effect. Consider the artist Rembrandt, heralded as the master of light and shadow. As beautiful as they are, the lighting in many of his paintings often makes no sense at all.

In one of his most famous paintings, *The Night Watch*, different characters are picked out by seemingly magical light sources shining from whatever angle he thought best showed them off. One character may be brightly lit from the right; the following four characters in the painting are barely lit, and the next one is lit from below. If it's good enough for Rembrandt, it's good enough for us. In his painting *The Conspiracy of the Batavians under Claudius Civilis*, the light seems to be coming from the tablecloth, catching everyone at the table under the chin. It makes the scene look exotic and mystical.

The second goal is to pre-visualize a lighting design, spurring inspiration before getting bogged down in details. The idea is to create a series of lighting storyboards, a series of preliminary sketches for each significant lighting moment in the show.

This calls for a little more adherence to properties of actual lighting, but since the goal is to create general impressions that will inform the creation of the light plot,

FIGURE 12.3 Virtual light at 5000 watts. a) The light going through a wall. b) Lighting the figure with a miraculous lack of overspill.

you don't have to worry too much about accuracy. Since it is always good not to design a show before you design it, shoot for overall impressions rather than getting hung up on specific details. In the pre-visualization stage, it's enough to know that the light is coming from high right, for example. Later, you can decide precisely which instruments to use and from where. Having a little leeway with how objects are being lit is forgivable. Precise beam angles and gel colors are all left for later.

The wonderful thing about doing lighting storyboards on the computer is that you can clearly depict highlights and shading on objects and plainly depict the shadows cast on the floor. When you look at a sketch and can see the attitude of the highlight and the direction of the cast shadows, it becomes clear where the intended instruments should be positioned in the theatre. Often, lighting storyboards are done in grayscale; other times, in color. It is good practice to start with the former and move to the latter. In color storyboards, if you are using materials in your computer model that approximate the materials and paint treatments of the finished scenery, you can get an excellent idea of how different colors of light will act on those textures and colors.

FIGURE 12.4 A complete lighting storyboard will guide all the steps in the design process that follow.

The final goal for lighting a computer model is visualization. Visualization is done very late in the process, after the plot and other paperwork have been finished, perhaps even as cues are being written. In the visualization workflow, you are more likely to give all the light sources realistic parameters and not let them perform the wild magic of the previous workflows.

Visualization may take the form of moving the light plot data into the 3D modeler to ensure all instrumentation is exactly positioned, focused, and gelled. Will that light go through the door and hit the rocking chair on the other side? Can you light the backdrop from the fourth electric? There are software tools that are designed for this purpose alone. The drafting package of choice is *Vectorworks*. *Vectorworks* has a built-in renderer provided by the makers of the 3D modeling program *Cinema 4D*. *Vectorworks* also has an export function to export the information of a light plot in *Cinema 4D* format. *Vectorworks* offers a separate visualization program called Vision, which is an all-in-one application. *WIZZYWIG* is a combination of a visualizer, a drafting program, and a paperwork generator. It lacks the ability to create 3D models. Those must be imported before there is anything for the visualizer to light. Similarly, *Capture* is a visualization program from Sweden that has similar capabilities.

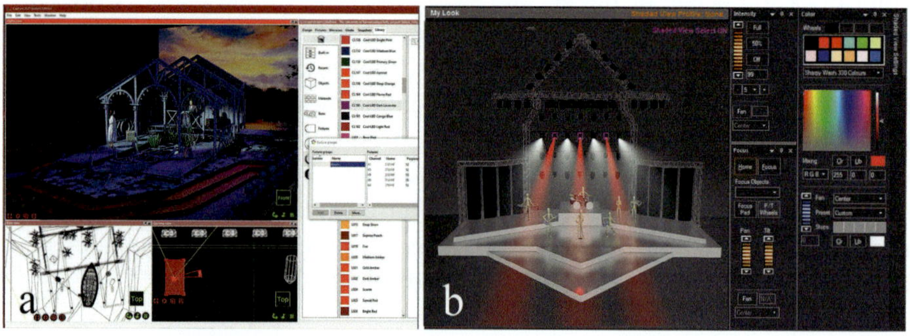

FIGURE 12.5 Two visualizer interfaces. a) *Capture*. b) *WIZZYWIG*.

Many modern light boards have visualization software included in their operating system. The ETC corporation makes some of the most advanced boards available today. Their built-in system is called *Augment 3D*. With *Augment 3D*, the user inputs a 3D model of the scenery and light design data from a program such as *Vectorworks*. After they're combined, one can see the show on a monitor and write cues before the lights are finished being hung. The virtual ETC light boards run on personal computers, allowing users to simulate a lightboard and the *Augment 3D* environment. On a home computer, drafts of the show's cues can be written before ever stepping into the theater.

LIGHT SOURCES (THE INSTRUMENTS)

All 3D modeling programs have a basic set of light sources. Some programs have a few interesting variations, but they are all based on the four essential types.

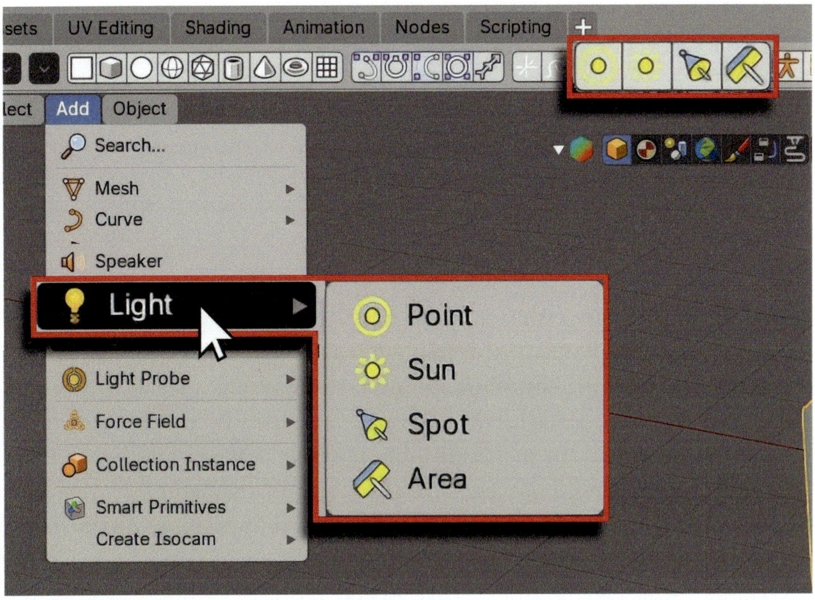

FIGURE 12.6 The light source palette in *Bforartists.*

Point Sources

The first is the point light or just light. The point source is precisely what it sounds like: a point in space from which light emanates in all directions. Think of it as a candle flame or a bare bulb. Like all light sources, the point source has no physical object, no lighting instrument that will appear in the final rendering. It is just an invisible point in space. Point sources can supply the light from a practical instrument such as a desk lamp or a candle. They can also be used as a quick fix for dark spots in your rendering. They can be tucked in just about anywhere to add a little light to an otherwise dark area. Think of Rembrandt and the painting *Night Watch*. The mysterious light sources on the faces he wanted to highlight are instructive in using point light sources.

Spotlights

The next light source is the spotlight. This is the closest source to the ellipsoidal reflector spotlight. That is the workhorse in all theater productions, just like the spotlights we are all familiar with. The width of its beam can be set to various degrees. If desired, it can be set to have the realistic characteristics of field and beam, making the outer parts of the beam darker than the bright center. It can be manipulated to have a soft edge, just as you would slide the barrel of a lip soil reflector spotlight. You can soften the focus of a virtual spotlight. It does not have the shutter handles we are accustomed to, so the beam cannot be easily trimmed, but it does have the uncanny ability to ignore objects that should not be lit.

It also does not have a physical manifestation, so it can be placed anywhere as needed. You can place a spotlight in the center of the scene, only feet from the actor's head.

Area Lights

The next light source is a rather unusual one. Referred to as an area light or an area source, it is a flat plane or disk that emanates light. You can make one as a rectangle, the width of the entire proscenium, to represent a wash from an overhead electric batten, or place a tall, narrow one vertically in the wings to serve as the light from a boom. In such a fashion, it does the work of a lighting boom that in a real theatre would use six, seven, or eight instruments.

The degree of the spread can be manipulated so that it shines either in a narrow beam, equal to its width, or spread wide to cover a large area. An entire color system, "Stage Right Blue," that would require 15 instruments, can be replaced by a single area light stretching across a lighting beam or port. You can also place the aerial light in the middle of the set, just above the actors, or on the floor to give some extra fill or create a special effect. In some programs, area lights can shine in both forward and backward directions. Think of Rembrandt's magic illuminating tablecloth. That great effect can be achieved by placing a rectangular area light just above the table.

Directional or Infinite Light

A final source is the directional light. In *Bforartists*, it is referred to as the sun, but it is simply a light source that shines over the entire scene from a specified angle. Once placed into the scene, it can be moved anywhere. Moving it to the side to get it out of the way does not affect the light at all. What matters is the angle of the beam. Using the rotate tool, you can turn the source in any direction, and the light over the entire scene will reflect the change.

This light shines in parallel beams, much like sunlight. Unlike sunlight, it does not have any diffuse light properties. So, using it as a sun source has the appearance of the sunlight you see on astronauts and spaceships in orbit: very bright light on one side and near-total darkness on the other. The sunlight that we all enjoy is a combination of sunlight and skylight. It is the sky, the diffuse sunlight that bounces through the atmosphere, that fills in the visual world from all angles.

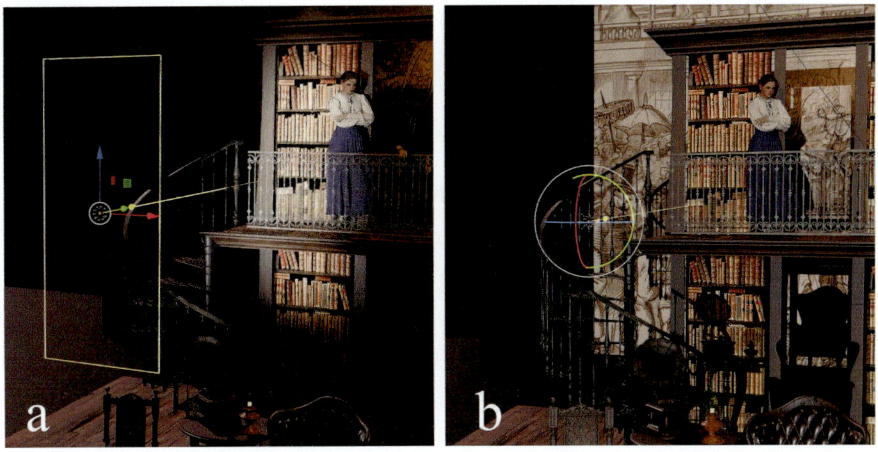

FIGURE 12.7 a) An Area light with 20° spread. b) A Directional light with .1° spread

LIGHTING A SCENE

To see the lights in your scene correctly, you must **change the Viewport Shading to Render Preview mode.**

Without this, the effect of the lighting will not appear in the viewport, and many light settings will not be visible in the properties panel. You can use one of two different rendering engines. The standard renderer in *Bforartists* is EVEE. EVEE works well enough for standard lighting. It renders the brightness, color, and direction for all the lighting instruments or sources that are placed in your scene. For more advanced visualization with effects such as patterns and projections, switch the rendering engine from EVEE to Cycles. Cycles is a physically based renderer and will not only display the physically based materials in their full glory, but will render the most intricate lighting effects. Physically based rendering puts a greater workload on the computer, and you may find that navigating in the viewport slows down. If this is the case, stay with the EVEE rendering engine until it is necessary to visualize an advanced lighting effect. At that point, you can switch to Cycles temporarily and back to EVEE.

If your computer is equipped with a GPU (Graphics Processing Unit), change the render setting from CPU to GPU. GPU chips are designed for physically based rendering when running advanced computer games with very elaborate visual effects. If your computer does not have a GPU, you may consider buying a GPU video card to speed up your viewport and final renders. If you are going to be rendering animations with hundreds or thousands of frames, a GPU-accelerated video card is almost mandatory.

The good news is that the price of video cards is coming down all the time. And, buying a unit that is a year or two old or not the latest generation is usually very affordable. As mentioned earlier, this type of upgrade can be purchased with an open box discount or as a used item (excuse me, "Pre-owned") on any of the web's many resale sites. Computer chips don't run badly because they are old or have some hours of use on them. They either work or they don't

Adding Lights

Adding lights is done with the same process and just as easily as adding primitive objects to a scene.

- Topbar > Light object icons.
- Select a light.
    - A light object will appear in the scene and the Organizer.
    - The row of light source icons in the topbar is found to the right of the primitive shapes icons. If you don't see it, it may be hidden. Click on the menu editing arrow next to the primitive shapes and check the Light box.

Or,

- Viewport menu > Add > "Lights".
- Select from the same options.

In the properties panel, a new icon has appeared. The Light Properties panel has an appropriate light bulb icon. Clicking on it will show you a new set of properties that are mostly the same for all light sources.

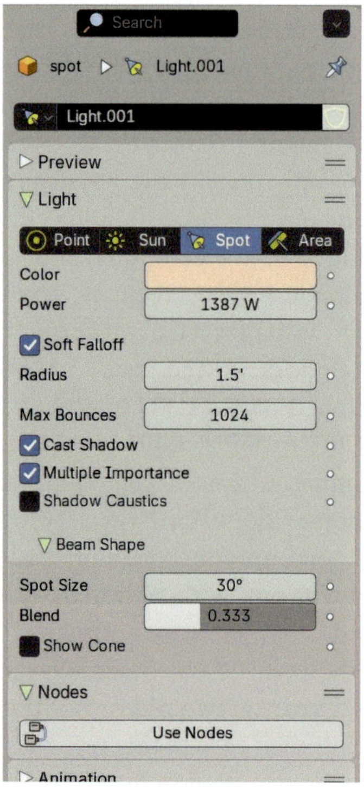

FIGURE 12.8 The Light Properties panel.

Color

The first is color. A new light source has no color, so the color swatch is white. Clicking on it brings up a typical color picker wheel, which you can use to pick virtually any color that you would need. When you are setting up lights to enhance a set rendering, you don't need to worry about any realistic color application. Just pick the color that you want. When you are using lighting in a pre-visualization stage, making lighting storyboards to guide you for the rest of the light design process, it is usually a good idea to pick the color that you want first and only later worry about how that will translate into gel colors. Make your artistic choices first and figure out a way to realize them afterward. There were so many gels from all of the various manufacturers that you would be hard-pressed to pick a color that can't be found in their inventories.

If you do wish to visualize a particular gel color, either in the pre-visualization stage or the later visualization stage, use the RGB input beneath the color wheel. There are editable fields for the red, green, and blue values of a color. Optionally, you can use the hexadecimal or hex code. Open that tab, and you'll be able to enter the six-digit alphanumeric code for available colors. Hexadecimal code was invented as a shortcut to use in designing web pages, but it can be employed by anybody who has an interest in using digital color designations.

3D modeling programs do not, in general, have any means of inputting gel numbers, but gel manufacturers do have an interest in having their colors used by software developers and users. Drafting programs like *Vectorworks*, *WIZZYWIG*, and *Capture* all need a means of displaying appropriate gel colors within their programs. With a bit of detective work, the RGB values for all color filters can be found, and from the RGB values, hexadecimal codes can be determined. An index to this book lists the RGB values and hex codes for a great many of the color filters that are available from the major manufacturers. Enter the red, green, and blue values or the hexadecimal code in the appropriate fields, and the color will closely approximate the gel.

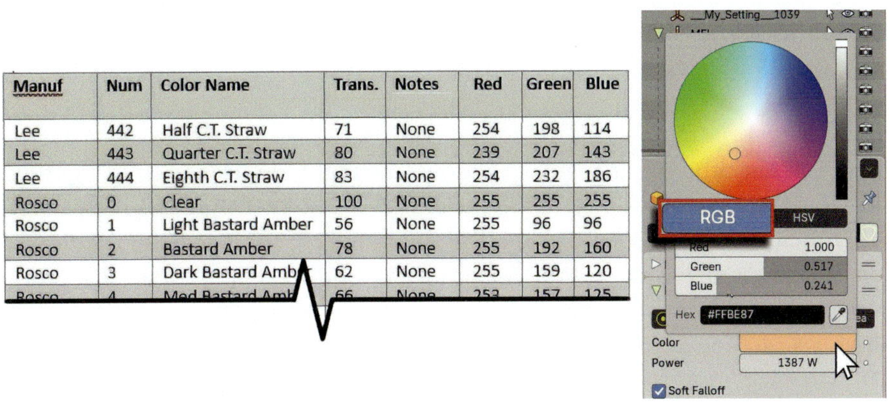

Manuf	Num	Color Name	Trans.	Notes	Red	Green	Blue
Lee	442	Half C.T. Straw	71	None	254	198	114
Lee	443	Quarter C.T. Straw	80	None	239	207	143
Lee	444	Eighth C.T. Straw	83	None	254	232	186
Rosco	0	Clear	100	None	255	255	255
Rosco	1	Light Bastard Amber	56	None	255	96	96
Rosco	2	Bastard Amber	78	None	255	192	160
Rosco	3	Dark Bastard Amb	62	None	255	159	120

FIGURE 12.9 Assign Gel colors to digital lights.

Intensity/Power/Brightness

The next property that can be manipulated is intensity. This is handled in a slightly different way by each modeling program, but the application is very straightforward. The higher the number, the brighter the lights. In *Bforartists*, there is a W designation as if the number in that field had something to do with the wattage of the light source. This, of course, is a fantasy, so we can just ignore the W. It is possible to type in any value from zero to infinity. Try typing in the value of 500,000 watts and see what happens. It will work. The scene will turn completely white, or perhaps your computer will burst into flames with the power of the sun lighting the scene. Rather than just resigning yourself to having God-like control over the brightness of your light sources, limit your brightness to a manageable range. One to 1,000 is a good range for lighting power. If that does not light up the scene enough, or if an instrument at 1,000 watts does not resemble the brightness that you would expect from a similar instrument in a real theater, adjust the exposure value in the rendering settings.

Once the exposure is set for the brightest instrument, any other light sources at lower settings should fall into reasonable approximations. Near the exposure setting is the gamma setting. If you have experience in using gamma settings, slight changes to this value can be used instead of exposure.

Soft Falloff

Below the power setting is the checkbox for Soft Falloff. This is a property that is unique to *Bforartists (Blender)*. For the purposes of rendering stage lighting, it is best to just leave this turned on.

Radius

The Radius parameter is used to soften the edges of light. The effect is most obvious in spotlights, but it does have some use in other light sources as well. The higher the value, the softer the edge of the lit area will become. If the light source is being used to project a gobo, slide, or video clip, it will become blurry and unfocused.

Shadows

Next is a checkbox that toggles Shadow Casting. One neat trick of lighting in a computer simulation is that lights don't have to cast shadows if we don't want them to. For the sake of realism, most lights will be casting shadows, but if you simply want to add some upstage fill to a scene and you don't want ugly shadows running downstage towards the audience, just turn the shadows off.

Distance

The distance property is another that separates computer lighting from the real thing. Check the box marked custom distance, and the light will stop rather suddenly at whatever distance you type into the value. If you want to light something on stage right and not have the light go across to stage left, type in the value of 15 feet, and the light will miraculously stop. Wouldn't it be nice if real stage lights could do that?

Hanging and Focusing Virtual Lights

Start with a Point Light

- Select a source from the toolbar icons or the Add menu. Like any object, it will first appear at the location of the 3D cursor.
- Use the move tool to place it anywhere in your project, a location that matches the location of an actual lighting position, or anyplace it looks good.

To hang and focus a Point source, you can use the usual tools: move, rotate, and scale. However, with a point source, rotating has no effect because it is emitting light in all directions. Scaling a light source also doesn't do any good.

A Spotlight light source has a visible cone coming from the negative Z axis. It is standard across all 3D modeling to use the negative Z as the direction of light. In *Bforartists*, spotlights have two control handles that other objects don't.

The yellow dot is a focusing handle.

- Click and drag it around the light. The light's beam will follow.
  Very cool, but it can be misleading. Remember to check the focus from different viewing angles.
  The blue arrow is a quick zooming tool.
- Drag the blue arrow closer or farther from the source. The beam will narrow or widen.
  Use a shortcut.
- Press Shift + T. Then, move the cursor around the viewport. The light will follow.

The yellow line of the Z axis will indicate the direction of focus, but it is still a good idea to occasionally change your viewpoint.

The best way to know if the beam is pointing at the desired target is to bring up its power and watch the effect of the light. Just like in a real focusing session, it often helps to narrow the beam and illuminate the target before widening it to the desired beam spread.

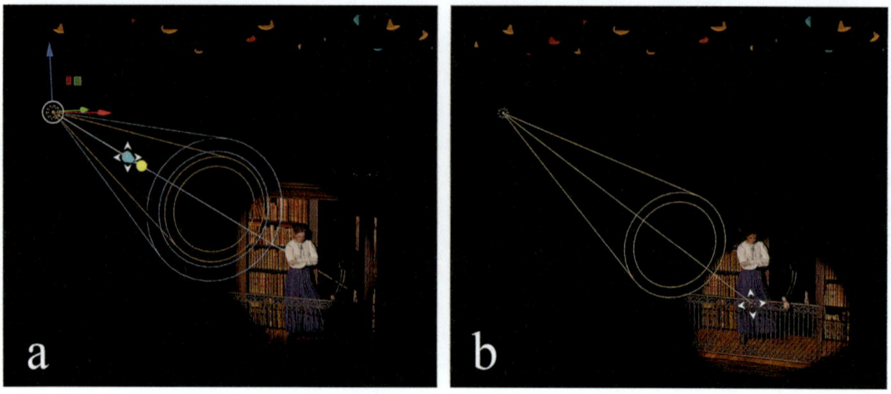

FIGURE 12.10 Spotlights have additional controls for focusing. a) Drag the blue arrow to zoom. b) Drag the yellow dot to aim.

Chain a Light to its Target

Here's a neat trick to ensure the target is well-lit. Light sources can be connected to a target so that the target will always be the center of focus, even if it is moved. The target could be a platform, a wagon, or a figure. Should you move the target, the light source will track like a good follow spot. An empty object can also be used as a target and serve as a quick-focusing aid. Instead of rotating the light, just move the empty object-target to a new position. Better yet, several light sources can be linked to the same target and follow it from multiple angles.

- Select the spotlight.
- Open the restraints tab in the Properties panel.
- Click "Add Restraint" to open the menu.
- Select "Track To".
- Click in the "Target" field and select a target from the list of objects in the scene. (See why it is important to name everything?)
  - Or, use the eyedropper to select a target in the viewport or in the Outliner.
- Because light shines from the negative Z-axis of the source, set "Track Axis to -Z".
- Set "Up" to either X or Y. An object that tracks another needs an "up" vector to keep it from rotating around its own Track axis.

Aim a Follow Spot

Another neat way to focus a light is to aim it like a follow spot. When running a follow spot, you aim by sight, and it is possible to do the same with virtual lights.

First, use the light as a camera.

- Select the spotlight.
- View menu > Cameras > Set "Active Object as Camera".
- View menu > Align View > "Active Camera to View".
  - Or, press "." On the number pad, to toggle from regular viewport to Camera view.

Next, make the light/camera move with the view in the viewport.

- Viewport sidebar View > Camera Lock = "Camera to View".
  - Or, click on the "Lock Camera to View" icon either in the Align View options of the Toolbar or in the view icons floating in the Viewport.

Now, any rotation in the viewport will be reflected in the light's focus. Just rotate the view in the usual manner until the aiming point is dead-center. Keep in mind that any panning or zooming of the view will change the light's position. This could be quite handy for finding the best hanging position to light the target at the best angle.

To exit the camera view and return to the standard editing viewport, simply press the period key on the number pad again. To stop the light from functioning as a camera:

- Select a camera in the scene.
- View menu > Cameras > Set "Active Object as Camera".

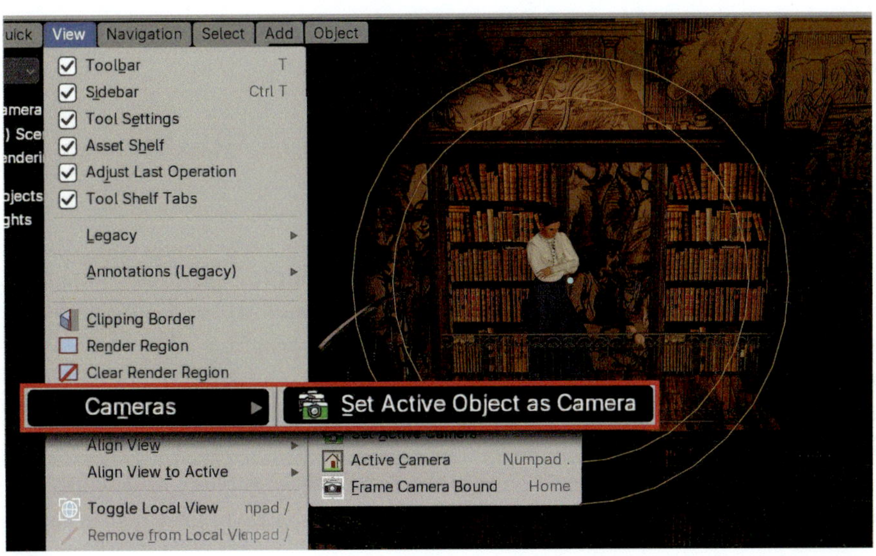

FIGURE 12.11 Focus a light as you would a follow spot.

Spotlights

Spotlights have the same basic principles as other light sources, with the addition of Beam Shape, Blend, and Radius.

Beam Shape

"Beam Shape" is located in the properties panel, and it primarily offers the option to change the spread of the instrument, measured in degrees. In a visualization model, you can match the degree of beam spread to the type of instrument that will be used, such as a 30-degree Source4, 50-degree, and so on.

Blend

The "Blend" modifier helps simulate the difference between "field" and "beam" found in real lighting instruments. Increasing the value of Blend makes the lighting pool dimmer near the edges and brighter in the center. It is labeled Blend because this setting allows lighting pools to overlap without creating overly bright areas where they intersect.

Radius

When using the Blend modifier, the effect of the "Radius" property becomes more visible. As you can see, the edges of the spotlight beam become softer as the value changes.

TEXTURING LIGHT

TO USE NODES, THE RENDERER MUST BE SET TO CYCLES.

Gobos

Since we have virtual spotlights, we must have the ability to use gobos. Patterned or textured lighting is often overlooked in early visualization. Using gobos in our computer spotlights is very simple. All modeling programs allow for the use of patterns in light sources. Often, it involves creating a material similar to the materials used on the faces of objects, but instead, that material is applied to a light source.

First, you need to find a good pattern for basic gobos. A black-and-white pattern is all that is needed, but you can use gobos with shades of gray just as easily.

Just like real gobos, the white areas will be the transparent sections that allow light to pass through, and the black areas will be opaque.

All major manufacturers of gobo templates offer catalogs online.

- Download the patterns that you want.
- Crop the gobo image to a 1 x 1 square aspect ratio.
- In the Render tab, set the Render Engine to "Cycles".
- In the Data (Light bulb) tab > Nodes, click "Use Nodes".
- Click the yellow dot of the Color node and select "Image Texture" from the pop-up menu.
- Same as always, click the folder icon and locate your gobo image.
- To rotate the gobo, rotate the entire light source on its Z axis.
- Use the "Radius" property of the spotlight to soften the focus and blur the gobo pattern.

Projecting Images

Spotlights also project images and even video clips. Images are loaded into an instrument just as one does a gobo pattern. Gobo patterns are typically round with a 1 x 1 aspect ratio. If you desire a projected image that is rectangular, that can be accomplished in a few ways.

The easiest is to frame the desired image in the middle of a square so that it fits entirely within the space of a gobo pattern.

It is also possible to assign a set of mapping controls for scale, rotation, and location, just as you can do for the mapping of materials. However, the resulting projections usually have edges that are slightly warped in a pillow effect.

There's a better, although unorthodox, method for projecting images that is faster and easier to control. Instead of a Spotlight, use an Area light as a projector. The light from an area light starts as a parallel beam.

If you want to fill a projection screen that is 20' x 15':

- Make an area light.
- Change the size to (you guessed it) 20' x 15'.
- Follow the steps listed for using a gobo.
- Adjust the Beam Shape to make the image larger.
  - The greater the angle, the more the image will blur.

Remember, you can place a virtual projector at any distance from the screen, 2' or 200', and it will look the same. Like all virtual lights, the projector has no geometry of its own and will not appear in a rendering. Another nice trick.

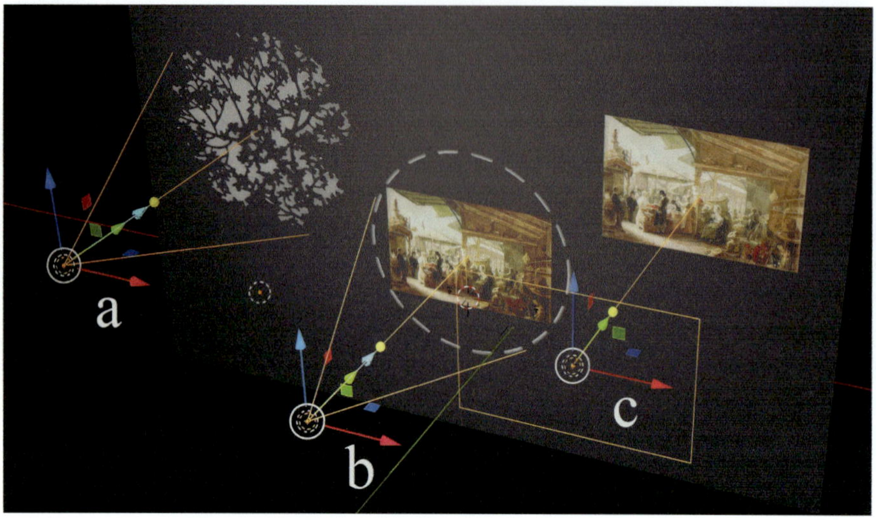

FIGURE 12.12 Three different methods of projecting patterns and images. a) A gobo from a spotlight. b) An image from a spotlight. c) An image from an area light.

WORKFLOWS

You can use those elements as templates in the future. Copy the light source, paste it into a blank document, and save it. You may want to save a template file containing various light sources that you have configured for future use.

You can then open a template file, copy a pre-configured lighting instrument, and paste it into the current project.

Work goes more quickly when you duplicate objects.

- Select a light.
- Press Shift + D.
  - The duplicate object will have the same gel color and focus properties as the original instrument. It'll also share any aiming points that belong to the original.
  - This is a quick method of setting up entire color systems.
  - Duplicate an object, then select those two and duplicate them again. Then select the resulting four, duplicate to eight, and again to 16, and onward to infinity.

Another incredibly useful option is to make an **instance** of a lighting instrument rather than a copy. Instances are clones of the original object placed at different locations.

- Select a light.
- Press Alt + D instead of Shift + D.
  - Instances can all be controlled by using the properties of a single one. Gel color, beam spread, focus, or Radius of all instances can be tweaked at once.

- **If you raise the light intensity of one, it raises the intensity of all other instances.** This is analogous to setting up control groups in a lightboard. Writing virtual cues for your scene goes that much quicker. Pick a lead instrument, and the others will follow along, like good little instances.
- Instances have the additional benefit of not increasing the file's size because they don't have all the data of a lighting instrument, only the location and rotation.

13 Rendering the Scene

FIGURE 13.1 A finished rendering captures a dramatic moment in the play, showcasing the shape of the space, colors, and materials, as well as the use of lighting that highlights the action.

Once you have completed the modeling, adjusted the materials to your satisfaction, and ensured that the lights are correctly positioned and focused, it is time to render the scene. Rendering can be complex, but it doesn't have to be. There are three key elements necessary for achieving good renders: lighting, camera settings, and render settings.

When everything looks good in the viewport, the modeling, materials, and lighting are ready to go; the next step is to create a gorgeous rendering. It's always beneficial to conduct test renders throughout the process to monitor

DOI: 10.4324/9781003571742-13

your progress before committing to a high-resolution render, as these can be time-consuming.

THE CAMERA

If you've established some constraints on the lighting, keeping the brightness between 0 and 1,000 lumens, then we can move forward without further adjustments to the lighting.

By now, you may have noticed that when you render the scene, the render engine uses a different viewpoint than the one you see in the viewport. A common feature in all 3D modeling programs is the existence of a separate camera object that provides the viewpoint from which scenes are rendered. This is very useful because you can position the camera in the best possible rendering location and then return to the viewport to move around and edit. As you work, you can move, orbit, and zoom to the view that works best for editing. When you hit the render command again, the scene will be rendered from that pre-selected optimal viewpoint.

It is also possible to set up multiple cameras at different locations throughout the scene. For example, you might place one camera on the balcony, another on the left side of the house, and another on the right side. If you preset the views, as you get closer to rendering, it's much easier to switch between cameras than to continually adjust a single camera's position. To avoid mistakes, lock each camera in position.

- Select a camera.
- Viewport sidebar > Item tab > Transform.
- Click the "Lock" icons behind the Location and Rotation fields.

FIGURE 13.2 Setting up cameras in anticipation of making final renderings.

However, aligning the camera to the correct angle can be challenging if you are not viewing the scene through it. Fortunately, there is a way to address this. Every program offers a method to create a camera or adjust one to match the current viewport position.

- View menu > Align View > "Active Camera to View".
- Press "." on the number pad to toggle from regular viewport to Camera view.

If you then lock the camera to your view, any rotation, panning, or zooming you perform in the viewport will be reflected in the camera's position. To exit the camera view and return to the standard editing viewport, simply press the period key on the number pad again.

- Press "." on the number pad to enter "Camera view".
- Viewport sidebar View > Camera Lock = "Camera to View".

Or,

- Click the "Lock Camera to View" icon that appears in the toolbar when in Camera View.

If you frequently use the "Active Camera to View" command to align the active camera to your view, you might want to create a keyboard shortcut for it. This way, you won't need to keep going back to View menu > Cameras. **To create any shortcut, locate it in the menu, right-click on it, and choose "Create Shortcut".** You will be prompted to select a key. Choose one that isn't already in use for another function; for instance, the zero key on the keypad is a good option since other numbers are already assigned to switch views. Or use a combination of the Control key and a keypad number to make it more unique.

While in the camera view, you'll notice a dotted line and a dotted square box in the center of the screen. This box corresponds to the dimensions you've set in the output tab. For example, if you have set the output resolution to 1080p, the box will match that size. This dotted view can be quite distracting, but you can address this in the View menu by selecting Cameras, then Frame Camera Balance. This will expand the dotted view to cover the entire screen.

In physically-based rendering, the camera behaves similarly to a real-life camera. You can modify the exposure settings to reflect those of a 35mm camera. Some programs go so far as to include the ISO, film type, film speed, aperture settings (F-stop), and shutter speed. In any case, the goal is to replicate a physical camera as part of the physically-based rendering and materials approach. To start, set the camera according to standard parameters, such as using a 50mm lens, and leave the sensor size and attitude at the defaults. Once you have these initial settings in place, you can adjust the render settings to produce a good

FIGURE 13.3 The dotted rectangle or "Render view" shows the area that will be captured in the rendering. The gray area outside the Render view is the "Passepartout". The darkness can be controlled in the Camera properties.

image. Given the overwhelming number of options available in the render settings, the key is to keep things as simple as possible, especially since time is of the essence and renderings need to be produced quickly.

RENDER ENGINES

Rendering is performed by a component of the software known as a render engine. All 3D programs typically include at least two built-in render engines. The first is a standard render engine, which is used for everyday rendering tasks that do not require special effects. Standard render engines are not physically based, meaning that using PBR materials does not provide any advantage. Features like displacement and alpha channels will not be visible in standard rendering. However, standard rendering is faster, making it a useful option for quick test renders as you work towards the final product.

The second type of render engine found in most programs is the physically-based render engine. This engine utilizes the properties of physically-based materials and supports advanced lighting techniques, such as gobos, projections, and volumetric or fog lighting. PBR materials are fully supported, revealing many of the most subtle qualities of light, diffusion, reflection, gloss, refraction, absorption, etc. If your materials include alpha channels, you will need to use physically-based rendering to make them appear correctly. Be aware that all of these wonderful qualities come at the cost of longer rendering time.

FIGURE 13.4 a) Standard rendering is fast and works well in some situations. b) Physical rendering is needed to show advanced materials and lighting techniques.

There are differences among physically-based render engines; some are CPU-based, while others are GPU-based. For instance, the physical renderer in *Cinema 4D* is CPU-based, whereas Cycles in *Bforartists* is GPU-based. If you want to take advantage of GPU rendering, you must use the Cycles render engine by setting the "Device" property to "GPU Compute". The primary advantage of having a Graphics Processing Unit (GPU) in your computer is its speed. GPUs are designed for running games and can render scenes at 30 frames per second or higher. While games do not utilize all the properties of physically-based materials, they do employ most of them.

There are also third-party render engines that can be integrated as plugins into your primary software, allowing you to operate them directly from the program's user interface. Other third-party render engines are stand-alone programs that require you to export your file, adjust the materials and lights, and add cameras before rendering it separately.

Third-party render engines can vary greatly in their capabilities. Most are GPU-based, which is why users might choose to invest in them. Ideally, the settings from the modeling program should transfer seamlessly. If something works in a test render, it should work in the third-party renderer as well; unfortunately, that's not always the case. Third-party products often have specific requirements; you may be expected to use a special set of lighting instruments and cameras and to reformat materials to suit their engine before achieving the desired results.

Cloud-based render engines are another option. These services allow you to buy rendering time by purchasing credits; the more time your project takes to render, the more credits you will use. None of these cloud-based renderers is free. Some may offer discounts for students, but they still charge. Students often take longer to render because they may perform multiple passes or set up complex animations, consuming a lot of processing time that must be paid for. The advantage of cloud-based rendering is that it frees up your computer, allowing you to work on other projects while the rendering is done remotely.

Cycles is a decent renderer. While it isn't the fastest renderer available, it performs well. *Cinema 4D* comes with the *Redshift* renderer, which is also owned by the Maxon company. *3DS Max* includes *Arnold*, a powerful rendering engine. Many of the primary render engines available can be quite expensive, although some offer student discounts. These render engines are primarily used by animation studios that require dedicated computers for rendering tasks, thereby alleviating the workload on computers designated for modeling and texturing.

Redshift is one of the fastest third-party renderers available and is particularly well-suited for creating game environments. It provides impressive rendering results, characterized by vibrant colors and enhanced contrast. However, to achieve your desired look with *Redshift*, you may need to fine-tune your scene, making adjustments to materials, lighting, and camera settings. While *Redshift* works exceptionally well with existing objects in your scene, it does have a subscription cost of $22 per month for non-students.

Other third-party render engines include:

D5 GPU renderer
D5 offers a free community version that can be used for an unlimited period. Rapidly refreshes effects when the user changes a parameter, moves an object, or tweaks it.

LuxCoreRender GPU renderer
Although not well known, *LuxCoreRender* is a free, open-source renderer that can compete with commercial solutions.

RenderMan CPU + GPU

Developed by Pixar, this is another excellent renderer that offers quality comparable to Cycles. It is known for producing very high-quality results, having been used by Pixar for most of its major motion pictures. However, *RenderMan* has a steeper learning curve due to its greater number of settings, and it may not always integrate smoothly with all 3d modeling applications.

SETTINGS

Output Settings

When it's time to render, there are two main sets of properties in the properties panel that need to be addressed. The first is the Output tab, indicated by a small printer icon. Begin by entering resolution settings for test renders. A resolution of 720p is suitable for testing, but for final prints, a much higher resolution is recommended. Try to stay with a standard aspect ratio, either 16:9 or 4:3. Note

TABLE 13.1 Standard resolutions for standard aspect ratios.

2:3	3:4	9:16
2000 x 3000	2250 x 3000	720 x 1280
2500 x 3750	3240 x 4320	768 x 1366
2880 x 4320	3400 x 4400	900 x 1600
3000 x 4500	3750 x 5000	1080 x 1920
3600 x 5400	5400 x 7200	1440 x 2560
4320 x 6480	6480 x 8640	2160 x 3840
4800 x 7200	9000 x 13500	2700 x 4800
6000 x 9000		3240 x 5760
7200 x 10800		3600 x 6400

that the Aspect setting pertains to the dimensions of the pixels rather than the image itself, so it's typically best to leave these settings alone. Don't worry about Frame rate since you're not creating an animation, and the Frame range is not a concern either. At this stage, stereo settings are also not relevant.

In the output settings, the first field prompts you to choose a folder for saving the finished render. For file format, you will usually select either PNG or JPEG. The color mode can be set to RGB. The color depth is generally set to 8 bits, but can be adjusted to 16 bits if needed; however, keep in mind that 16-bit files are significantly larger and slower to process. The Compression setting is the inverse of the Quality settings found in other programs. For example, a Compression of 60% equals 40% Quality, whereas a Compression of 20% corresponds to 80% Quality. Most of the other options are self-explanatory.

The Transparent checkbox may be necessary if there are objects in the scene that should be invisible. While it's usually not essential, including it doesn't hurt. If you're rendering glass in your scene, it's advisable to also check the transparent glass option. You can enter any desired information in the metadata field, as it serves as a header for the image and does not significantly affect the rendering process. Post-processing should not be required for the types of renders we are performing.

Render Settings

The second set of settings to consider is found under the render tab, labeled "Render Settings". There is a wide array of options here, many of which may have different names in other programs. It is best to leave most settings at their default values until you become familiar with the rendering process and decide to implement specific changes. At the top of the settings, ensure that the render engine is set to "Cycles" with the feature set as "Supported". When selecting between CPU and GPU, note that some render engines allow both to run simultaneously, but Cycles does not offer this option. When you are ready to render, you can access the render icon in the top toolbar for rendering the active scene (shortcut: F12). Alternatively, you can click on the little camera with a flash icon or navigate to the render menu at the top row to render either an image or an animation.

In Bforartists, the camera does not have dedicated exposure controls. The only adjustable F-stop is related to the "depth of field" effect, and there is no option for shutter speed. Therefore, instead of trying to mix and match settings between the camera and the lighting, it's faster and easier to set the overall exposure in the render settings for both the Cycles renderer and Eevee.

In the Color Management dropdown in the Render tab, you can find exposure controls.

- Render tab > Color Management > Exposure.
- Adjust the Exposure sliders.
  - o To see the effect before rendering, the viewport shading must be set to "Render Preview".
  - o The gamma settings can be adjusted similarly.

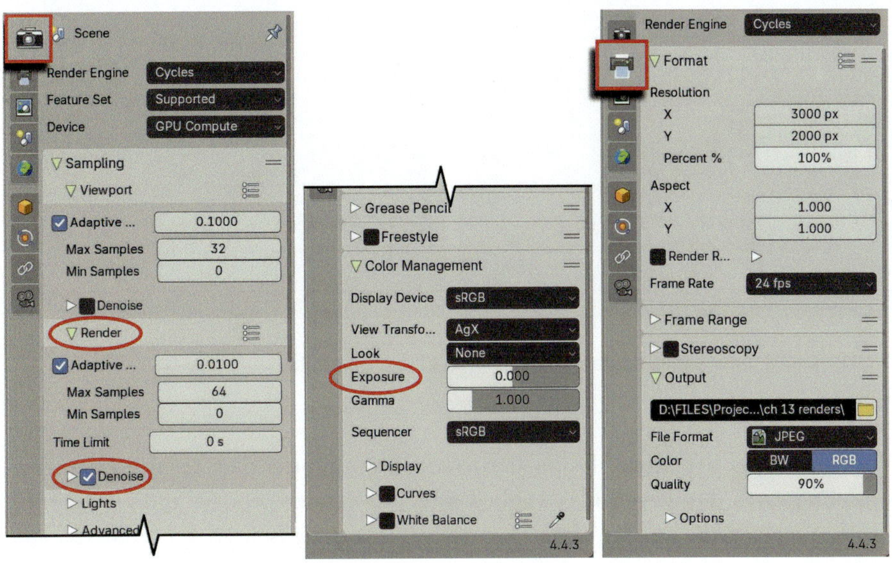

FIGURE 13.5 The main rendering settings are found in the "Render" and "Output" tabs.

Exposure controls affect the overall brightness of the scene, while gamma settings influence a combination of brightness and contrast. If you use a standard camera and standardize the brightness levels of lighting instruments, you can find exposure settings that work for you and save them for all future projects.

Additionally, the Cycles renderer provides an extra exposure control in the Film dropdown menu. Although this feature may not always be particularly useful, it's good to know that there are multiple ways to manage lighting and rendering in Cycles.

The sampling settings are crucial for achieving optimal performance. If the settings are too high, the program may slow down significantly during both viewport rendering and final rendering. Conversely, if the samples are set too low, the resulting images will appear very grainy and of low quality.

In *Bforartists*, you can configure rendering samples to be different for the viewport and final renders. Start with a reasonable Max Sample value of around 128 for the final render. After rendering, check the image quality to ensure it is not unacceptably grainy, and note the time it takes to complete the render. Adjust the sample value up or down as needed. For the viewport settings, start with a value around 32, and similarly evaluate the quality and speed to determine if adjustments are necessary. There is also an option for denoising that can be checked.

FIGURE 13.6 Low sample rates result in "Noise" in a rendering.

Denoising is a feature designed to reduce graininess that results from low sampling rates. However, it is applied after the render process and can significantly increase the render time. Typically, denoising is used for final renders rather than for viewport rendering. You can access detailed Denoising settings through a dropdown menu. It's best to leave the settings as they are, but please note the option to utilize your GPU. If your computer has a GPU, select this option for improved performance.

For lights, it is advisable to retain the default settings. Leave the options for light paths, volumes, and curves unchanged for now.

14 Design Presentation

FIGURE 14.1 Using different media makes for exciting ways to present and sell your designs, as well as offer new methods of collaboration.

Now that you've created fantastic, dynamic images, presenting them effectively to colleagues and collaborators is essential. Printing your costume and set renderings can enhance production meetings and job interviews as part of your portfolio.

While most portfolios are digital, high-quality prints are invaluable during in-person interactions. Aim for large, high-resolution prints (11" x 14" or larger) to maximize impact, as standard desktop printers often fall short for these needs. Large-format printing options include local print shops or online services, but for urgent needs, local is best. Using an office color copier can also be effective for creating ledger-size copies suitable for smaller meetings.

When printing, choose the right paper – avoid standard printer paper. Opt for photo-grade or bright-white coated paper for vibrant images, as high-gloss paper, though striking, can smudge easily. Satin photo paper is a durable alternative that can maintain quality without the issues of gloss. If using a copy

DOI: 10.4324/9781003571742-14

machine, you may need to supply high-quality paper yourself, particularly for larger sizes. For larger prints, consider mounting them on mat board using permanent spray adhesive for a professional finish.

Avoid using plastic protective sleeves, as they can reflect light and look cheap. For long-term displays, mounting prints under glass will enhance their appearance and durability.

VIDEO CLIPS

One innovative option for presentations is creating a video showcase of your scenic models. This method highlights set changes, transitions, and lighting cues, enabling you to navigate the house and stage with fluidity.

Many modern 3D modeling programs include built-in video creation features, making it easier for stage designers to present their work. However, it's crucial to stay focused on the presentation's effectiveness rather than getting bogged down in film production details.

In your video, you can animate objects in your scene to simulate set shifts or actor movements. The camera can zoom, pan, and move vertically, while you can also animate properties like lighting intensity, color, and movement of intelligent fixtures. Projections can be included for added dynamism.

The key to efficient presentations lies in animating each object and property individually, which simplifies the process. For example, you could animate a curtain rising over three seconds, followed by furniture sliding in from stage right in five seconds. The next three seconds cover the lighting cue, brightening as the action unfolds.

Having a clear outline of the total animation is essential. When you plot the individual actions, it is less likely that any will be left out. By identifying where they overlap, you can better divide the project into smaller clips.

FIGURE 14.2 Start with an outline of the entire clip. A storyboard works very well.

Each clip should be kept to 3 to 10 seconds for efficiency. After creating several short clips, you can merge them together using a video editing program. Simple joining can often be done using free utilities, sparing you the expense of buying software like Adobe *Premiere Pro*.

One limiting factor is the time it takes to render video clips. In standard video production, 30 frames per second is considered the minimum, while 60 frames per second is seen as high quality. In the traditional standard definition, 24 frames per second was the minimum. Even at that, a five-second clip would equal 120 frames. Reducing it to 20 frames per second still results in 100 frames, which you need to check to determine if you can live with that frame rate. For a three-second clip at 24 frames per second, there would be 72 frames total.

Set up a sample video clip. You might start with something simple, like raising the curtain. Set the animation to five seconds at 20 frames per second, which means testing 100 frames. The output resolution is crucial. If you plan to project on a screen or large television during a meeting, 720p is a minimum, with 1080p being preferable if your computer can handle it.

- **Save a copy of the project and use the current one for animation only.**

The animation timeline is at the bottom of the viewport.

- Drag the top edge upward to open the animation working area.
- Enter the Start and End points of the clip in the header of the timeline (frame 0 to 100, 4 seconds at 25 frames per second?)
- In the scene Output tab > Format > "Frame Rate" = 25 fps.
- Select the first object to animate.
- Move the animation slider to the point where the movement is to begin.
- Click the "Insert keyframe" button in the header.
- Move the slider to the point where the motion is to stop, rest, or change direction.
- Insert another keyframe.
- Move the slider back to the beginning or click the "Rewind" button.
- Click the "Play" button and watch it go!

Next,

- Return the slider to start.
- Select the next object to be animated.
- Set more keyframes while moving or changing properties.
  - Remember, almost any property can be animated: scale, rotation, light color, and intensity.
  - If you want an object to appear or disappear magically, change the Alpha value of its material to 0, and POOF, it's gone.

Rendering Video

Rendering a video clip is not much different than rendering a single image. Of course, the output format is different.

- Output tab > Set a folder where the video clip will be saved.
- Output tab > "File Format" = FFmpeg.

New, video-specific options will appear.

- > Encoding > "Container" Select your favorite video format. MPEG-4 (mpg4) is the most commonly used. It is a good compromise between quality and compression, and it is easily edited and compiled.
- > Video > "Video Codec" H.264 is the most universal. H.265 is a bit faster if your computer uses an Nvidia video GPU.
- For a trial run, set up your project to render around 200 frames at 720p.

FFmpeg is an open-source video application that compiles all the separate frames of an animation into a finished video.

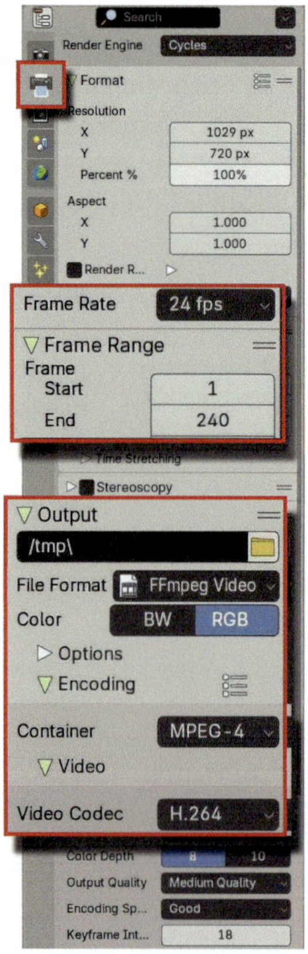

FIGURE 14.3 Typical output settings for video clips.

- To start the render, click on the "Render Video" (the clapperboard) button, next to the usual "Render" button.

You can watch each frame in the render window. When finished, the total rendering time is listed at the top of the window. This will help you determine the length of animation you want to create. You may need to speed up the process by reducing the length of each clip, the image resolution, the sampling rate, or the output quality. Turning off "Denoise" in the Render settings will also gain some speed.

You don't have to create a video covering the entire show. Just a few moments that best illustrate how clever you are and how much they are going to love your design. These moments can be patched, end-to-end, or separated by sexy transitions. If you like to add music behind it or give it a title and credit opening, knock yourself out. It wouldn't be a bad idea to put the director and producer's names right up front. They will love it.

Cropping and Editing

Assembling the short, rendered clips together into a finished video presentation is quite simple. There are numerous easily accessible video editing programs available online, and many of the free options are just as effective as expensive commercial packages.

If you have experience and already own a commercial video editing program, such as Adobe *Premiere Pro*, that's fantastic. However, several very good free software packages will work equally well.

- DaVinci *Resolve* is a bit of overkill; it's so full of advanced features that it's hard to believe it's free. The learning curve is a little steeper, so if you don't want to add a lot of special effects, one of the other options might work better for you.
- There is a streamlined Adobe product called Adobe *Premiere Rush*. It only has basic functionality, but it operates similarly to its bigger counterpart, *Premiere Pro*.
- *OpenShot* is another program that will get the job done, and there are probably 10 more options available.

Most of these programs operate with a simple drag-and-drop input process. You simply drag each video clip into the program, and it will place it on a timeline. Once you have all the clips arranged in order, you can add transitions between them, or you can leave them as is, if the clips are designed to flow smoothly into one another. To finish, just set the parameters for format and quality, export the completed video, and voila, it's all done!

360° PANORAMAS!

Now that other stuff was fun, but this is absolutely a gas. To convince people that you are a wizard of great power, show them 360° panoramic renderings.

These renderings are becoming more popular, and even the average smartphone today can create a complete 360° panorama by taking a series of pictures in all directions and using the built-in software to stitch them all together.

It is now a standard feature of 3D modeling programs, making it fairly easy. After you have set up the scene for regular rendering, creating a 360° panorama is simply a matter of adjusting a few settings. A panorama is a single image displayed in a window that can be panned right or left, up or down, allowing the view to be rotated as if the viewer were standing in one place and spinning in a circle. This includes looking straight up and straight down, a complete sphere of vision.

FIGURE 14.4 A panoramic rendering of the scene.

Most of the magic lies in the Camera and Output settings.

- Camera tab > Lens > Type > "Panoramic".
  - Panorama Type > "Equirectangular".
- Output tab > Format > Y (height) = a big number, X (wide) 2 x the big number.

Increase the resolution to some very large number. The standard for panoramic rendering is images that are twice as wide as they are tall, a two-to-one ratio. This is called the equirectangular format.

These high-resolution images are necessary because, in the viewing window, the user only sees one small slice of the rendering. Looking in any direction, you see about a tenth of the entire spherical rendering. Looking up and down, other small portions are visible. The rendering includes the area that is being seen and all that is "behind" the viewer as well. Some parts may not be seen at all if the viewer doesn't pan the image in that direction.

The high resolution will increase the rendering time significantly. You can create a small test render at about 1,000 pixels high and 2,000 pixels wide. When viewed as a 360° image, that image will be grainy, but it at least confirms that the system is working. The final rendering should be 2,500 x 5,000 pixels. If the viewing window is relatively small, it could go as low as 1,500 x 3,000 pixels.

The settings that accompany the equirectangular Panorama type define the extent of the spherical rendering. Looking all the way up and down puts the latitude at 90° (up) and -90° (down). Turning all the way around means the Longitude is 180° (left) and -180° (right).

Creating a 360° spherical image for a proscenium set design can be somewhat of a waste, as most of what you'll see when turning around is just the darkness behind and to each side. For that reason, there is another format for panoramas, 180°, in which only the front half of the viewing sphere is viewable. The longitudinal angles stay the same, but the side rotation, the angles of latitude, are reduced to plus and minus 90°.

For optimal functionality, position the camera very close to the scene or even place it on stage. This creates a unique panoramic view, simulating the perspective of an actor in the heart of the set. Panoramic rendering really shines in an arena-style theater format. You can place the camera position at the corner of the stage or right in its center for a more immersive experience.

FIGURE 14.5 An arena or theatre-in-the-round production makes full use of a panoramic rendering.

Adding audience members to the scene can make it feel even more alive. Choose low-polygon seated characters for efficiency, arrange them in multiple rows, and repeat the process on each side until you assemble approximately

100 spectators. To maintain focus on the performance, you could darken the audience textures or even make them partially transparent, ensuring they fade into the background. Excluding the audience from some lighting sources will also help, giving the audience a subtle presence without overpowering the scene.

Once you've created a 360° rendering, the fun begins.

Facebook, Google Photos, and YouTube enable you to upload these immersive images, allowing visitors to scroll around and explore every angle with ease. For YouTube, you must stretch the image into a short video clip using video editing software, converting it into a panoramic clip that is perfect for virtual reality viewing and sharing. Furthermore, embedding your panorama in your webpage is straightforward; simply use the embedded link from Google Photos or Facebook and integrate it into your site using services like Wix or Squarespace, which are already equipped for such functionalities.

To view your panoramic image on a computer, use a panorama-capable image viewer.

- *LizardQ Viewer*, *Richo Theta, Insta360 Studio*, *Panorado*, and *Lux*.

On a smartphone, panoramas can be viewed by visiting Facebook or Google Photos, or the images can be sent directly to the user and viewed using 360° viewing apps. The best apps differ between Android and iOS, but the *Panorama 360* and camera-based *Riccho360* apps are a good place to start.

EXIF Editing

Some of these viewing applications and websites will display panoramas just as they were rendered, but others cannot distinguish between a regular image and a panorama. For this reason, the image file's EXIF information needs to be edited. This embedded data provides essential details about your image, such as resolution, format, and – most importantly – whether the image is a panorama and its orientation (360° or 180°). If spherical images or videos are edited in programs like *Photoshop* or *Premiere Pro*, options can be set to save the images with correct panoramic Exif data in the files. Otherwise, the job can be accomplished easily with free utilities.

- *Exif Fixer* or exiffixer.com
    - o Exif Fixer has online and downloadable versions of the application. Open your file, select the type of image it is, and click on FIX. Nothing to it.
- *Hugin*

Hugin is a free application that creates panoramas by stitching together photos. It can also be used to simply inject panorama EXIF data into an image.

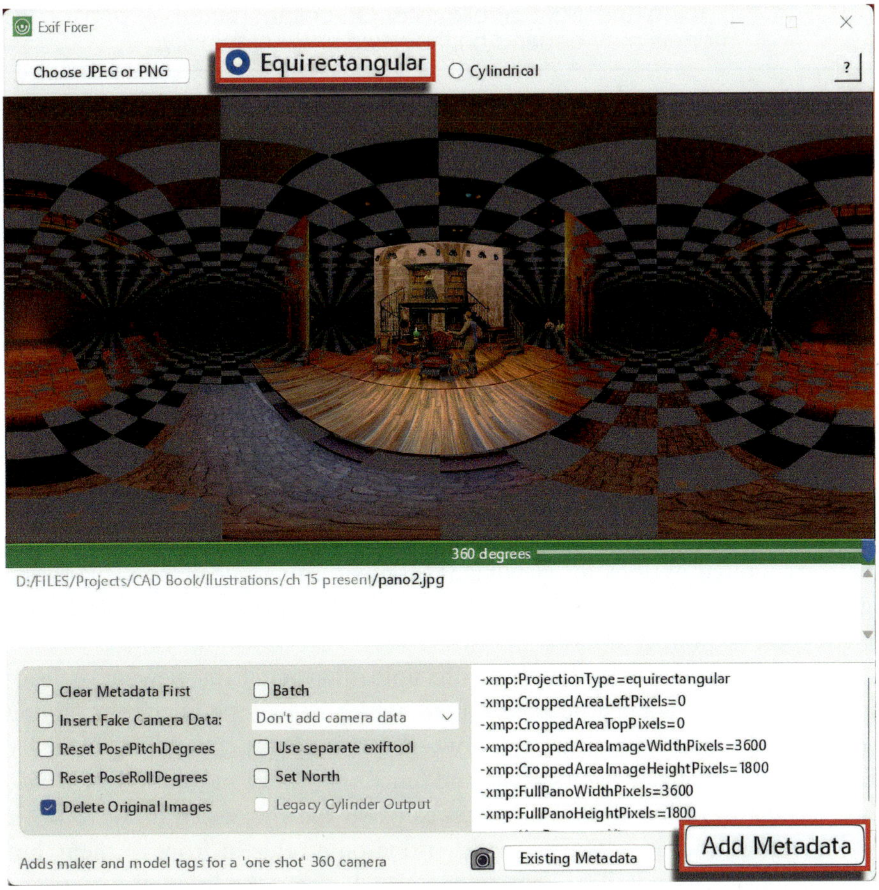

FIGURE 14.6 *Exif Fixer* is a tool for injecting panoramic EXIF data with two clicks.

3D MODEL VIEWERS

A fantastic way to share a 3D set design is by providing collaborators and colleagues the opportunity to manipulate the model on their own devices. Some 3D Model viewers for desktop computers include:

There are a few websites that allow you to share and host 3D models on their servers. Facebook, SWIFT XR, Meta, and Autodesk Viewer are services that let you upload and share 3D models. However, there are some significant limitations to what they accept.

There are limits on file size, and supported formats are limited to a few, particularly STL and GLB. They also permit OBJ files, which are slightly more convenient. Most websites that allow uploads tend to run best with GLB files, as this format was specifically developed for 3D gaming, particularly online gaming.

TABLE 14.1 Finding the right application for collaborative viewing of 3D models may depend on their size and complexity.

Applications	Type	Source
F3D	Desktop App	f3d.app
Modelo	Online	modelo.io/3d-viewer
Autodesk Viewer	Online	viewer.autodesk.com
FBX Review	Desktop App	autodesk.com/products/fbx/fbx-review
Facebook	Online	
Meta	Online	
SwiftXR	Online	home.swiftxr.io

Mobile Devices

There are limited options for viewing 3D content on mobile devices due to the significant variation in capabilities between different brands and models. Fortunately, there is another solution.

There are websites that allow users to upload a model for viewing. A leading platform for this purpose is *Sketchfab*, which has a long history of serving the 3D modeling community. It is now owned by Epic, the gaming industry giant, and eventually, all of its assets and functions will be moved to Epic's Fab.com. Once a model is uploaded, others can visit the site, zoom in, or rotate it as if it were a traditional scenic model sitting on a table in front of them, but now enhanced with excellent lighting and visual effects. Additionally, users can engage with the model using a VR feature, allowing them to enter the model and explore it as if they were an actor on stage.

Posting models on Sketchfab is very easy and even better; it's free. Many users utilize the platform to sell their models, while others simply share them or offer them for free download. After uploading a model to Sketchfab, users can customize its properties, apply cool lighting, and then share the web address with others for viewing. Furthermore, this link can be embedded in a webpage, allowing people to access it directly from a production website or page of your online portfolio.

Users can expand the view to full screen, offering a fantastic desktop VR interface. With a single click, they can switch from a detached, third-person viewpoint to a first-person, interactive view of a VR experience. This feature enables them to traverse the model and view it at eye level. Sketchfab is well-suited for portable devices like phones and tablets, and functions smoothly without significantly slowing down the device.

Users equipped with VR headsets, such as the popular Quest models from Meta, can access the site through a built-in web browser or via a standalone app developed by Sketchfab. This allows them to become completely immersed in the virtual set and even interact with it to some extent, such as changing texture patterns or adjusting lighting elements.

FIGURE 14.7 Sketchfab in the Meta Quest headset.

VIRTUAL REALITY

One of the most sophisticated ways to view your creation is by utilizing virtual reality (VR) technology. While VR collaboration tools can be remarkable, many directors and scenographers may not have the time or resources to invest in them. Setting up VR requires significant effort, making it a more personal tool for designers. However, experiencing your set design in VR can be incredibly beneficial, allowing you to immerse yourself in the environment before it is physically built. Plus, it's a lot of fun!

Creating virtual reality models parallels building theater sets. Both transport people to fictional locations, offering an ephemeral experience that only exists during the performance or simulation. At its core, virtual reality is about crafting an illusion that convinces your senses you're in a place that doesn't exist in real life.

What's exciting about VR is its versatility; it can adapt to various creative needs. With enthusiastic collaborators, there are countless possibilities to explore. Once limited to pioneers, VR has now become accessible to anyone with a headset, inviting everyone to jump into this immersive world.

The range of VR experiences available online is astounding – there are scores, if not hundreds, to choose from. Even within a single platform like Meta, the definitions of what constitutes VR vary widely. The liberating aspect of this technology is that you have the creative freedom to design whatever you envision and label it as VR without hesitation (or AR, MR, or the catchall, XR).

Stereoscopic Rendering 3D!

One of the first challenges to be tackled is stereo rendering. Adding stereo effects to standard perspective renderings can create the impression of depth, enhancing the experience significantly. This technique can be applied just as easily to 360° panoramas. While you will need some type of viewing apparatus to truly appreciate these renders, options abound, from the classic turn-of-the-century stereopticon or View-Master toy to modern VR headsets. A smartphone is an excellent platform for viewing 3D images.

Stereoscopic rendering is the practice of creating two views of a scene that are slightly offset from one another. One view represents that of the right eye, while the other view is captured by moving the camera a small distance to the left, rendering the view from the left eye. When viewed through special equipment that presents these images separately to each eye, it creates a convincing illusion of three-dimensionality.

In the past, this technique was demonstrated using the famous stereoscope device, which utilized what amounted to a 3D postcard with right and left-eye views, viewed through a charming wooden and metal viewer. It was common for people to build extensive collections consisting of hundreds of stereoscope cards.

Later, the technology evolved and was popularized with the View-Master toy, which gained popularity among children in the 1960s and 70s. The View-Master used reel discs that contained separate right and left-eye views on opposite sides of the disc, enabling users to view up to seven pairs of stereo images.

All modern 3D modeling programs have stereoscopic rendering capabilities integrated into their standard feature sets. Typically, this involves converting a camera into a stereo camera, which is really two cameras to represent the viewer's two eyes. Rendering in stereo after this conversion is relatively simple, requiring only two extra render settings.

The first of these is the interpupillary distance, or the space between the pupils of the right and left eyes. That measurement determines the distance between the two cameras.

The second measurement is the convergence distance. As the right and left eye views are angled, or toed, slightly towards the center, the distance from your eyes to the point where their sight lines cross, or converge, is the convergence distance. Any objects in the model that are beyond that convergence point will seem to be farther away. Any objects in front of that convergence point will appear to be emerging from the 3D view towards the viewer. Once the camera settings are entered, set the output settings so that the program knows how to render using the stereo format. The standard format is side-by-side for a basic stereo, with the right channel on the right and the left channel on the left. There are a few exceptions to that.

The 4:3 ratio is the standard for stereo rendering. It can be done in a widescreen format, but that makes it more challenging to bring the two images closer together and achieve the desired illusion.

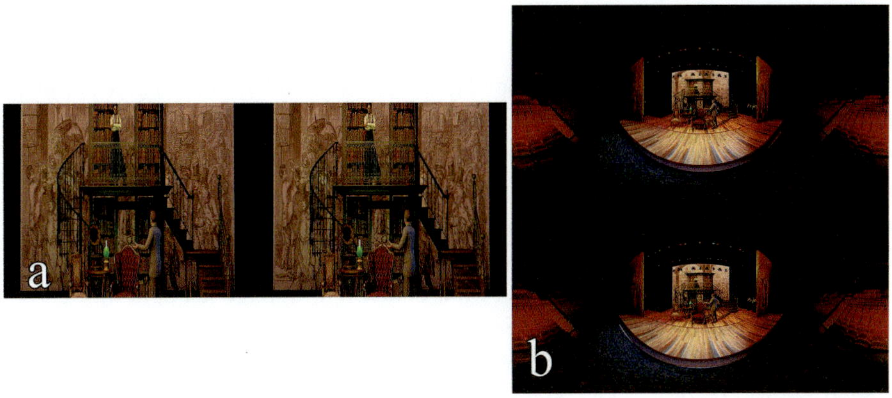

FIGURE 14.8 a) A stereo render. b) A stereo panorama.

Stereo Rendering

- Output Tab > Check the "Stereoscopy" box.
  - New options will appear in several panels.
- Stereo 3D, both right and left.
- Format > "Resolution" – For SBS stereo, double the width of the rendering.
- Output tab > Output > Options > Views.
  - "Views Format" = "Stereo 3D".
  - "Stereo Mode" = "Side-by-Side".
- Camera tab > Stereoscopy > "Mode" Set this to "Off-Axis".
- Convergence Plane.
- "Interocular Distance" = 63mm or 2.5 inches (average distance between one's pupils).
  - If the 3D effect needs a little boost, increase the distance by about 1/2 inch. Experiment.
- Viewport Sidebar > View tab > "Stereoscopy".
  - Select "3D".
  - Display Cameras and Plane.
  - Set "Stereo 3D" = "Side-by-Side" and click "Set".

Viewing Stereo Images in 3D

Stereo images can be viewed in various ways. There are devices that allow you to view images on a monitor, but these can be somewhat awkward as they require you to lean in close.

If you make small-sized prints, they can be mounted in a format that resembles a modern-day stereoscope. Although 35mm slides are now considered outdated, that format was wonderfully suited for use in 3D viewers. Perhaps the best technology for viewing stereo images today is the smartphone.

The Google *Cardboard* phone app aligns the right and left images at the appropriate distance on the phone's screen. The *Cardboard* viewing device holds the smartphone at the right distance from the user's eyes and uses simple lenses that enable the user to focus on the screen, only inches away. The *Cardboard* device earned its name because it is made of cardboard and is available online for around $5. In addition to these basic viewers, there are numerous high-tech versions of smartphone viewers that feature adjustable controls and stereo headphones. These enhanced versions of Google Cardboard cost between $20 and $200.

The most sophisticated technologies for viewing stereo images are consumer virtual reality headsets. The Meta Quest family of products includes software that can view stereo images downloaded from websites or directly from the headset's internal memory.

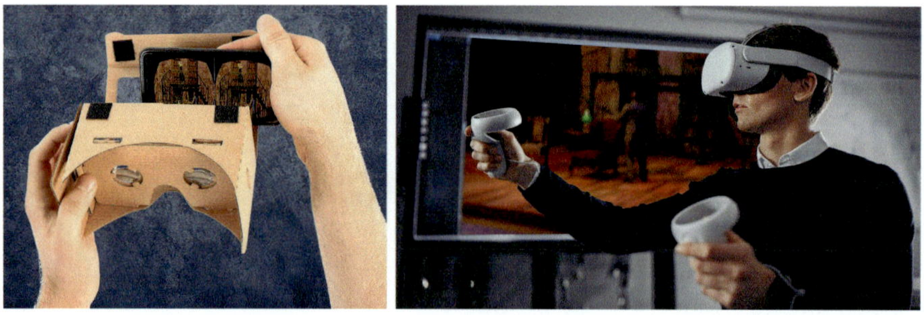

FIGURE 14.9 3D and VR viewing devices can be as simple as the "Carboard" or as sophisticated as Meta's Quest systems.

Full Interactive VR

This is the VR where you can actually roam through a space, weaving around furniture and peering down from different angles, or striding alongside Alfred Doolittle through the streets, or exploring various corners of the embassy ballroom. But don't get too excited – this requires a special toolkit. You'll need to import 3D models from programs like *Bforartists*, *3ds Max*, or *Cinema 4D* into platforms that can handle real-time experiences.

SketchFab allows users to marvel at 3D models in all their glory while also immersing themselves as a virtual observer within the scene. Game navigation here is a breeze. With a quick push of the arrow or WASD keys, you can glide across the scene while your mouse lets you gaze in every possible direction. Please note that, since this is a web-based solution, it has some limitations. Sorry, picking up objects or opening doors isn't part of the package. That level of interaction is reserved for a more advanced experience.

Various modeling programs have dedicated VR software that's compatible and can import directly from your design tools. A solid option is *Simlab*, which is not only affordable but also free to students for a full two years. It's designed for ease of use and boasts built-in features for animating characters, syncing music, and implementing real-time effects like fire and water.

15 Digital Scenography

FIGURE 15.1 CGI is an exciting medium when used in live theatre production. Zero is in his version of heaven in *ADD1NG MA¢H1N3: A MU$1¢AL*.

DOI: 10.4324/9781003571742-15

Now firmly established as a scenographic tool in the planning of productions, CAD scenography is currently moving from that stage to that of being a participating ingredient in the final production.

THE NEED FOR A NEW SCENOGRAPHY

Even a cursory examination of art within the context of historical periods reveals that scenography is closely linked with styles, reflecting the tastes of the era. Concurrent with movements such as Romanticism, Expressionism, Symbolism, and Realism, the theatre incorporated the prevailing style and created works that spoke in the language of its contemporary audience. Recently, however, we may be in a period in which scenography has not kept pace with popular culture.

Many newer scripts call for a completely new setting for each of many short scenes, changing both the time and place rapidly with little regard for the physical limitations of production. These plays reflect the current culture in that they are rich in information and use a multitude of visual images and multiple storylines. This new style of presentation is similar to the dissemination of information through electronic media and is suited to the talents of a population that can simultaneously watch two television shows and a football game while avoiding commercial breaks.

Production teams face the challenge of creating a production design comparable to that of a feature film, but with budgets that are only a fraction of what a film can command. Unable to produce the number and intricacy of settings called for in a script, we often opt for a nearly bare stage that, with a change in lighting or a few props, can represent many locales or, at least, the general moods or themes of the play. Fortunately, the advances in lighting technology and control have made it possible for the lighting to serve this expanded function as a scene changer.

Now we are at the threshold of being able to employ technology that will better realize the intentions of today's playwrights and better reflect the culture that has inspired the play. The visual language of our culture is to saturate the viewer with overlapping ideas through complex images and sounds. With CGI and other new media, we can employ stagecraft that will allow us to jump from place to place with the same ease evident in motion pictures. Similarly, we can make jumps in time and create fantastic spaces that are not compatible with the physical laws of the universe. We can create fluid, ever-changing environments that present settings for expressionist works in the same capricious manner in which thoughts are formed.

This form of cinematic staging is exactly what many new playwrights had envisioned while writing their plays. During several experimental productions at the University of Kansas that employ new media as a scenic device, the playwrights involved confirmed this.

Modern audiences have become accustomed to accepting information through electronic media to the point where they often discount traditional media.

People now get more news of the outside world through electronic media than from newspapers. Recent studies indicate that the average American watches approximately 3 hours and 45 minutes of television each day.

Television watchers are accustomed to having a narrative interrupted by unrelated information and then resumed. Computer users utilize hypertext documents, such as pages on the internet's websites, that promote the idea of linking a variety of information sources in a loose, non-linear manner.

Almost 50 years ago, the noted stage designer, Robert Edmund Jones, wrote and lectured on the topic of a new scenography that would merge elements of film and live performance. As he put it, "The business of workers in the theatre is, as I see it, to express timeless themes by means of the tools of one's own time."[1] His proposed technology would use cinematic elements to reveal the inner, emotional life of characters and other expressionistic functions.

Incorporating digital images into your scenography is only limited by your imagination. The design-audience interface can be mediated through the most complex modern entertainment systems or as simply as a slideshow of images and a digital projector. One of the most effective applications I have seen simply used a pair of projectors and images animated with PowerPoint. Another used two pairs of live cameras and projectors.

i.e.VR

In the mid-1990s, our group started a series of experimental theater productions that featured new technologies, media, and computer graphics. Over the next 20 years, we expanded to create a substantial body of work across a series of productions that utilized various technologies and interfaces with the audience. We were dedicated to communicating with a modern audience in a visual language they are accustomed to using technologies that cross barriers and bridge the differences between live theater, real-time computing, film, and video. With each production, we experimented with new technology as it became available, aided by the help and generosity of numerous corporations, software developers, and hardware manufacturers.

The productions were spaced a year or two apart, allowing time for technical innovations in the computer environment or for us to become aware of different tech that showed promise of utility in live stage production. At the same time, each production advanced the methods and tech that had proved successful in previous productions.

Another aspect of the series of experiments, another aim we sought to accomplish, was to make the technology and technicians part of the event, to feature them in the publicity for the show, and inform the expectations of the theatergoers, that they would know what they were in for, or at least had a general idea of the unique nature of the event before they entered the theater.

As the experiments progressed, we found new ways to allow the technicians to be visible to the audience as they went about their work. We made no bones about the fact that the images presented were media-enhanced or mediated images. We were always striving to highlight the fact that the images on the screen were being produced in real-time and not pre-recorded, which gave the computer operators a role akin to that of the cast – essentially, they became actors themselves.

Simultaneously, while designing our productions around the use of technology, we remained dedicated to addressing the dramatic needs of the play. All the new tech would be of little use if it only served for its own sake.

Our first production was Elmer Rice's *The Adding Machine*. *Adding Machine* is an episodic play with a series of scenes, each set in a new and different location, providing us a chance to experiment with stagecraft illusions in a variety of ways and look for opportunities to use technology for seamless changes from one scene to the next, similar to the scene transitions of movies or television shows. *The Adding Machine* is also considered one of the few true examples of expressionism in American theater, with scenes that exhibit elements that are somewhat fantastic or surrealistic. This presented the opportunity to use virtual reality to portray things that would be very difficult to achieve through standard stagecraft.

Some of the production elements were cutting-edge. For the first time, we attempted to project digital images using a polarized stereo system, which required two separate projectors and necessitated that the audience be outfitted with polarized 3D glasses. A decade later, this would become very popular in cinema and movie theaters. We beat them to the punch by nearly a decade (Polar Express by IMAX 2004).

Other aspects of the technology were very old-school stagecrafty. We used improvised lenses in front of the video cameras and projectors on occasion. We often combined a live feed from video cameras with computer-generated images.

3D Projection

Projecting images or videos in stereoscopic 3D can be a very complex matter, or it can be surprisingly simple. Using the procedures outlined in the previous chapter, stereo images are created in the side-by-side format. Then the computer's display settings are set for dual-monitors, or in this case, dual-projectors. A single desktop, or the stereo images, are stretched across both.

Polarizing filters are placed in front of the projectors' lenses, and they are ready to go. One caveat is that some projectors emit light already polarized. If the light is not polarized in a plane or direction that works with the audience's 3D glasses, it can be depolarized simply by using almost any clear filter. Or, the direction of polarization can be "turned" with a special clear filter called a half-wave plate.

Some rear-projection screens work with polarized light, and any surface painted with a metalized paint will work for front projection.

The next show was *Wings* by Arthur Kopit. In this production, we took a great leap when we discovered that the first commercial head-mounted display was being introduced to the public. Each member of the audience wore one of these HMDs, which allowed them to see both the real-time images within the headset and the live actors on stage simultaneously.

This is similar to the technology we would today call augmented reality. We found that by varying the brightness of the stage lights and the images within the headsets, we could draw the audience's attention to either one or the other, or a combination of both. The headsets also included a pair of stereo earphones, which allowed us to send stereo sound effects directly to each individual audience member.

The play was again an episodic adventure, this time following the journey of an elderly woman as she suffers a stroke at the beginning of the play, then goes through the fear of the experience and the hospital emergency system. Then, as she recovers, her brain forces her to see different versions of reality and various types of hallucinations. We piped these experiences directly to the audience's perceptions, so rather than having a purely sympathetic experience of watching the woman's ordeal from a distance, they were having the empathic experience of sharing it with her.

This was a very intense experience for the audience and an immense amount of work for the stage crew. There were 10 people at different stations in the control room. One was generating computer imagery in real time, and two more were switching the video feeds of offstage actors dressed as doctors, technicians, and social workers. There was another person redirecting the output to the head monitor displays and various onscreen projectors, with yet another person handling sound playback from recorded music and effects. There was also someone in charge of switching between recorded effects and live effects from actors on and off stage, redirecting them to house speakers or head-mounted displays.

Following an interval was *Machinal* by Sophie Treadwell. We had acquired a new generation of projectors and computers, along with virtual simulation software, yielding a much more polished, realistic, and high-quality look with detailed scenes. We also experimented with a different projection method, where a central screen displayed most of the real-time rendering, while two, higher, side screens carried peripheral information. This setup allowed us to reveal the technicians and backstage workings of the show, as the sightlines were left open below the side screens, so the audience could see the operators at their computers and the actors standing before cameras while their live images were projected.

Tesla Electric was a relatively new script by Canadian playwright David Fraser, a semi-biographical, dramatic story about Nikola Tesla. It seemed fitting to utilize new technologies to tell the story of the man who was largely responsible for the world's technological growth in the 20th century, having invented AC power along with the accompanying generators and motors, as well as a host of other wildly imaginative items. *Tesla Electric* took a different approach in creating images. We formed a partnership with Illuminating Engineers, who were experts in the computer science of Radiance rendering,

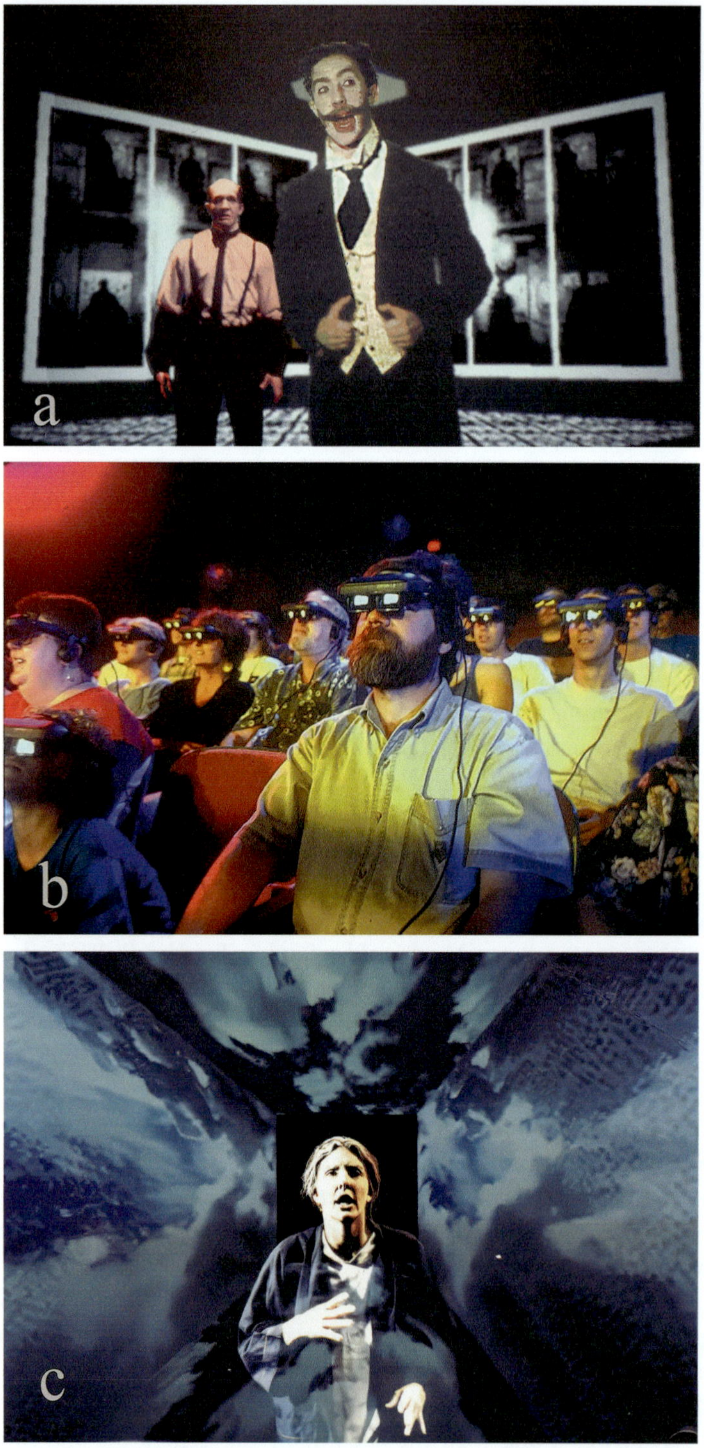

FIGURE 15.2 a) *The Adding Machine,* The Office, the Boss fires Zero. b) *Wings,* The audience was equipped with head-mounted displays. c) *Wings,* Emily experiences a vision.

and secured time on a local mainframe that was necessary to achieve the high degree of sophistication required to render all the images in the project's timeframe.

These images were projected on three screens connected to form a continuous, semi-cylindrical surface that filled the audience's view, spanning 120° in width. The result, when married with the 3D stereoscopic projection, was incredibly realistic and immersive.

The next production was, *A Midsummer Night's Dream*, produced at the University of Canterbury in Kent, UK. It was time to experiment and discover how well Britons would react to a new media production of their beloved bard.

Among the new tricks we tried out for this production was capturing actors live on camera in stereoscopic 3D by placing a beam splitter in front of the camera lens to collect right and left views and merge them into the two sides of a standard video picture. We then sent that image to front-of-house projectors, where the side-by-side images would be split, polarized, and overlapped using another set of beam splitters in front of the projection lens.

While the idea was certainly innovative, it was executed with the typical improvised stagecraft of mirrors, plywood, Velcro, foam rubber, and some drywall screws. At one point, the center projection screen was raised, and the acting area was filled with stage fog, allowing the actors to move in and out of tunnels created when the projected lines and shapes formed seemingly three-dimensional shapes in the smoke channels.

The next year featured a children's production, *Dinosaurus*. The original production had the dinosaurs inhabiting underground caverns brought to life with simple shadow puppets on a rear-projection screen, while a narrator stood in front and provided their voices. In our production, the dinosaurs were computer-generated, 3D puppets on an RP screen, controlled with joysticks and keyboard strokes.

The biggest concern, and area of greatest interest, was whether the kids could grasp the idea of a projected onscreen dinosaur that looked mostly like a real dinosaur, paired with a live actor in front giving it voice and emotion. The kids understood perfectly, and they cheered, laughed, and yelled, having a grand old time – one of the best audiences we ever had.

This was followed by *The Magic Flute* in 2003. This was perhaps our most grandiose project. The ambitious parts were very successful, while other parts didn't hit the mark. The main experiment here was to move the projected images away from the environment/backdrop position to a location on stage where actors and performers could interact with them more directly. In the first scene, the magic dragon appeared on a small screen. As it battled Prince Tamino, it moved around the stage thanks to a pair of "Mozart" stagehands. The image was projected from a data projector, rigged to work much like a follow spot. The projector, its operator, and the computer operator who brought the dragon to life were positioned in the orchestra pit and visible to the audience.

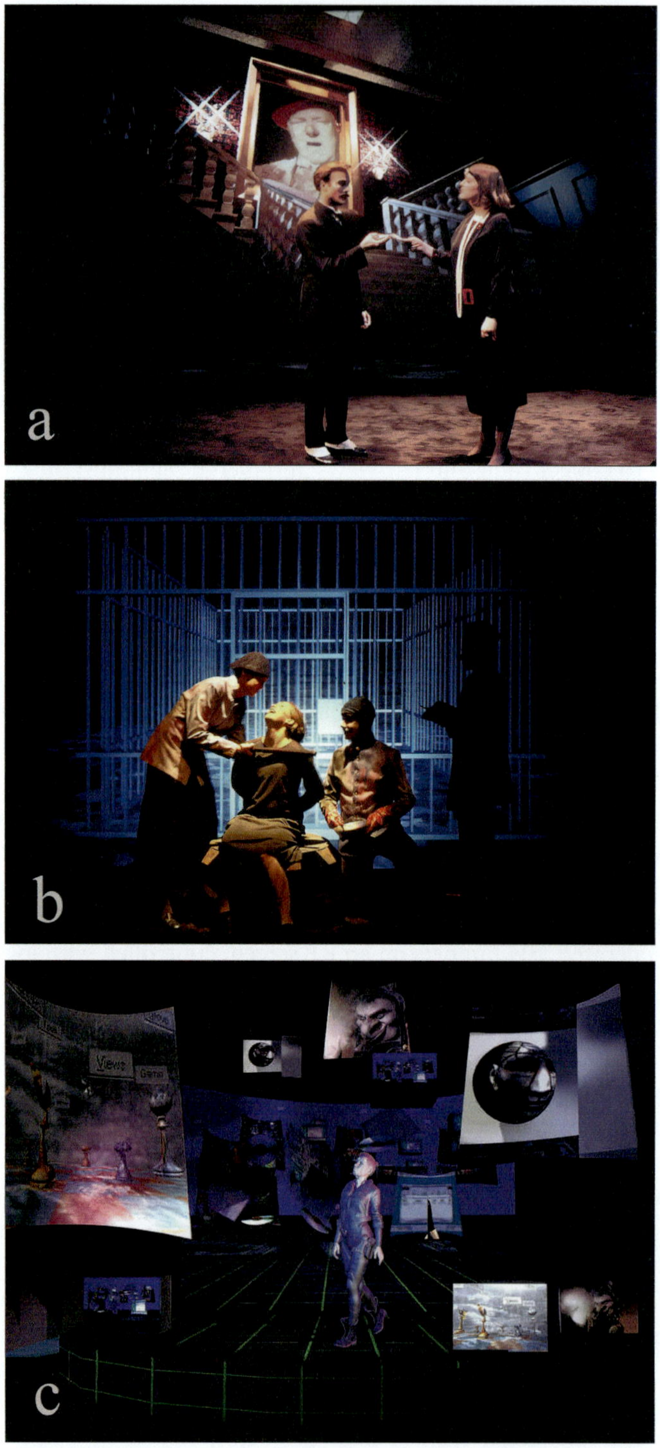

FIGURE 15.3 a) *Machinal,* Helen and her Mother at home. b) *Tesla Electric,* Nikola Tesla, in the home of J. P. Morgan. c) *A Midcyber Night's Dream,* The young lovers in the "forest."

FIGURE 15.4 a) *Dinosaurus,* Two dinosaurs facing off. b) *The Magic Flute,* Tamino is pining for the princess. c) *Rhinoceros,* Society is descending into fascism.

In the next scene, Papageno, the bird catcher, arrives on stage and comes across a tree carried by another "Mozart" stagehand, with a flock of digital birds perched on the branches in the form of half a dozen small screens hanging from the tree. In other scenes, wagons rolled on with screens mounted to their fronts, both tall and short. A large circular screen was attached to a staircase holding the Queen of the Night. Images were projected onto performers' bodies, on fabric with holes for the singers' faces. The final scenes of the play were more abstract, as the prince and princess moved through valleys of water and fire. Their voices were captured by stage microphones and transformed into pulsating seas and great, circling globes of fire, based on their sound waveforms.

This was followed by an original project called *The Tree of Life*. This mostly focused on different types of environments. A realistic tree was projected on layers of shark-tooth scrim hanging above a tree trunk assembled by dancers on stage. Afterward, other performers represented evolving life emerging from a wave-filled ocean simulated in real-time around and behind them.

Then came a reprise of *The Adding Machine*. This time, *The ADD1NG MA¢H1N3: A MU$1¢AL*. The production employed many of the techniques and technologies used previously, but was enhanced with new upgrades in hardware and software. We further experimented with techniques using data projectors for front-of-house lighting. Pools of light from the projectors behaved like those of a follow spot, reacting to inputs from the operator via a joystick and mouse. This evolved to incorporate digital images and video clips projected onto the performers.

Rhinoceros was the last big production, a political protest play by Eugene Ionesco that tells the story of a young man dedicated to standing up to fascism, where fascists are depicted as rhinoceroses. We built a multimedia library of video clips, animations, newspaper headlines, tweets, and blurbs – parts of the script, all projected and pullable at any moment by the crew in the control room. This required a significant investment in learning and refining animation techniques. The four-legged rhinoceroses and a few two-legged politicians all donned matching headgear.

For more information on these productions and other projects using virtual reality and scenography, visit the Institute for the Exploration of Virtual Reality: www.ievr.org

NOTE

1 Jones, Robert Edmund, *Towards a New Theatre: The Lectures of Robert Edmund Jones*, Ed. Delbert Unruh, Limelight Editions, New York, 1992.

Appendix A: Gel Color to Approximate RGB Equivalent

Manuf	Num	Color Name	Transmission	Red	Green	Blue
Gam	105	Antique Rose	58	188	251	147
Gam	106	1/2 Antique Rose	75	165	183	205
Gam	107	1/4 Antique Rose	79	180	252	247
Gam	108	1/8 Antique Rose	83	255	171	160
Gam	110	Dark Rose	22	233	33	163
Gam	120	Bright Pink	21	237	61	149
Gam	130	Rose	36	241	90	154
Gam	140	Dark Magenta	10	185	13	164
Gam	150	Pink Punch	27	192	0	96
Gam	155	Light Pink	71	251	170	210
Gam	160	Chorus Pink	62	252	163	209
Gam	170	Flesh Pink	47	250	103	180
Gam	180	Cherry	27	249	28	94
Gam	190	Cold Pink	51	252	141	174
Gam	195	Nymph Pink	53	253	145	183
Gam	220	Pink Magenta	18	206	4	75
Gam	235	Pink Red	18	249	53	72

(*Continued*)

(Continued)

Manuf	Num	Color Name	Transmission	Red	Green	Blue
Gam	245	Light Red	13	208	6	21
Gam	250	Med Red	XT8	116	0	16
Gam	260	Rosy Amber	50	252	124	153
Gam	270	RedOrange	17	111	0	0
Gam	280	Fire Red	26	255	9	9
Gam	290	Fire Orange	28	230	17	0
Gam	305	French Rose	70	254	150	171
Gam	315	Autumn Glory	37	253	71	62
Gam	320	Peach	47	252	85	37
Gam	323	Indian Summer	46	255	32	32
Gam	325	Bastard Amber	72	254	173	150
Gam	330	Sepia	37	182	119	109
Gam	335	Coral	44	159	0	0
Gam	340	Light Bastard Amber	78	254	208	167
Gam	343	Honey	62	112	16	0
Gam	345	Deep Amber	41	255	0	0
Gam	350	Dark Amber	51	252	103	39
Gam	360	Amber Blush	73	240	206	179
Gam	363	Sand	85	255	223	175
Gam	364	Pale Honey	82	223	147	64
Gam	365	Warm Straw	79	240	206	179
Gam	370	Spice	21	112	80	80
Gam	375	Flame	72	252	123	54
Gam	380	Golden Tan	36	124	82	69
Gam	385	Light Amber	77	253	180	136
Gam	390	Walnut	11	54	39	41
Gam	420	Med Amber	71	253	202	96
Gam	440	Very Light Straw	83	254	232	186
Gam	450	Saffron	83	230	157	23
Gam	460	Mellow Yellow	83	248	252	82
Gam	470	Pale Gold	87	239	255	57
Gam	480	Med Yellow	88	245	235	27
Gam	510	No Color Straw	90	252	249	186

(*Continued*)

(Continued)

Manuf	Num	Color Name	Transmission	Red	Green	Blue
Gam	520	New Straw	85	198	255	167
Gam	535	Lime	86	96	255	137
Gam	540	Pale Green	75	145	255	92
Gam	570	Light Green-Yellow	46	26	226	10
Gam	650	Grass Green	6	0	106	0
Gam	655	Rich Green	12	0	12	0
Gam	660	Med Green	36	0	179	4
Gam	680	Kelly Green	35	38	181	113
Gam	685	Pistachio	30	0	44	16
Gam	690	Bluegrass	17	0	56	32
Gam	710	Blue Green	14	58	118	97
Gam	720	Light Steel Blue	56	119	227	255
Gam	725	Princess Blue	32	0	88	112
Gam	730	Azure Blue	27	0	102	123
Gam	740	Off Blue	17	0	167	230
Gam	750	Nile Blue	14	0	130	168
Gam	760	Aqua Blue	14	34	111	119
Gam	770	Christel Blue	19	47	152	164
Gam	780	Shark Blue	27	54	176	190
Gam	790	Electric Blue	40	104	157	255
Gam	810	Moon Blue	11	0	62	176
Gam	815	Moody Blue	20	0	52	108
Gam	820	Full Light Blue	50	147	185	255
Gam	830	North Sky Blue	51	219	198	255
Gam	835	Aztec Blue	6	0	0	92
Gam	840	Steel Blue	19	94	0	249
Gam	842	Whisper Blue	44	0	138	255
Gam	845	Cobalt	4	0	0	88
Gam	847	City Blue	13	0	0	96
Gam	848	Bonus Blue	14	0	0	108
Gam	850	Blue (Primary)	5	64	0	170
Gam	860	Sky Blue	28	152	89	255
Gam	870	Winter Blue	76	0	211	255

(*Continued*)

(Continued)

Manuf	Num	Color Name	Transmission	Red	Green	Blue
Gam	880	Daylight Blue	22	88	0	236
Gam	882	Southern Sky	24	0	28	72
Gam	885	Blue Ice	60	0	132	160
Gam	888	Blue Belle	31	0	24	56
Gam	890	Dark Sky Blue	3	2	9	136
Gam	905	Dark Blue	1	0	0	108
Gam	910	Alice Blue	11	16	0	100
Gam	915	Twilight	4	12	0	92
Gam	920	Pale Lavender	63	241	219	255
Gam	925	Cosmic Blue	2	0	0	12
Gam	930	Real Congo Blue	2	0	0	16
Gam	940	Light Purple	20	7	26	190
Gam	945	Royal Purple	2	69	2	108
Gam	948	African Violet	4	12	0	32
Gam	950	Purple	7	65	2	98
Gam	960	Med Lavender	22	138	4	210
Gam	970	Special Lavender	32	175	34	251
Gam	980	Surprise Pink	52	224	170	253
Gam	990	Dark Lavender	15	105	4	159
Gam	995	Orchid	6	36	0	28
Gam	1510	UV Shield	90	255	255	255
Gam	1514	.15 ND	66	199	184	189
Gam	1515	.3 ND	52	160	160	144
Gam	1516	.6 ND	23	116	116	116
Gam	1517	.9 ND	13	100	100	100
Gam	1518	1.2 ND	6	16	16	16
Gam	1520	Extra Blue CTB	13	0	0	120
Gam	1523	Full Blue CTB	24	0	0	96
Gam	1526	3/4 Blue CTB	31	0	24	136
Gam	1529	1/2 Blue CTB	44	20	20	220
Gam	1532	1/4 Blue CTB	60	112	160	22
Gam	1535	1/8 Blue CTB	76	104	104	217
Gam	1540	Extra CTO	44	255	0	0

(Continued)

(Continued)

Manuf	Num	Color Name	Transmission	Red	Green	Blue
Gam	1543	Full CTO	62	233	24	0
Gam	1546	3/4 CTO	65	215	32	0
Gam	1549	1/2 CTO	73	92	32	0
Gam	1552	1/4 CTO	82	184	88	4
Gam	1555	1/8 CTO	85	252	132	44
Gam	1556	CTO/.3 ND	36	61	30	30
Gam	1557	CTO/.6 ND	21	30	8	8
Gam	1558	CTO/.9 ND	11	16	8	8
Gam	1560	Y-1	89	225	225	92
Gam	1565	MTY	64	255	33	0
Gam	1570	MT2	72	208	47	0
Gam	1575	1/2 MT2	78	202	104	0
Gam	1580	Minusgreen	58	104	16	48
Gam	1581	3/4 Minusgreen	69	104	16	48
Gam	1582	1/2 Minusgreen	75	255	64	236
Gam	1583	1/4 Minusgreen	79	255	97	127
Gam	1584	1/8 Minusgreen	83	255	129	184
Gam	1585	Plusgreen	75	56	80	8
Gam	1587	1/2 Plusgreen	86	142	170	0
Gam	1588	1/4 Plusgreen	89	130	160	0
Gam	1589	1/8 Plusgreen	91	130	160	0
Gam	1590	Fluorofilter CW	46	96	0	0
Lee	2	Rose Pink	33	217	0	145
Lee	3	Lavender Tint	75	219	177	255
Lee	4	Med Bastard Amber	64	255	125	63
Lee	7	Pale Yellow	85	255	255	157
Lee	8	Dark Salmon	35	255	39	28
Lee	9	Pale Amber Gold	71	255	160	64
Lee	10	Med Yellow	87	255	220	0
Lee	13	Straw Tint	72	255	181	98
Lee	15	Deep Straw	61	253	130	0
Lee	19	Fire	19	252	1	7
Lee	20	Med Amber	51	255	155	106

(*Continued*)

(Continued)

Manuf	Num	Color Name	Transmission	Red	Green	Blue
Lee	21	Gold Amber	31	253	92	15
Lee	22	Dark Amber	24	223	32	32
Lee	24	Scarlet	19	223	0	0
Lee	26	Bright Red	9	202	0	0
Lee	27	Med Red	4	66	0	8
Lee	35	Light Pink	61	255	92	130
Lee	36	Medium Pink	33	255	98	133
Lee	46	Dark Magenta	6	96	0	0
Lee	48	Rose Purple	15	96	0	92
Lee	52	Light Lavender	45	99	0	173
Lee	53	Paler Lavender	62	162	192	255
Lee	58	Lavender	9	64	0	128
Lee	61	Mist Blue	62	89	219	251
Lee	63	Pale Blue	54	0	160	223
Lee	68	Sky Blue	13	0	0	147
Lee	79	Just Blue	6	11	11	153
Lee	85	Deeper Blue	3	0	0	66
Lee	89	Moss Green	30	0	159	0
Lee	90	Dark Yellow Green	11	4	61	0
Lee	101	Yellow	80	255	191	0
Lee	102	Light Amber	75	251	210	17
Lee	103	Straw	82	255	222	181
Lee	104	Deep Amber	64	249	163	34
Lee	105	Orange	41	253	121	2
Lee	106	Primary Red	9	128	0	0
Lee	107	Light Rose	48	255	79	109
Lee	109	Light Salman	55	241	103	103
Lee	110	Middle Rose	47	255	104	168
Lee	111	Dark Pink	32	236	55	150
Lee	113	Magenta	11	176	0	0
Lee	115	Peacock Blue	35	21	155	141
Lee	116	Med Blue-Green	19	0	79	32
Lee	117	Steel Blue	55	0	223	255

(*Continued*)

(Continued)

Manuf	Num	Color Name	Transmission	Red	Green	Blue
Lee	118	Light Blue	24	17	118	255
Lee	119	Dark Blue	3	0	16	128
Lee	120	Deep Blue	1	35	29	118
Lee	121	Lee Green	64	0	191	0
Lee	122	Fern Green	52	0	232	0
Lee	124	Dark Green	31	0	164	0
Lee	126	Mauve	4	96	0	112
Lee	127	Smokey Pink	12	112	48	64
Lee	128	Bright Pink	14	204	19	116
Lee	129	Heavy Frost	7	255	255	255
Lee	130	Clear	95	255	255	255
Lee	132	Med Blue	9	0	0	192
Lee	134	Golden Amber	38	254	116	69
Lee	135	Deep Golden Amber	19	159	34	34
Lee	136	Pale Lavender	43	175	128	223
Lee	137	Special Lavender	26	83	41	207
Lee	138	Pale Green	80	128	255	32
Lee	139	Primary Green	15	0	80	0
Lee	141	Bright Blue	18	0	48	208
Lee	142	Pale Violet	21	48	0	176
Lee	143	Pale Navy Blue	16	1	135	150
Lee	144	No Color Blue	32	0	112	223
Lee	147	Apricot	53	255	118	72
Lee	148	Bright Rose	14	221	2	96
Lee	151	Gold Tint	69	255	185	168
Lee	152	Pale Gold	71	255	201	174
Lee	153	Pale Salmon	65	255	166	184
Lee	154	Pale Rose	73	255	204	191
Lee	156	Chocolate	26	120	92	92
Lee	157	Pink	36	224	0	80
Lee	158	Deep Orange	30	253	94	40
Lee	159	No Color Straw	89	255	255	202

(*Continued*)

(Continued)

Manuf	Num	Color Name	Transmission	Red	Green	Blue
Lee	161	Slate Blue	25	16	48	144
Lee	162	Bastard Amber	78	255	160	128
Lee	164	Flame Red	18	227	0	0
Lee	165	Daylight Blue	20	0	64	255
Lee	166	Pale Red	25	235	3	102
Lee	170	Deep Lavender	26	181	0	219
Lee	174	Dark Steel Blue	30	0	69	253
Lee	176	Loving Amber	50	239	112	96
Lee	179	Chrome Orange	54	255	125	47
Lee	180	Dark Lavender	7	111	0	223
Lee	181	Congo Blue	1	13	4	113
Lee	182	Light Red	11	144	0	0
Lee	183	Moonlight Blue	19	32	96	255
Lee	184	Cosmetic Peach	57	255	239	223
Lee	185	Cosmetic Burgundy	52	192	159	160
Lee	186	Cosmetic Silver Rose	51	255	160	207
Lee	187	Cosmetic Rouge	54	255	155	134
Lee	188	Cosmetic Highlight	56	255	210	200
Lee	189	Cosmetic Silver Moss	61	213	255	181
Lee	190	Cosmetic Emerald	60	255	244	215
Lee	191	Cosmetic Aqua Blue	53	96	255	223
Lee	192	Flesh Pink	35	223	32	96
Lee	193	Rosy Gold	36	255	81	103
Lee	194	Surprise Pink	22	96	64	191
Lee	195	Zenith Blue	3	0	16	96
Lee	196	True Blue	27	0	64	255
Lee	197	Alice Blue	10	32	64	191
Lee	200	Double C.T. Blue	16	36	1	201
Lee	201	Full C.T. Blue	34	0	128	25
Lee	202	1/2 C.T. Blue	55	0	128	191

(*Continued*)

(Continued)

Manuf	Num	Color Name	Transmission	Red	Green	Blue
Lee	203	1/4 C.T. Blue	69	215	243	255
Lee	204	Full C.T. Orange	55	254	153	86
Lee	205	1/2 C.T. Orange	71	255	171	87
Lee	206	1/4 C.T. Orange	79	255	194	134
Lee	212	L.C.T. Yellow	89	255	255	157
Lee	213	White Flame Green	89	192	255	128
Lee	218	1/8 C.T. Blue	81	223	223	22
Lee	219	Lee Fluorescent Green	32	0	136	113
Lee	223	1/8 C.T. Orange	85	255	216	176
Lee	226	Lee U.V.	92	255	255	255
Lee	230	Super Correct L.C.T. Yellow	42	166	131	83
Lee	232	Super White Flame	37	198	135	149
Lee	236	H.M.I. To Tungsten	58	255	96	0
Lee	237	C.I.D. To Tungsten	39	253	92	15
Lee	238	C.S.I. To Tungsten	30	201	67	56
Lee	241	Fluorescent 5700K	27	13	152	155
Lee	242	Fluorescent 4300K	37	50	181	135
Lee	243	Fluorescent 3600K	46	0	206	114
Lee	244	Lee Plus Green	74	112	223	64
Lee	245	Half Plus Green	82	192	255	128
Lee	246	Quarter Plus Green	85	203	255	151
Lee	247	Lee Minus Green	59	255	0	128
Lee	248	Half Minus Green	72	255	0	255
Lee	249	Quarter Minus Green	82	255	128	192
Lee	278	Eighth Plus Green	88	220	255	151

(*Continued*)

(Continued)

Manuf	Num	Color Name	Transmission	Red	Green	Blue
Lee	279	Eighth Minus Green	87	255	128	255
Lee	281	3/4 C.T. Blue	46	0	24	136
Lee	285	3/4 C.T. Orange	61	215	32	0
Lee	328	Follies Pink	20	204	0	43
Lee	332	Special Rose Pink	11	195	0	75
Lee	343	Special Med Lavender	6	32	0	128
Lee	344	Violet	20	32	32	191
Lee	353	Lighter Blue	41	27	136	219
Lee	354	Special Steel Blue	39	0	223	223
Lee	363	Special Med Blue	4	0	0	96
Lee	441	Full C.T. Straw	57	255	96	0
Lee	442	Half C.T. Straw	71	254	198	114
Lee	443	Quarter C.T. Straw	80	239	207	143
Lee	444	Eighth C.T. Straw	83	254	232	186
Rosco	0	Clear	100	255	255	255
Rosco	1	Light Bastard Amber	56	255	96	96
Rosco	2	Bastard Amber	78	255	192	160
Rosco	3	Dark Bastard Amber	62	255	159	120
Rosco	4	Med Bastard Amber	66	253	157	125
Rosco	5	Rose Tint	80	254	190	209
Rosco	6	No Color Straw	92	253	255	215
Rosco	7	Pale Yellow	96	255	255	176
Rosco	8	Pale Gold	86	239	207	143
Rosco	9	Pale Amber Gold	74	253	183	79
Rosco	10	Med Yellow	92	255	255	32
Rosco	11	Light Straw	82	253	204	36
Rosco	12	Straw	88	239	255	0

(*Continued*)

(Continued)

Manuf	Num	Color Name	Transmission	Red	Green	Blue
Rosco	13	Straw Tint	78	254	198	114
Rosco	14	Med Straw	68	254	171	48
Rosco	15	Deep Straw	65	248	149	1
Rosco	16	Light Amber	68	255	96	0
Rosco	17	Light Flame	56	239	63	32
Rosco	18	Flame	56	240	16	0
Rosco	19	Fire	20	255	4	4
Rosco	20	Med Amber	54	253	140	66
Rosco	21	Golden Amber	43	236	96	2
Rosco	22	Deep Amber	26	253	64	49
Rosco	23	Orange	32	253	108	66
Rosco	24	Scarlet	22	191	0	0
Rosco	25	Orange Red	14	255	0	0
Rosco	26	Light Red	12	159	0	0
Rosco	27	Med Red	4	96	0	0
Rosco	30	Light Salmon Pink	44	254	101	88
Rosco	31	Salmon Pink	46	254	99	134
Rosco	32	Medi Salmon Pink	28	252	1	57
Rosco	33	No Color Pink	65	255	128	160
Rosco	34	Flesh Pink	45	255	32	64
Rosco	35	Light Pink	66	255	164	175
Rosco	36	Med Pink	46	232	91	137
Rosco	37	Pale Rose Pink	56	255	128	175
Rosco	38	Light Rose	49	255	96	175
Rosco	40	Light Salmon	34	255	0	0
Rosco	41	Salmon	24	239	0	16
Rosco	42	Deep Salmon	8	144	0	0
Rosco	43	Deep Pink	28	255	0	112
Rosco	44	Middle Rose	26	223	0	112
Rosco	45	Rose	8	144	0	32
Rosco	46	Magenta	6	96	0	0

(*Continued*)

(Continued)

Manuf	Num	Color Name	Transmission	Red	Green	Blue
Rosco	47	Light Rose Purple	16	64	0	64
Rosco	48	Rose Purple	16	183	2	183
Rosco	49	Med Purple	4	112	0	80
Rosco	50	Mauve	14	112	0	0
Rosco	51	Surprise Pink	54	255	128	255
Rosco	52	Light Lavender	26	175	16	239
Rosco	53	Pale Lavender	64	191	192	255
Rosco	54	Special Lavender	50	192	160	255
Rosco	55	Lilac	37	109	79	255
Rosco	56	Gypsy Lavender	4	64	0	128
Rosco	57	Lavender	24	64	0	128
Rosco	58	Deep Lavender	10	64	0	128
Rosco	59	Indigo	2	48	0	80
Rosco	60	No Color Blue	62	128	192	255
Rosco	61	Mist Blue	66	80	192	208
Rosco	62	Booster Blue	54	80	144	191
Rosco	63	Pale Blue	56	16	144	191
Rosco	64	Light Steel Blue	26	0	80	240
Rosco	65	Daylight Blue	35	0	64	255
Rosco	66	Cool Blue	67	0	192	192
Rosco	67	Light Sky Blue	26	0	96	255
Rosco	68	Sky Blue	14	0	0	208
Rosco	69	Brilliant Blue	18	0	64	223
Rosco	70	Nile Blue	45	16	160	176
Rosco	71	Sea Blue	30	0	128	144
Rosco	72	Azure Blue	44	0	160	207
Rosco	73	Peacock Blue	28	16	144	144
Rosco	74	Night Blue	4	0	0	176
Rosco	76	Light Green-Blue	9	0	128	144
Rosco	77	Green-Blue	9	0	128	223
Rosco	78	Trudy Blue	19	32	16	176
Rosco	79	Bright Blue	8	0	0	208

(*Continued*)

(Continued)

Manuf	Num	Color Name	Transmission	Red	Green	Blue
Rosco	80	Primary Blue	9	0	0	128
Rosco	81	Urban Blue	10	36	1	201
Rosco	82	Surprise Blue	6	16	0	112
Rosco	83	Med Blue	4	0	0	96
Rosco	84	Zephyr Blue	14	30	1	163
Rosco	85	Deep Blue	3	0	0	96
Rosco	86	Pea Green	56	0	143	0
Rosco	87	Pale Yellow Green	85	192	255	128
Rosco	88	Light Green	82	128	255	80
Rosco	89	Moss Green	45	0	122	0
Rosco	90	Dark Yellow Green	13	16	95	0
Rosco	91	Primary Green	7	0	64	0
Rosco	92	Turquoise	59	0	191	127
Rosco	93	Blue Green	35	0	176	96
Rosco	94	Kelly Green	25	46	135	104
Rosco	95	Med Blue Green	15	0	96	80
Rosco	96	Lime	98	191	255	0
Rosco	97	Light Gray	50	192	192	192
Rosco	98	Med Gray	25	112	112	112
Rosco	99	Chocolate	35	144	112	96
Rosco	120	Red Diffusion	12	142	0	0
Rosco	121	Blue Diffusion	8	0	0	205
Rosco	122	Green Diffusion	13	0	72	0
Rosco	123	Amber Diffusion	32	255	45	45
Rosco	124	Red Cyc Silk	12	151	0	0
Rosco	125	Blue Cyc Silk	8	0	0	198
Rosco	126	Green Cyc Silk	13	0	62	0
Rosco	127	Amber Cyc Silk	32	255	26	26
Rosco	128	Magenta Silk	6	81	0	61
Rosco	129	Sky Blue Silk	14	0	0	251
Rosco	130	Med Blue Green Silk	15	0	89	74
Rosco	131	Med Amber Silk	54	253	126	0

(*Continued*)

(Continued)

Manuf	Num	Color Name	Transmission	Red	Green	Blue
Rosco	150	Hamburg Rose	80	254	203	218
Rosco	151	Hamburg Lavender	26	197	56	250
Rosco	152	Hamburg Steel Blue	26	0	0	191
Rosco	304	Pale Apricot	79	255	160	128
Rosco	305	Rose Gold	75	255	128	96
Rosco	312	Canary	85	252	223	90
Rosco	317	Apricot	51	239	16	0
Rosco	321	Soft Golden Amber	39	223	32	0
Rosco	337	True Pink	55	255	138	197
Rosco	339	Broadway Pink	15	255	0	144
Rosco	342	Rose Pink	16	207	0	80
Rosco	344	Follies Pink	21	224	0	128
Rosco	355	Pale Violet	20	64	32	160
Rosco	356	Middle Lavender	27	174	53	255
Rosco	357	Royal Lavender	5	48	0	112
Rosco	358	Rose Indigo	5	32	0	80
Rosco	359	Med Violet	5	16	0	96
Rosco	378	Alice Blue	15	80	0	208
Rosco	383	Sapphire Blue	4	26	0	130
Rosco	385	Royal Blue	4	0	0	79
Rosco	388	Gaslight Green	76	0	224	0
Rosco	389	Chroma Green	40	0	127	0
Rosco	397	Pale Gray	70	224	224	224
Rosco	3102	Tough MT2	66	255	96	0
Rosco	3106	Tough MTY	57	239	63	32
Rosco	3107	Tough Y-1	93	253	255	215
Rosco	3114	Tough UV Filter	93	255	255	255
Rosco	3134	Tough MT 54	83	239	207	143
Rosco	3202	Full Blue (CTB)	36	96	0	223
Rosco	3203	Three-Quarter Blue CTB)	41	0	24	136

(*Continued*)

(Continued)

Manuf	Num	Color Name	Transmission	Red	Green	Blue
Rosco	3204	Half Blue (1/2 CTB)	52	128	96	255
Rosco	3206	Third Blue (1/3 CTB)	64	176	176	240
Rosco	3208	Quarter Blue (1/4 CTB)	74	191	223	255
Rosco	3216	Eighth Blue (1/8 CTB)	81	223	223	223
Rosco	3220	Double Blue (2x CTB)	10	36	1	201
Rosco	3304	Tough PlusGreen	76	112	223	
Rosco	3308	Tough Minusgreen	55	255	0	128
Rosco	3310	Fluorofilter	36	255	39	28
Rosco	3313	Tough 1/2 Minusgreen	71	255	0	255
Rosco	3314	Tough 1/4 Minusgreen	81	255	128	192
Rosco	3315	Tough 1/2 Plusgreen	90	192	255	128
Rosco	3316	Tough 1/4 Plusgreen	92	203	255	151
Rosco	3317	Tough 1/8 Plusgreen	93	220	255	185
Rosco	3318	Tough 1/8 Minusgreen	89	255	128	255
Rosco	3401	RoscoSun 85	58	239	80	0
Rosco	3405	RoscoSun 85N.3	33	144	112	96
Rosco	3406	RoscoSun 85N.6	17	112	80	80
Rosco	3407	RoscoSun (CTO)	47	191	64	0
Rosco	3408	RoscoSun (1/2 CTO)	73	255	128	0
Rosco	3409	RoscoSun (1/4 CTO)	81	255	191	143
Rosco	3410	RoscoSun (1/8 CTO)	92	255	224	192
Rosco	3411	RoscoSun (3/4 CTO)	58	215	32	0
Rosco	3441	Full Straw (CTS)	50	255	96	0

(*Continued*)

(Continued)

Manuf	Num	Color Name	Transmission	Red	Green	Blue
Rosco	3442	Half Straw (1/2 CTS)	73	254	198	114
Rosco	3443	Quarter Straw (1/4 CTS)	81	239	207	143
Rosco	3444	Eighth Straw (1/8 CTS)	92	254	232	186
Rosco	3761	Roscolex 85	58	255	96	32

Index

Notes: Page numbers in *italic* refer figures and **bold** tables in the text.